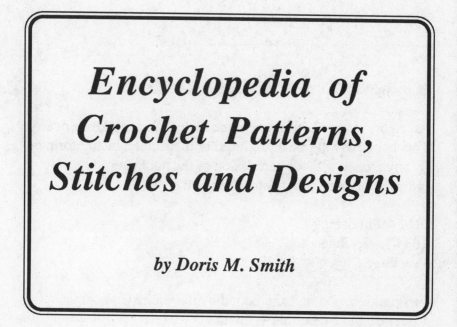

Encyclopedia of Crochet Patterns, Stitches and Designs

by Doris M. Smith

About the Author

Doris Smith lives in a rural Georgia community with her husband and owns and operates a craft store. Crafts have always been a very important part of her life, particularly painting and crocheting.

At a very early age, she learned to crochet from her mother who in turn had learned from her mother. Nearly everyone in her family crocheted so it was natural and fun for her to learn. Over the years, she has taught many of her friends and acquaintances to crochet, sharing with them many of the old patterns handed down by her family from generation to generation. She is now teaching her granddaughter to crochet.

The background on the cover of the book is a piece designed and crocheted by Mrs. Smith's grandmother.

Acknowledgements

There are many people who gave of their time and energy to prepare this book. You have my earnest thanks.

A very special thank you:

To my husband Edgar, for his love and support through the long hours.

To my children for their encouragement.

To Frank and Gayle for the idea and for making it all possible.

To Linda Sciullo for your fine editing skills and helpful ideas.

To Jan Lycans for your long hours of camera work and for putting the puzzle pieces together.

To Jan Ulery, Diane Keith, Jo Bauer, Joan Richardson, and Kathy Carringer for filling in the gaps.

To our Lord and Saviour Jesus Christ who gave us strength and patience through the long hours.

"He has filled them with skill to do all manner of work . . . —
those who do every work and those who design artistic works."
                                                    Ex. 35:35

The heavens declare the glory of God; And the firmament
shows His handiwork.
                                                    Ps. 19:1

Trust in the Lord with all your heart, and lean not to your own
understanding; In all your ways acknowledge Him, And He
shall direct your paths.
                                                    Prov. 3:5,6

Table of Contents

Introduction 7
Chapter I 9
               Basic Crochet Stitches 9
               Abbreviations 12
               International Crochet Symbols . . . 13
Chapter II . . . . . . Chain, Picot and Single
               Crochet 15
Chapter III . . . . . . Chain, Picot, Single and
               Half-Double Crochet 23
Chapter IV . . . . . . Double Crochet 27
Chapter V . . . . . . Treble Crochet 49
Chapter VI . . . . . . V-Stitch and Shell 59
Chapter VII . . . . . Relief Stitch 81
Chapter VIII . . . . Puff Stitch 89
Chapter IX . . . . . . Popcorn Stitch 97
Chapter X . . . . . . Cluster Stitch 107
Chapter XI . . . . . . Dropped Stitch 119
Chapter XII . . . . . X-Stitch 125
Chapter XIII . . . . Wraparound Stitch 133
Chapter XIV . . . . Y-Stitch 137
Chapter XV . . . . . Motifs 139
Chapter XVI . . . . Edgings and Trims 177
Four Ways to Join Crochet Items 240

Introduction

Crochet is an ancient craft that has been handed down from generation to generation. The art of crochet was often passed on from grandmother to grandchildren. But in our modern world, grandma usually lives miles away, and her skills and expertise often are lost.

Some of the most beautiful lace in the world was, at one time, hand-produced in Italy and Ireland. Until machine crochet was introduced, crochet was all hand done. In China, doilies and tablecloths are still hand crocheted in factories. However, as labor costs continue to rise and new machinery is introduced, the fine craft of hand crochet is in danger of dying out. Machine-crochet techniques are used to make lace, doilies, afghans, intricate trims and sometimes large items such as sweaters. Most people agree that it's just not quite the same as what grandma used to make.

Now, more and more people are rediscovering the wonderful art of hand crochet. Recently with the popularity of antiques, crochet is making a comeback. A fine antique graced with a beautiful doily or an afghan placed over the back of a chair is both useful and decorative. Trimming pillowcases and dresser scarves with crochet and dressing up plain outfits with frilly lace collars and cuffs have become very popular.

The "Encyclopedia of Crochet Patterns, Stitches and Designs" starts with the basics. It shows how to combine basic stitches to make beautiful and unique designs. The beginner can use these patterns as a guide for other projects; the expert can use them in creating original designs.

Chapter XV includes motifs such as Granny-Square Wheel, Old American Square, Geometric Circle, Wreath and Shamrock. By using one or more of these motif designs, you can create original bedspreads, tablecloths, dresser scarves, dressy collars and afghans.

The chapter on trims and edgings will show you how to give your work a neatly finished, decorative edge. Lace or trim may be added to many plain items for that special look. A pillow case trimmed with lace is not only beautiful, but it makes a wonderful gift. A tablecloth looks elegant with a bit of lace around the edge, and you can trim your napkins for a real treat.

The instructions you find in the "Encyclopedia of Crochet Patterns, Stitches and Designs" will provide you with some good, old-fashioned know-how. Use the photos and drawings only as a guide. All handwork is unique and varies somewhat in appearance and size. Remember, the size of the crochet hook, the weight of the thread, and how tightly you crochet will determine the size of your finished stitches.

The diagrams used in this book are based on a European code called the International Crochet Symbols. This set of symbols is often used in craft books and magazines in Europe and, increasingly in the USA. When you learn them, they should be a useful tool to guide you in pattern directions. Some people have become so good at using them that they can crochet a whole piece with only these diagrams as a guide. Most people will need the combination of photo, instructions and symbols to master the more difficult patterns.

If you are just beginning to crochet, don't be overwhelmed by the directions. Just take it one step at a time, following each instruction. Punctuation is important! Many crocheters find it helpful to check off each step at the punctuation mark as they complete it. Practice, practice, practice . . . and in no time at all, you will have mastered the art of crochet.

Chapter I

Basic Crochet Stitches, Abbreviations and Symbols

Foundation Chain

Knot a loop onto hook. Put hook in your right hand, the end of yarn extending from the loop in your left hand, and the yarn over the forefinger of your left hand. Place yarn over hook and pull the yarn through to make the first chain. Repeat to make chain as long as desired.

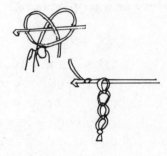

Slip Stitch

Make a chain. Place hook in chain and yarn over hook. Pull through chain and loop on hook.

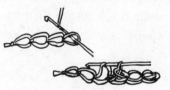

Single Crochet

Make chain. Put the hook into the 2nd chain. Place yarn over hook and pull the yarn through the 2 loops, leaving 1 loop on hook.

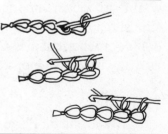

Half Double Crochet

Make chain. Place yarn over hook. Put hook into stitch. Place yarn over hook again. Now pull the yarn through all 3 loops leaving 1 loop on

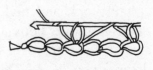

hook.

Double Crochet

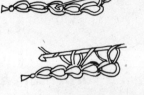

Make chain. Place yarn over the hook. Put the hook into the chain. Place the yarn over the hook again and pull the yarn through 2 loops on hook, leaving 2 loops on hook. Place yarn over hook and pull through 2 loops leaving 1 loop on hook.

Treble Crochet

Make chain. Place yarn over hook twice. Put hook into 5th chain from hook. Place yarn over hook and pull yarn through 2 loops. Place yarn over hook again and pull through 2 loops, leaving 2 on hook. Place yarn over hook and pull through the last 2 loops, leaving 1 on hook

Popcorn Stitch

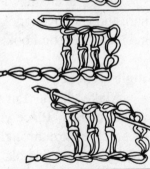

Make chain. Crochet 3 or more double crochet in same chain. Turn and slip stitch in the chain after the 1st double crochet, chain 1. Can work with as many as 2 to 6 loops.

Puff Stitch

Make chain. Place the hook into the 3rd chain from hook. Place yarn around hook and pull yarn through. Place yarn over hook and insert hook again. Put yarn over hook as many times as you desire. Then pull the yarn

through all the loops, leaving 1 loop on hook. Can use from 2 to 6 loops.

Cluster Stitch

Make chain. Place yarn over hook. Put hook in chain. Place yarn over hook, pulling yarn through loop. Place yarn over hook and pull through 2 loops. Put yarn over hook and into same chain stitch, pull yarn through 2 loops, leaving 3 loops on the hook. Now pull yarn through all loops, leaving 1 on hook. Can use from 2 to 6 loops.

Treble X-Stitch

Make chain. Place yarn around hook twice. (Make a treble crochet). Put hook in chain and pull yarn through chain. Place yarn over hook and pull through 2 loops, leaving 3 on hook. Start next treble crochet in 2nd chain and pull yarn through 2 loops 4 times. Chain 1 and make 1 double crochet in the middle of the 2nd treble crochet.

Y-Stitch

Make chain. Place yarn over hook twice, like making a treble crochet. Pull yarn through 3 times. Place yarn over hook once. Insert hook in the middle of the treble crochet and make a double crochet. Start next stitch.

Inverted V or Shell Stitch

Make chain. Start double crochet in

3rd chain from hook. Place yarn over hook and pull through 2 loops, leaving 1 loop on hook. Make as many double crochets as you like. Then place yarn over hook and pull yarn through all the loops.

Relief Double Crochet

Follow directions for double crochet stitch, except instead of inserting the hook into the hole, circle the post of the previous crochet stitch. You can either circle the post from the front and out again or from the back and out again.

front

Back

Increasing Crochet Stitches

Increasing involves the work of 2 stitches in the same stitch. This is done by making an extra stitch of the same pattern in the same stitch. You can increase in the beginning or at the end of the crochet row.

Decreasing Crochet Stitches

Decreasing involves the working off of 2 stitches as 1, thus losing 1 stitch. You can decrease in the beginning or at the end of the crochet row.

Overcast Stitch*

To join crochet pieces together — Lay pieces to be joined together, right side up. With a blunt sewing needle and the same thread used to crochet piece, sew the pieces together by passing the needle from left to right through the crochet stitches on the outer edge.

Whip Stitch*

To join crochet pieces together — Using a blunt sewing needle and the same thread used to crochet, sew right sides of the crochet pieces together, using the back loops.

*For more information on joining pieces together see page 240.

Abbreviations

beg	beginning
bl	block
ch	chain
cl	cluster
dc	double crochet
dec	decrease
dtr	double triple crochet
F.O.	fasten off
fol	following
grp	group
hdc	half double crochet
inc	increasing
lp(s)	loops
mc	main color
pat	pattern
pc	popcorn
rem	remaining
rep	repeat
rnd(s)	rounds
sc	single crochet
sk	skip
sl st	slip stitch
sp	space
st(s)	stitch(es)
tog	together
trc	treble crochet
yo	wrap yarn over hook
*	repeat from * as indicated
( )	repeat between ( ) as indicated
[ ]	repeat between [ ] as indicated

International Crochet Symbols

chain stitch

slip stitch

single crochet

half-double crochet

double crochet

treble crochet

picot

popcorn
(3-looped)

puff stitch
(2-looped)

cluster stitch
(2-looped)

treble X-stitch

V-stitch

shell (3-looped)

inverted V-stitch
(3-looped)

4-looped shell
with chains

wraparound stitch

Y-stitch

Chapter II

Chain, Picot and Single Crochet

1. Multiples of any number plus 1.

Row 1: Sc in 2nd ch, continue across to end of row, turn, ch 1.
Row 2: Sc across row, ch 1, turn.

2. Multiples of 8 plus 2.

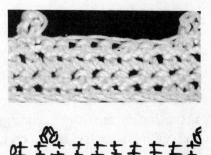

Row 1: Sc in the 2nd ch and in each ch across the row, ch 1 and turn.
Row 2: Sc in the 1st sc and in each sc. across the row, ch 1, turn.
Row 3: Sc in the 1st two sc. * work 4-ch picot, sc in the next sc and the next 7 sc, rep from *, ending row with 8 sc.

3. Multiples of 8 plus 4.

Row 1: Sc in the 2nd ch and in each of the next 2 chs, * ch 7 and sc in the 6th ch, sc in each of the next 2 chs, rep from *, ending row with sc in each of the last 3 chs, ch 1, turn.

Row 2: Sc in the 1st two sc, * ch 4, work sc in the middle of the 7 ch, work 4-ch picot, ch 4, sc in the 2nd sc, rep from * ending row with sc in each of the last 2 sc.

4. Multiples of 3 plus 2.

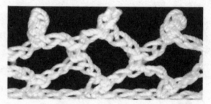

Row 1: Sc in 2nd ch, * ch 5, sc in the 3th ch, rep from *, ending row with last sc, ch 5, turn.

Row 2: Sc in the sc, * ch 2, work 3-ch picot, ch 2, sc around the middle of the 5 ch, rep from *, ending rnd with last sc, ch 1 and sc in the last sc.

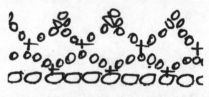

5. Multiples of 2 plus 2.

Row 1: 2 sc in the 4th ch,* 2 sc in the 2nd ch, rep from *, ending row with 2 sc in last stitch, ch 1, turn.

Row 2: 2 sc in the 2nd stitch, * 2 sc in the 2nd stich, rep from *, ending row with 2 sc in last stitch, ch 2, turn.

6. Multiples of 5 plus 2.

Row 1: 1 sc in the 2nd ch and in each ch across the row.
Row 2: 1 sc in the 1st sc, * ch 2, work 1 3-ch picot, ch 2, 1 sc in the 5th sc, rep from *, ending row with sc, ch 1, turn.
Row 3: * sc in the sc, ch 3, work 3-ch picot, ch 3, rep from *, ending row with last sc.

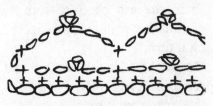

7. Multiples of 4 plus 2.

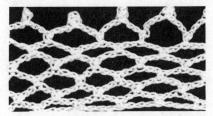

Row 1: Sc in 2nd ch, * ch 5, sc in the 4th ch, rep from *, ending row with last sc, ch 5, turn.
Row 2: * sc in 3rd ch, ch 5, rep from *, ending row with sc in last 5-ch, ch 2, dc in last sc, ch 1, turn.
Row 3: Sc in dc, * ch 5, sc in 3rd ch, rep from *, ending row with sc in last ch, ch 5 and turn.
Row 4: * Sc in the middle of the 5-ch, ch 5 rep from *, ending row with 2 chs and 1 dc in the last sc, ch 1, turn.
Row 5: * ch 5 and sc in the middle of the 5-ch, rep from *, ending row with sc in the last ch, ch 4, turn.
Row 6: * work 3-ch picot, ch 3, sc in the middle of the 5-ch, ch 3, rep from *, ending row with

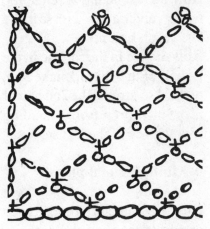

sc in the middle of the last 5-ch, ch 3 and dc in the last sc.

8. Multiples of 6 plus 2.

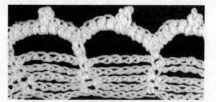

Row 1: Sc in the 2nd ch, * ch 5, sc in the 6th ch, rep from *, ending row with sc in the last ch, ch 1, turn.

Row 2: * sc in the sc, ch 5 and rep from *, ending row with sc in the last sc, ch 1, turn.

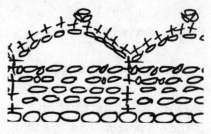

Row 3: * sc in the sc, ch 7, rep from *, ending row with sc in the last sc, ch 1, turn.

Row 4: * sc in the sc, ch 8, rep from * ending row with sc in the last sc, ch 1, turn.

Row 5: * sc in the sc, ch 9, rep from *, ending row with sc in the last sc, ch 1, turn.

Row 6: * sc in the sc, 5 sc in the lst half of the 9th-ch, make 3-ch picot, 4 sc around the 2nd part of the 9th-ch, rep from *, ending row with sc in the last sc.

9. Multiples of 8 plus 4.

Row 1: Sc in 2nd ch and in each ch across the row, ch 1, turn.

Row 2: Sc in lst sc and in each of next 2 sc, * ch 8, sc in 6th sc and in each of the next 2 sc, rep from *, ending row with sc in each of the last 3 sc, ch 1, turn.

Row 3: Sc in 1st sc and next sc, * make 3 sc around the beginning of the 8-ch, make a 3-ch picot, work 3 sc around the same 8-ch, make another 3-ch picot, work 3 sc around the same 8-ch, make a 3-ch picot, work 3 sc around the same 8-ch, work 1 sc in 2nd sc, rep from *, ending row with sc in each of the last 2 sc.

10. Multiples of 3 plus 1.

Row 1: 1 sc in 2nd ch, * ch 5, 1 sc in the 3rd ch, rep from *, ending row with 1 sc, ch 4, turn.

Row 2: 1 sc in the middle of the 5-ch, * ch 2, 1 sc in the middle of the 5-ch, rep from *, ending row with 1 ch and 1 dc, ch 1, turn.

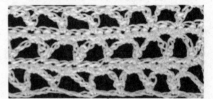

Row 3: 1 sc in dc, 1 sc in the 1-ch, * ch 2, 1 sc in the 2-ch, rep from *, ending row with 1 sc in the last ch, ch 5, turn.

Row 4: 1 sc in 2-ch, ch 5, rep from *, ending row with 2 chs and 1 dc, ch 1, turn.

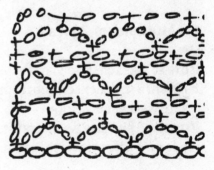

Row 5: 1 sc in dc, * ch 2, 1 sc in middle of the 5-ch, rep from *, ending row with 1 sc, ch 1, turn.

Row 6: 1 sc in 1st sc, ch 1, * 1 sc in 2-ch, ch 2, rep from * ending row with a sc, ch 1, turn.

11. Multiples of any number.

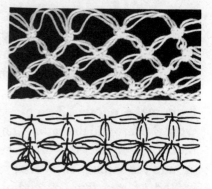

* draw a 1/4 inch loop on hook, yarn over and pull through ch, sc in single loop, sc in 1st ch, repeat from *, ending row with sc. To turn, pull another loop on hook, sc in center of loop, sc in middle of loop in first row.

12. Multiples of 2.

Row 1: Ch 1, 1 sc in 2nd ch, * 1 dc in next ch, 1 sc in next ch, repeat from * across row, ending with 1 dc in last ch, ch 1 turn.
Row 2: * 1 sc in next dc, 1 dc in next sc, Repeat from * across row, ch 1, turn.

13. Multiples of 2 plus 2.

Row 1: Sk 3 ch, 2 sc in next ch, * sk 1 ch, 2 sc in next ch, rep from * across row, ch 2, turn.
Row 2: * sk 1 st, 2 sc in next st, rep from * across row, ch 2, turn.

14. Multiples of 2 plus 2.

Row 1: Sk 2 ch, 1 sc in next ch *1 dc, 1 sc, rep from * across row, 1 dc, ch 2 turn.
Row 2: Sk 1st dc, * 1 dc in sc of 1st row, 1 sc in dc of 1st row, rep

from * across row, 1 dc in ch 2 of
1st row, ch 2, turn.

15. Multiples of 4 plus 1.

Row 1: Ch 3, (1 sc, ch3, 1 sc) in
4th ch from hk, picot made, * ch
5, sk 3 ch, 1 picot in next ch,
repeat from * across row, 1 sc in
last ch, ch 5, turn.

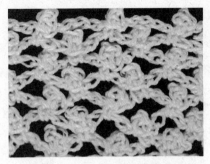

Row 2: Sk, 1 sc, 2 ch, * 1 picot in
next ch, ch 5, sk (2 ch, 1 picot, 2
ch), rep from *, ending with 1 sc
in last ch of prev row, ch 5, turn.
Repeat row 2 for pattern.

16. Multiples of 9.

Row 1: Ch 1, 1 sc in 2nd ch from
hk, 1 sc in each of the next 2 ch,
* ch 7, sk 2 ch, 1 sc in the next 7
chs, rep from * across row, ending with 1 sc in each of the last 4
chs, ch 1, turn.

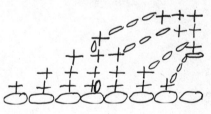

Row 2: Sk 1st sc, 1 sc in each of
the next 2 sc,* ch 3, sk 3 ch, 1 sc,
1 sc in the next 5 sc, rep from *
across row, ending with 1 sc in
the last 2 sc, ch 1, turn.

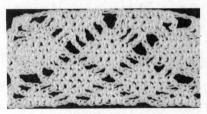

Row 3: Sk 1st sc, 1 sc in next sc,
* ch 3, sk 2 ch, 1 sc in next ch, 1
sc in next sc, 1 sc in next ch, ch 3,
sk 2 ch, 1 sc, 1 sc in each of the
next 3 sc, rep from * across row,
ending with 1 sc in last sc, ch 4,

turn.

Row 4: * Sk 1 sc, ch 2, 1 sc in the next ch, 1 sc in each of the next 3 sc, 1 sc in the next ch, ch 3, sk 2 ch, 1 sc, 1 sc in next sc, ch 3, rep from * across row, ending with 1 sc in last sc, ch 3, turn.

Row 5: * Sk 1 sc, 2 ch, 1 sc in next ch, 1 sc in each of next 5 sc, 1 sc in the next ch, ch 7, sk 2 ch, rep from * across row, ending with ch 3, 1 sc in 1st ch of last ch of the prev row, ch 4 turn.

Row 6: Sk 1 sc, ch 3, 1 sc, * 1 sc in the next 5 sc, ch 3, sk 1 sc, 3 ch, 1 sc in in the next ch of 7, ch 3, sk 3 ch, 1 sc, rep from * across row, ending with ch 3, 1 sc in last ch of prev row, ch 1, turn.

Row 7: 1 sc in 1st sc, 1 sc in 2nd ch, * ch 3, sk 2 ch, 1 sc, 1 sc in the next 3 sc, ch 3, sk 1 sc, 2 ch, 1 sc in each of next ch, 1 sc in the next sc, 1 sc in the next ch, rep from * across row, ending with ch 3, sk 1 sc, 2 ch, 1 sc in the last 2 chs, ch 1, turn.

Row 8: 1 sc in each of the 1st 2 sc, * 1 sc in the next ch, ch 3, sk 2 ch, 1 sc, 1 sc in the next sc, ch 3, sk 1 sc, 2 ch, 1 sc in next ch, 1 sc in the next 3 sc, rep from * across row, ending with 1 sc, in the last 2 sc, ch 1, turn.

Row 9: 1 sc in each of 1st 3 sc, sk ch 3, 1 sc, 2 ch, * ch 7, 1 sc in next ch , 1 sc in the next 5 sc, 1 sc in next ch, sk 2 ch, 1 sc, 2 ch, rep from * across row, ending with ch 7, 1 sc in next ch, 1 sc in the last 3 sc, ch 1, turn.

Repeat rows 2-9 for pattern.

Chapter III

Chain, Picot, Single and Half-Double Crochet

1. Multiples of any number

Row l: Ch 2, 1 hdc in 3rd ch from hook,* 1 hdc in next ch, repeat from *, across row, ch 2 turn.
Row 2: Crochet 1 hdc across row, ch 2, turn.
Repeat for desired size.

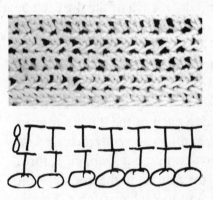

2. Multiples of 3 plus 2.

Row 1: 1 hdc in 4th ch from hk, * ch 1, skip 1 ch, 1 hdc in next ch, repeat from *, across row, ch 3 turn.
Row 2: * Skip 1 hdc, 1 hdc in next ch-1 st, ch 1, repeat from * across row, ending with 1 hdc in last ch of row, ch 3, turn.
Repeat for pattern.

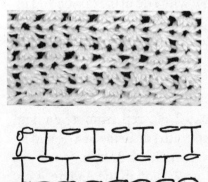

3. Multiples of 15 plus 3.

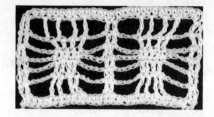

Row 1: 1 hdc in the 5th ch and in each st across the row, ch 3, turn.
Row 2: 1 dc in the 2nd hdc * ch 3, 1 trc in the 4th hdc, ch 1, 1 trc in the 2nd hdc, ch 1, 1 trc in the 2nd hdc, ch 3, 1 dc in the 4th hdc and the next hdc, rep from *, ending row with 2 dc in the last ch, turn.
Row 3: 1 dc in the 2nd dc, * ch 5, 1 dc in each of the 4 trc, ch 5, 1 dc in each of the 2 dc, rep from *, ending row with 1 dc in the last dc and 1 in the last ch, ch 3, turn.

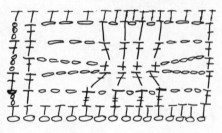

Row 4: 1 dc in the 2nd dc, * ch 5, 1 sc in each of the 4 dc, ch 5, 1 dc in each of the 2 dc, rep from *, ending row with 1 dc in the last dc and in the last ch, ch 3, turn.
Row 5: 1 dc in the 2nd dc, * ch 5, 1 sc in each 4 sc, ch 5, 1 dc in each 2 dc, rep from *, ending row with 1 dc in the last dc and in the last ch, ch 3, turn.
Row 6: 1 dc in the 2nd dc, * ch 3, 1 dc in the 1st sc, ch 1, dc in the next sc, ch 1, dc in the next sc, ch 1, 1 dc in the sc, ch 3, 1 dc in the next 2 dc, rep from *, ending row with 1 dc in the last dc and in the last ch, ch 3, turn.
Row 7: 1 dc in the 2nd dc, * ch 3, 1 trc in the dc, ch 1, trc in the dc, ch 1, trc in the next dc, ch 1, trc in the next dc, ch 3, 1 dc in the next 2 dc, rep from *, ending row with 1 dc in the last dc and in the last ch, ch 3, turn.
Row 8: Repeat row 1 except make 1 hdc in each ch across the row.

Repeat for pattern.

4. Multiples of 2.

Row 1: 1 sc in the 2nd ch and across row, ch 1, turn.
Rows 2 & 3: Same as row 1.
Row 4: 1 hdc in 3rd sc, * ch 1, 1 hdc in 2nd sc, rep from *, ending row with 1 hdc, ch 1, turn.

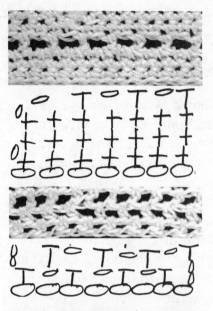

5. Multiples of 2.

Row 1: * 2 hdc in 2nd ch, skip 1, repeat from *, ending with 2 hdc in last ch, ch 2, turn. Repeat for desired size.

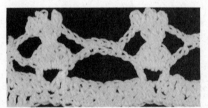

6. Multiples of 10 plus 4.

Row 1: Dc in 4th ch from hk and across ch, ch 1, turn.
Row 2: 1 hdc in 1st dc and in next 3 dc, * ch 6, hdc in next 10 dc, rep from *, ending row with hdc in last dc, ch 6, turn.
Row 3: Sc in the 6th ch, in the same 6 ch, * 1 sc, 1 hdc, 1 dc, 2 trc, 1 dc, 1 hdc, 1 sc, ch 8 and rep from *, ending row in last 6 ch, ch 3, dc in last ch, ch 1, turn.
Row 4: Sc in the dc,* ch 3, dc in the 3rd dc, ch and dc in the same dc, ch 3, dc in the same dc, ch 3, sc in the 1st part of the 8-ch, ch 3, and sc in the last part of the 8-ch, rep *, ending row with sc in the

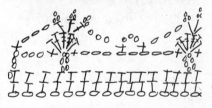

last ch.
Repeat for pattern.

7. Multiples of 2 plus 1.

Row 1: Sk 1 ch, * 1 sc in each ch, rep from * across row, ch 1, turn.
Row 2: 1 hdc, * sk 1 st, 1 hdc in next st, 1 hdc between the 2 preceding hdc, rep from * across row, sk 1 st, 1 hdc in ch at start of row, ch 1, turn.
Row 3: * 1 sc, insert hook through front loop of each st in prev row, rep from * across row, ch 1, turn.
Repeat row 2.

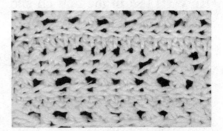

8. Multiples of 8 plus 5.

Row 1: Ch 1, 1 sc in 2nd ch from hk, * 1 sc in next ch, rep from * across row, ch 3, turn.
Row 2: 1 hdc in each of next 5 sc, * ch 1, sk 1 sc, 1 hdc in next sc, ch 1, sk 1 sc, 1 hdc in each of next 5 sc, rep from * across row, ch 1, turn.
Row 3: 1 sc in each hdc and each ch-1 sp across row, ch 4, turn.
Row 4: Sk 2 sc, 1 hdc in next sc, * ch 1, sk 1 sc, 1 hdc in each of the next 5 sc, ch 1, sk 1 sc, 1 hdc in next sc, rep from * across row, end with ch 1, sk 1 sc, 1 hdc in last sc, ch 1, turn.

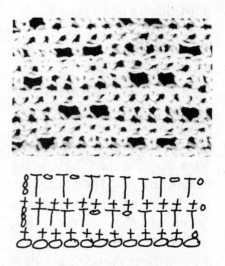

Row 5: 1 sc in each hdc and ch-1 sp across row, end with 2 sc in the last ch of prev row, ch 3, turn.
Repeat rows 2-5 for pattern.

Chapter IV

Double Crochet

1. Multiples of any number.

Row 1: Ch 2, 1 dc in 3rd ch from hook, * 1 dc in next ch, repeat from * across row, ch 2 , turn.
Row 2: 1 dc in each st across row, ch 2, turn.
Repeat for pattern.

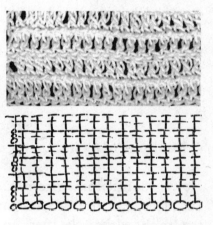

2. Multiples of 2 plus 6.

Row 1: 1 dc in the 5th ch, * ch 1, 1 dc in the 2nd ch, rep from *, ending row with last dc, ch 4, turn.
Repeat pattern. Can use in filet crochet.

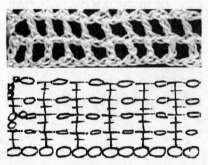

3. Multiples of 3 plus 4.

Row 1: 1 dc in the 5th ch and in each ch across the row, ch 4, turn.

Row 2: 1 dc in the 3rd dc, * ch 1, 1 dc in the 2nd dc, rep from *, ending row with 1 ch and 1 dc in the last ch, ch 3, turn.

Row 3: 1 dc in each ch and in each dc across the row, ch 3, turn.

Row 4: 1 dc in the 2nd and 3rd dc, * ch 1, 1 dc in the 2nd dc and the next 2 dc, rep from *, ending row with 1 dc in the last ch, ch 3, turn.

Repeat pattern by using rows 1-4.

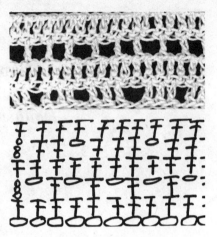

4. Multiples of 6 plus 2.

Row 1: 1 dc in the 5th ch from hk, 1 dc in the next ch, * ch 3, 1 dc in the 4th ch and the 2 chs after, rep from *, ending row with 3 chs, and 1 dc in the last ch, ch 3, turn.

Row 2: 3 dc in 3-ch space, * ch 3, 3 dc in the next 3-ch space, rep from *, ending row with 3 ch-5 and 1 dc in the last ch, ch 3, turn.

Repeat pattern by using rows 1-2

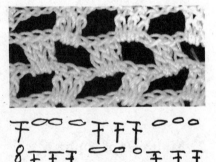

5. Multiples of 6 plus 3.

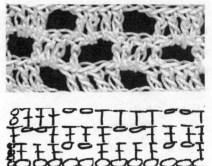

Row 1: Dc in 5th ch from hk, 3 dc in the 1st 3 chs,* sk 2, ch 2, 4 dc in the next 4 chs, rep from *, end with 1 dc in last ch, ch 3, turn.

Row 2: Ch 5, * dc in 1st dc of the prev row, 2 dc in 2 ch space of prev row, rep from * ending with 1 dc in the last ch, ch 3, turn. Repeat row 2 for pattern.

6. Multiples of 3 plus.

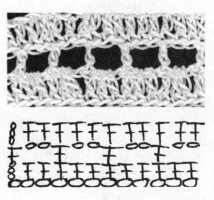

Row 1: Dc in the 5th ch and in each ch across the row, ch 5, turn.

Row 2: Dc in the 4th dc, * ch 2 and dc in the 3rd dc, rep from *, ending row with dc in the last ch, ch 3, turn.

Row 3: Dc in each ch and in each dc across the row. Repeat rows 2-3 for pattern.

7. Multiples of 9 plus 4.

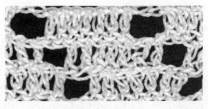

Row 1: Dc in the 5 ch and the next ch, * ch 2, dc in the 3rd ch, dc in each of the next 6 chs, rep from *, ending row with 1 dc in each of the last 5 chs, ch 3, turn.

Row 2: 1 dc in the 2nd dc, * dc in each of the next 3 dc, dc in each of the next 2-ch, ch 2, dc in the 3rd dc and the next dc, rep from *, ending row with 2 chs and 1 dc in the last ch, ch 3, turn.

Row 3: * dc in each of the 2-ch, dc in each of the next 5 dc, ch 2, rep from *, ending row with 1 ch and 1 dc in the last ch, ch 3, turn.

Row 4: Dc in the 1-ch, * ch 2, dc in the 3rd dc and dc in each of the next 4 dc, dc in each of the next 2-chs, rep from *, ending row with 6 dc, the last in the last ch.

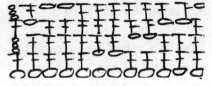

8. Multiples of 3 plus 1.

Row 1: Ch 2, (1 dc, ch 3, 1 dc) in 3rd ch from hook, * sk 2 ch, (1 dc, ch 3, 1 dc) in the next ch, repeat from * across row, ch 2, turn.

Row 2: * (1 dc, ch 3, 1 dc) in next ch 3 sp, repeat from * across row, ch 2 turn.

Repeat row 2 for pattern.

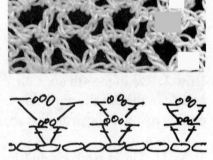

9. Multiples of 20 plus 4

Row 1: 1 dc in the 5th ch and the 8 chs after, * ch 4, 1 dc in the 5th ch, ch 4, 1 dc in the 5th ch and the 9 chs after, rep from *, ending row with 4 chs and 1 dc in the 5th and last ch, ch 1, turn.

Row 2: 1 sc in the dc, ch 4, * 1 dc in each of the 1st-4 dc, ch 2, dc in

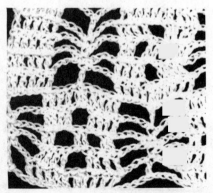

the 3rd dc and the 3 dc after, ch 4, 1 sc in the dc, ch 4, rep from *, ending row with 3 dc and 1 in the last ch, ch 3, turn.

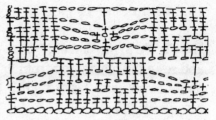

Row 3: 1 dc in the 2nd dc, ch 2, 1 dc in each of the 2-chs, ch 2, 1 dc in the 3rd dc and the dc after, * ch 4, 1 sc in the last of the 4-chs, ch 1, 1 sc in the lst of the 4-chs, ch 4, 1 dc in each of the lst 2 dc, ch 2, 1 dc in each of the 2-chs, ch 2, 1 dc in the 3rd dc and the dc after, rep from *, ending row with sc in the sc, ch 1, turn.

Row 4: Sc in the sc, ch 4, * 1 dc in each of the 2 dc, 1 dc in each of the 2-chs, ch 2, 1 dc in each of the 2-chs, 1 dc in each of the 2 dc, ch 4, 1 sc in the 1-ch, ch 4 and rep from *, ending row with 1 dc in the last ch, ch 3, turn.

Row 5: 1 dc in the 2nd dc and the next 2 dc, 1 in each of the 2-chs, 1 in each of the 4 dc, * ch 4, 1 dc in the sc, ch 4, 1 dc in each of the 4 dc, 1 in each of the 2-chs and 1 in each of the 4 dc, rep from *, ending row with 1 dc in the sc, ch 3, turn.

Row 6: 5 dc in the 4-ch, * ch 4, 1 dc in the 5th dc, ch 4, 5 dc in the 4-ch, 5 dc in the next 4-ch, rep from *, ending row with 1 dc in the last ch, ch 7, turn.

Row 7: Sk lst dc, 1 sc in the dc, ch 4, * 1 dc in each of the next 4 dc, ch 2, 1 dc in the 3rd dc and the 3 dc after, ch 4, 1 sc in the dc, ch 4 and rep from *, ending row with 1 dc in the last ch, ch 3, turn.

Row 8: 1 dc in the 2nd dc and the 4 dc after, * ch 4, 1 sc in the end of the 4-ch, ch 1, 1 sc in the lst of the 4-ch, ch 4, 1 dc in the dc and the next, ch 2, 1 dc in each of the 2-chs, ch 2, 1 dc in the 3rd dc and the next dc, rep from *, ending row with 1 dc in the last ch, ch 7, turn.

Row 9: 1 sc in the 1-ch, ch 4, * 1 dc in each of the 2 dc, 1 dc in each of the 2-chs, ch 2, 1 dc in each of the 2-chs, 1 dc in each of the 2 dc, ch 4, 1 sc in the 1-ch, ch 4, rep from *, ending row with 1 ch and 1 dc in the last ch, ch 3, turn.

Row 10: 1 dc in the 1-ch and 1 dc in each of the 4 dc, * ch 4, 1 dc in each of the 4 dc, 1 dc in each of the 2-chs, 1 dc in each of the 4 dc, rep from *, ending row with 1 dc in the last ch.

Repeat pattern by rows 1-10.

10. Multiples of 12 plus 2.

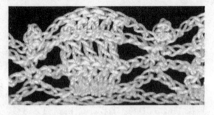

Row l: Sc in the 2nd ch, * ch 5, and sc in the 6th ch, rep from *, ending row with last sc, ch 3, turn.

Row 2: * 5 dc in the 5-ch, ch 3, sc in the middle of the next 5-ch, ch 3, rep from *, ending row with 5 dc and l dc in the last sc, ch 3, turn.

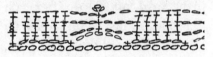

Row 3: Sk l dc, * dc in the next 5 dc, ch 3, sc in the next sc, ch 3, rep from *, ending row with 5 dc and l dc in the last ch, ch 3, turn.

Row 4: Sk lst dc, * dc in each of the next dc, ch 3, sc in the next sc, make 3-ch picot, ch 3, rep from *, ending row with 5 dc and l dc in the last ch.

11. Multiples of 5 plus 4.

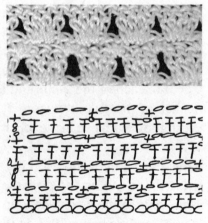

Row l: l dc in the 5th ch and l dc in the next 3 chs, * ch 1, l dc in the 2nd ch and dc in the next 3 chs, repeat from *, ending row with last set and l dc, ch 1, turn.

Row 2: l sc between the lst and the 2nd dc, * ch 4, l sc in the l-ch, rep from *, ending row with l sc in the last ch, ch 3, turn.

Repeat pattern by rows 1-2.

12. Multiples of 10 plus 7.

Row 1: 1 dc in the 11th ch, * 1 dc in the next 2 chs, ch 3, 1 dc in the 4th ch, ch 3, 1 dc in the 4th ch, rep from *, ending row with 3 chs, 1 dc, ch 5, turn.

Row 2: * 1 dc in the 3rd ch, 1 dc in each of the next 3 dc, 1 dc in next ch, ch 5, rep from *, ending row with 2 chs, 1 dc in the last ch, ch 3, turn.

Row 3: Sk 1 dc, * 1 dc in the 2nd dc and the next 2 dc, ch 3, 1 dc in the 3rd ch of the 5-chs, ch 3, rep from *, ending row with 3 chs and 1 dc in the last ch, ch 3, turn.

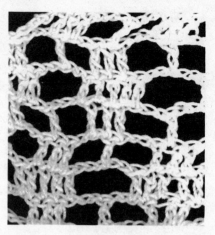

Row 4: 1 dc in the 2nd ch, * ch 3, 1 dc in the 2nd dc, ch 3, 1 dc in 3rd ch, 1 dc in the dc, 1 dc in the 1st ch after the dc, rep from *, ending row with 2 dc in the last ch, ch 3, turn.

Row 5: 1 dc in the 2nd dc, * 1 dc in the ch after the dc, * ch 5, 1 dc in the last ch before the dc and the 3 dc, and in the 1st ch after the 3 dc, rep from *, ending row with 1 dc in the last ch before the dc and in the last ch, ch 3, turn.

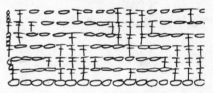

Row 6: 1 dc in the 2nd dc, * ch 3, 1 dc in the 3rd ch of the 5-chs, ch 3, 1 dc in the 2nd dc and the next 2 dc, rep from *, ending row in 2 dc, ch 6, turn.

Repeat pattern by rows 1-6.

13. Multiples of 9 plus 6.

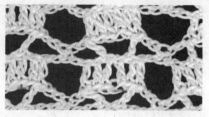

Row 1: 1 dc in 9th ch, * 1 dc in the next 5 chs, ch 5, 1 dc in 4th ch, rep from *, ending row with 2 chs and 1 dc in the last ch, ch 1, turn.
Row 2: 1 sc in the 1st dc, * ch 3, 1 dc in the 1st dc, ch 1, 1 dc in the 5th dc, ch 3, 1 sc in the 3rd ch of the 5-ch, rep from *, ending row.
Row 3: Same as row 1.
Repeat pattern by rows 1-2.

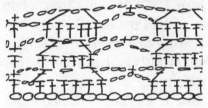

14. Multiples of 8 plus 5.

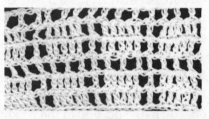

Row 1: 1 dc in the 7th ch,* ch 1, 1 dc in the 2nd ch, rep from * across row, ch 4 turn.
Row 2: 1 dc in the 2nd dc, ch 1, * 1 dc in the dc, 1 dc in the ch, dc in the dc, 1 dc in the ch, dc in the dc, ch 1, dc in the next dc, ch 1, rep *, ending row with 1 dc in the last ch, ch 4, turn.
Row 3: Same as row 2.
Row 4: Same as row 1.
Repeat pattern by rows 1-4.

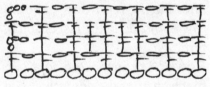

15. Multiples of 34 plus 4.

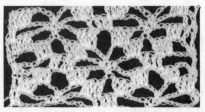

Row 1: 1 dc in the 5th ch, * ch 5, 1 sc in the 6th ch and in the 2 chs after, ch 5, 1 dc in the 6th ch and in the 3 chs after, rep from *, ending row with 2 dc in the last

2 chs, ch 3, turn.

Row 2: 1 dc in the 2nd dc and 3 dc in the ch after, * ch 4, 1 sc in the 2nd sc, ch 4, 3 dc in the last ch, 1 dc in the 1st dc, ch 3, 1 dc in the 3rd dc and 3 dc in the 1st ch, rep from *, ending row with 3 dc in the ch and 1 dc in the last ch, ch 1, turn.

Row 3: 1 sc in the 1st dc, * ch 4, 1 dc in the 4th dc of the group, 3 dc in the 1st ch, ch 2, 3 dc in the last ch before the 4 dc, 1 dc in the 1st dc, ch 4, 1 sc in the 3-ch, rep from *, ending row with 4 chs and 1 sc in the last ch, ch 8, turn.

Row 4: * 4 dc in the 2-ch, ch 5, 1 sc in the last of the 4-ch, 1 sc in the sc, 1 sc in the 1st of the next group of 4-ch, ch 5, rep from *, ending row with 1 dc in the sc, ch 1, turn.

Row 5: 1 sc in the dc, * ch 4, 3 dc in the last part of the 5-ch, 1 dc in the 1st dc, ch 3, 1 dc in the 3rd dc and 3 dc in the 1st part of the next 5 ch, ch 4, 1 sc in the 2nd sc rep from *, ending row with 4 chs and 1 sc in the last ch, ch 5, turn.

Row 6: * 3 dc in the last part of the 4-ch, 1 dc in the 1st dc, ch 4, 1 sc in the 3-ch, ch 4, 1 dc in the last of the next group of dc, 3 dc in the 1st part of the 4-ch, ch 2, rep

from *, ending row with 4 dc and 1 trc in the last ch, ch 3, turn.
Repeat pattern by rows 1-6.

16. Multiples of 24 plus 5.

Row 1: 1 dc in the 5th ch, ch 1, 1 dc in the 2nd ch, rep from * ending row with dc in the last ch, ch 4, turn.

Row 2: Sk 1 dc, dc in the next dc, ch 1 and dc in the next 6 dc, 1 dc in the 1-ch, dc in the next dc, ch 1 and dc in the 6 dc, ch 1 and dc in the last ch, ch 4, turn.

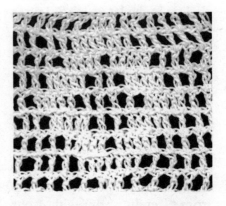

Row 3: Sk 1st dc, dc in the dc, ch 1 and dc in each of the 5 dc, dc in the 1-ch, dc in the dc, ch 3, dc in the 2nd dc, dc in the 1-ch, dc in ch 1, and dc in the 5 dc, ch 1, and dc in the last ch, ch 4, turn.

Row 4: Sk the 1st dc, dc in the dc, ch 1 and dc in the 4 dc, dc in the 1-ch and in the next dc, ch 3, sc in the 3-ch, ch 3, dc in the 3rd dc, dc in the 1-ch and the next dc, ch 1 and dc in the 4 dc, ch 1 and dc in the last ch, ch 4, turn.

Row 5: Sk 1st dc, dc in the next dc, ch 1, dc in the 3 dc, dc in the 1-ch, dc in the dc, ch 4, sc in the last of the 3-ch, sc in sc, sc in 1st sc, ch 4, dc in the 3rd dc, dc in the 1-ch, dc in the dc, ch 1, dc in the last ch, ch 4, turn.

Row 6: Sk 1st dc, dc in the dc, ch 1 and dc in the 1-ch, dc in dc, ch 4, sc in the last 4-ch, sc in each of the 3 sc, sc in the 1st of the 4-ch, ch 4, dc in the 3rd dc, dc in the 1-ch, dc in the dc, ch 1 and dc in the 2 dc, ch 1 and dc in the last ch, ch 4, turn.

Row 7: Sk 1st dc, dc in the dc, ch 1 and dc in the 2 dc, 1 dc in each of the 1st 2 chs, ch 4, sc in the 2nd sc and the next 2 sc, ch 4, 1 dc in each of the last 2 chs, dc in the dc, ch 1 and dc in the 2nd dc, ch 1 and dc in the 2 dc, ch 1, and dc in the last ch, ch 4, turn.

Row 8: Sk 1st dc, dc in the dc, ch 1 and dc in the 3 dc, ch 1, dc in the 2nd dc, 1 dc in each of the next 2 chs, ch 3, sc in the 2nd sc, ch 3, l dc in each of the last 2 chs, dc in the dc, ch l, dc in the 2nd dc, ch l, dc in the 3 d, ch 1, 1 dc in the last ch, ch 4, turn.

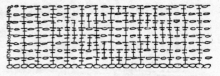

Row 9: Sk l dc, dc in the dc, ch l and dc in the 4 dc, ch l and dc in the 2nd dc, l dc in each of the lst 2 chs, ch 1, l dc in each of the last 2 chs, dc in the dc, ch l, dc in the 2nd dc, ch l and dc in the 4 dc, ch l, dc in the last ch, ch 4, turn.

Row 10: Sk lst dc, dc in the 2nd dc, ch l and dc in the 5 dc, ch1 and dc in the 2nd dc, dc in the l-ch, dc in the dc, ch l, dc in the 2nd dc, ch l and dc in the 5 dc, ch l and dc in the last ch, ch 4, turn.

Row ll: Sk lst dc, dc in the dc, ch l and dc in the 6 dc, ch l and dc in the 2nd dc, ch l and dc in the 6 dc, ch l and dc in the last ch, ch 4, turn.

Row 12: Sk lst dc, dc in the dc, dc in the l-ch, dc in the dc, ch l, and dc in the 11 dcs, dc in the l-ch, dc in the dc, ch l and dc in the last ch, ch 3, turn.

Row 13: Sk lst dc, dc in the l-ch, dc in the dc, ch 3, dc in the 2nd dc, dc in the l-ch, dc in the dc, ch l and dc in the 9 dc, dc in the l-ch, dc in the dc, ch 3, dc in the 2nd dc and 2 dc in the last ch.

Repeat pattern by rows 1-ll.

17. Multiples of 4 plus 1.

Row 1: Ch 2, work (sc, 3 ch, sc) 1 picot, * ch 5, 1 dc, 1 picot, rep from * across row, ch 7, turn.
Row 2: * 1 dc, 1 picot, ch 5, rep from * across row.
Repeat rows 1-2 for pattern.

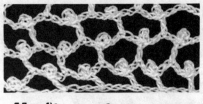

18. Multiples 4 plus 2.

Row 1: Sc in the 2nd ch and each ch across the row, ch 5, turn.
Row 2: Dc in the 3rd sc, * ch 1, dc in the 2nd sc, rep from *, ending row with dc in the last sc, ch 1, turn.
Row 3: Sc in the dc, * ch 5, sc in the 2nd dc, rep from *, ending row with 1 sc in last ch, ch 6, turn.
Row 4: * Sc in 3rd ch, ch 5, rep from *, ending row with last sc, ch 2, dc in the last sc, ch 1, turn.
Row 5: Sc in the dc, * ch 5, sc around the middle of the next 5-ch, repeat from * across row, ending with sc in the last ch, ch 1, turn.
Row 6: * Sc in the sc, make 1 hdc, 3 dc, 1 hdc in the 5-ch, rep from * , ending row with sc in the last sc.

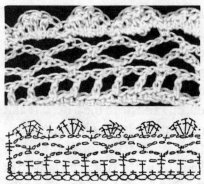

19. Multiples of 24 plus 4.

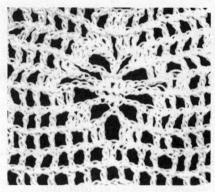

Row 1: 1 dc in the 7th ch, ch 1, 1 dc in the 2nd ch 6 times, 1 dc in the next 2 chs, ch 1, 1 dc in the 2nd ch 7 times, ch 4, turn.

Row 2: 1 dc in the 2nd dc, ch 1, 1 dc in the dc 5 times, 1 dc in the ch, 1 dc in each of the next 3 dc, 1 dc in the next 1-ch and in the dc, ch 1, 1 dc in the next dc 5 times, ch 1, 1 dc in the next dc 5 times, ch 1, 1 dc in the last ch, ch 4, turn.

Row 3: Sk 1st dc, dc in the next dc, ch 1 and dc in the dc 4 times, 1 dc in the 1-ch, 1 dc in each of the 3 dc, ch 1, 1 dc in the 2nd dc, 1 dc in each of the next 2 dc, dc in the 1-ch, dc in the dc, ch 1 and dc in the dc 4 times, ch 1 and dc in the last ch, ch 4, turn.

Row 4: 1 dc in the 2nd dc, ch 1, dc in the dc 3 times, dc in the 1-ch, 1 dc in each of the 3 dc, ch 1, dc in the 2nd dc, ch 1, dc in the dc, ch 1, dc 2nd dc, dc in the next 2 dc, dc in the 1-ch and the dc after, ch 1 and dc in the dc 3 times, ch 1 and dc in the last ch, ch 4, turn.

Row 5: Sk 1st dc, dc in the next dc, ch 1, dc in the dc, ch 1, dc in the dc, 1 dc in the 1-ch, 1 dc in each of the 3 dc, ch 1, 1 dc in the 2nd dc, ch 1 and dc in the dc 3 times, ch 1, dc in the 2nd dc, dc in the next 2 dc, dc in the 1-ch, dc in the dc, ch 1, dc in the dc, ch 1, dc in the dc, ch 1, dc in the last ch, ch 4, turn.

Row 6: Sk 1 dc, dc in dc, ch 1, 2 times, ch 1, dc in 2nd dc, and in next 2 dc, dc in 1-ch, dc in dc, ch 1, dc in dc 3 times, dc in 1-ch, dc in each of next 3 dc, ch 1, dc in 2nd dc, ch 1, dc in dc 2 times, ch 1, dc in last ch, ch 4, turn.

Row 7: Sk 1st dc, dc in the dc, ch 1 and dc in the dc 3 times, ch 1, 1 dc in the 2nd dc, 1 dc in each of the next 2 dc, dc in the 1-ch, dc in the dc, ch 1, dc in the next dc, dc in the 1-ch, 1 dc in each of the 3 dc, ch 1, dc in the 2nd dc, ch 1, dc in the dc 3 times, ch 1, dc in the last ch, ch 4, turn.

Row 8: Sk 1 dc, dc in the dc, ch 1 and dc in the dc 4 times, ch 1 and dc in the 2nd dc, 1 dc in each of the next 2 dc, dc in the 1-ch, 1 dc in each of the next 3 dc, ch 1 and dc in the 2nd dc, ch 1 and dc in the dc 4 times, ch 1, dc in the last ch, ch 4, turn.

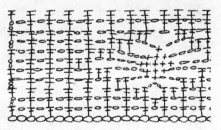

Row 9: Sk 1 dc, dc in the dc, ch 1 and dc in the dc 5 times, ch 1, dc in the 2nd dc, dc in each of the next 2 dc, ch 1, dc in the 2nd dc, ch 1, dc in the dc 5 times, ch 1, dc in the last ch.

Repeat pattern by rows 1-9.

20. Multiples of 18 plus 6.

Row 1: 1 dc in the 8th ch, * ch 2, 1 dc in the 3rd ch, ch 2, 1 dc in each of the following 9 chs, ch 2, 1 dc in the 3rd ch, rep from *, ending row with 10 dc, ch 3, turn.

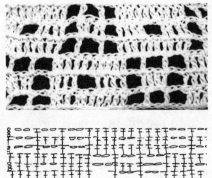

Row 2: 1 dc in the 2nd dc and the 2 dc after, * ch 2, 1 dc in the 3 dc, and the 3rd after, ch 2, 1 dc in the dc, 1 dc in each of the 2-chs, 1 dc in the dc, ch 2, 1 dc in the next dc and the 3 dc after, rep from *, ending row with 1 dc in the last ch, ch 5, turn.

Row 3: Sk 1 dc, * dc in the dc, ch 2, 1 dc in the 3rd dc, ch 2, 1 dc in the next dc and the 3 dc after, 1 dc in each of the 2 chs, 1 dc in each of the next 4 dc, ch 2, rep from *, ending row with 1 dc in the last ch, ch 5, turn.

Row 4: 1 dc in the 4th dc, * ch 2, 1 dc in the 3rd dc, ch 2, 1 dc in the 3rd dc, 1 dc in each of the next 2 chs, 1 dc in the dc, 1 dc in the 2 chs, 1 dc in the dc, 1 dc in the 2 chs and the next dc, ch 2, 1 dc in the 3rd dc, rep from *, ending row with 3 dc in the last ch, ch 3, turn.

Row 5: 1 dc in the 2nd dc and the next 2 dc, * ch 2, 1 dc in the 3rd dc and the 3 dc after, ch 2, 1 dc in the dc, 1 dc in each of the 2 chs, dc in the dc, ch 2, dc in the dc, and 1 in each of the 3 dc, rep from *, ending row with 1 dc in the last ch, ch 5, turn.

Row 6: Sk the 1st dc, * dc in the next dc, ch 2, 1 dc in the 3rd dc, ch 2, 1 dc in each of the next 4 dc, 1 dc in the 2-ch, 1 dc in each of the next 4 dc, ch 2, rep from *, ending row with 1 dc in the last ch.

Repeat rows 1-6 for pattern.

21. Multiples 10 plus 6.

Row 1: Sk 2 ch, 4 sc, * 5 dc, 5 sc, rep from * across row, ch 3, turn.
Row 2: Sk 1st st, 4 dc, * 5 dc, 5 sc, rep from * across row, make

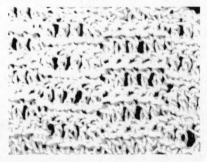

last dc in top of ch at beg of prev row, ch 2, turn.

Row 3: Sk lst st, 4 sc, * 5 dc, 5 sc, rep from * across row, make last sc in top of last ch, ch 3, turn.

Repeat from row 2 for pattern.

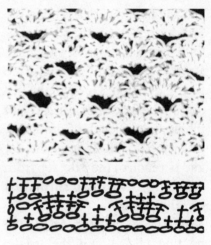

22. Multiples of 6 plus 8.

Row l: Sk 1 ch, 1 sc in each of the next 2 ch, * ch 3, sk 3 ch, 1 sc in each of the next 3 ch, rep from * across row, ch 3, sk 3 ch, 1 sc in each of last 2 chs, ch 1, turn.

Row 2: 1 sc in 2nd sc, * 1 dc in 3-ch sp, 1 sc in 2nd sc of 3-sc group, rep from * across row, turn.

Row 3: * ch 3, 1 sc in each of 3 center dc, rep from * across row, ch 2, 1 sc in last ch, ch 3, turn.

Row 4: 2 dc in 2-ch sp, * 1 sc in 2nd sc, 5 dc in 3-ch sp, rep from * across row, 1 sc in 2nd sc, 3 dc in 3-ch sp, ch 1, turn.

Row 5: 1 sc in each of lst 2 dc,* ch 3, 1 sc in each of the 3 center dc, rep from * across row, ch 3, 1 sc in last dc, 1 sc in last ch, ch 1, turn.

Repeat from row 2.

23. Multiples of 4 plus 6.

Row 1: Sk 3 ch, * 2 dc in next 2 ch, (1 dc, ch 3, 1 dc) in next ch, sk 1 ch, rep from * across row, 3 dc in last 3 ch, ch 3, turn.

Row 2: * (3 dc, ch 3, 1 sc) in each 3 ch sp, rep from * across row, 1 dc between last group of 3 dc and 1 in last ch, ch 3, turn.

Repeat from row 2.

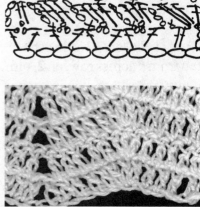

24. Multiples of 13.

Row 1: Sk 3 ch, 4 dc in next 4 ch, 3 dc in next ch, 5 dc in next 5 ch, * sk 2 ch, 5 dc in next 5 ch, 3 dc in next ch, 5 dc in next 5 ch, rep from * across row, ch 3, turn.

Row 2: Sk 1st st, 4 dc in next 4 sts, 3 dc in next st, 5 dc in next 5 sts, * sk 2 sts, 5 dc in next 5 sts, rep from * , ending with 4 dc, in the last group sk 1 dc, 1 dc in last ch, ch 3, turn.

Repeat from row 2.

25. Multiples of 2 plus 2.

Row 1: Sk 2 ch, 1 dc st (insert hook in ch, yo, pull through loop, insert hook in next ch, yo, pull through loop, yo and pull through all 3 loops), * 1 dc, insert hook 1st where 2nd yo was for

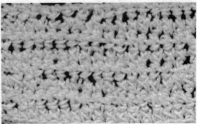

prev dc, rep from * across row, ch 2, turn.

Row 2: * 1 dc in each pair of sts, rep from * across row, 1 dc inserting hk in last ch and top of ch at beg, ch 2, turn.

Repeat row 2 for pattern.

26. Multiples of 4 plus l.

Row 1: Sk 1 ch, * 1 sc in each ch, rep from * across row, ch 2, turn.

Row 2: * sk 1 st, 1 dc in each of the next 3 sts, insert hk in last skipped st, yo and pull yarn through the loop, yo and pull through 2 loops, rep from * across row, 1 dc in last st, ch 1, turn.

Row 3: Sk 1 st, * 1 sc in each st, rep from * across row, 1 sc in last ch, ch 2, turn.

Repeat row 2

27. Multiples of 3 plus 2.

Row l: Sk 6 ch, 1 dc in next ch, ch 1, 1 dc in 4th ch from beg, cross over the 1st dc, * sk 2 ch, 1 dc, ch 1, 1 dc in 1st of the skipped ch, rep from * across row, 1 dc in the last ch, ch 4, turn.

Row 2: Sk 2 dc, 1 dc in next dc, ch 1, 1 dc in last skipped dc, * sk 1 dc, dc in next dc, ch 1, 1 dc in

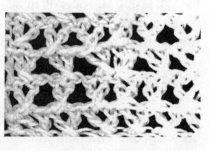

skipped dc, rep from * across row, 1 dc in 3rd ch of last ch, ch 4, turn.
Repeat row 2.

28. Multiples of 12 plus 4.

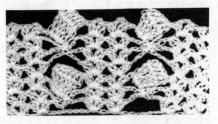

Row 1: 2 dc in the 4th ch, * ch 8, 2 dc in the 12th ch, ch 2, 2 dc in the same ch, rep from *, ending row with 3 dc in the last ch, ch 3, turn.

Row 2: 2 dc in the 1st dc, * ch 4, 1 sc worked around the middle of the 2 chs below, ch 4, 2 dc in the 2-ch, 2 dc in the 2-ch, rep from *, ending row with 3 dc in the last ch, ch 3, turn.

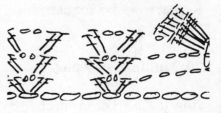

Row 3: 2 dc in the 1st dc, * ch 5, 1 sc in the sc, ch 3, work 5 dc around the 5-ch, ch 3, turn, 1 dc in the 2nd dc, 1 dc in the 3 dc after, 1 dc in the turning ch, 2 dc in 2-ch, ch 2, 2 dc in the same 2-ch, rep from *, ending row after the last group with 3 dc in the last ch, ch 3, turn.

Row 4: 2 dc in the 1st dc, * ch 8, 2 dc in the 2-ch, ch 2, 2 dc in the same 2-ch, rep from *, ending row with 3 dc in the last ch, ch 3, turn.

Row 5: 2 dc in the 1st dc, * ch 8, 2 dc in the 2-ch, 2 dc in the same 2-ch, rep from *, ending row with 3 dc in the last ch, ch 3, turn.

Row 6: 2 dc in the lst dc, * ch 5, 1 sc around the middle of the 2 chs below, ch 3, 5 dc around the 5-ch, ch 3, 1 dc in the 2nd dc, the next 3 dc and 1 in the turning ch, 2 dc in the 2-ch, ch 3, rep from * across row, dc in the last ch, ch 3, turn.

Rows 7 and 8: Same as row 1. Repeat rows 1-8 for pattern.

29. Multiples of 9 plus.

Row 1: Ch 3, 1 dc in 4th ch from hk, 1 dc in the next 2 ch, * ch 5, sk 4 ch, 1 dc in the next 5 chs, rep from * across row, ending with 1 dc in each of the last 4 chs, ch 3, turn.

Row 2: 1 dc in the next 2 dc, sk 2 dc, * ch 3, 1 dc in ch-5 sp, ch 3, sk 1 dc, 1 dc in each of the next 3 dc, sk 1 dc, rep from * across row, ending with sk 1 dc, 1 dc in each of the last 2 dc, 1 dc in the last ch of prev row, ch 3, turn.

Row 3: 1 dc in lst dc, sk 2 dc, * ch 3, 1 dc in the ch-3 sp, 1 dc in the next dc, 1 dc in the next 3-ch sp, ch 3, sk 1 dc, 1 dc in next dc, sk 1 dc, rep from * across row, ending with sk 1 dc, 1 dc in last dc, 1

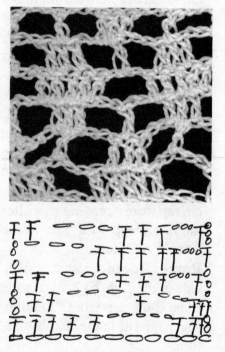

dc in last ch of prev row, ch 5, turn.

Row 4: Sk 1st 2 dc, 1 dc in ch-3 sp, *1 dc in each of the next 3 dc, 1 dc in the next ch-3 sp, ch 5, 1 dc in next ch-3 sp, rep from * across row, ending with ch 3, 1 dc in last ch of prev row, ch 3, turn.

30. Multiples of 20 plus 4.

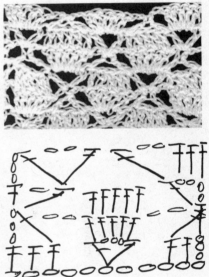

Row 1: 1 dc in the 5th ch, 1 dc in the 6th, * (1 dc, ch 3, 1 dc) in the 3rd ch, and 1 dc in each of the next 4 chs, rep from *, ending with 3 dc in the last 3 chs, ch 3, turn.

Row 2: 1 dc in 3rd dc, * ch 2, 5 dc around the 3-ch, ch 2, begin 1 dc in the 1st dc, begin 2nd in the 4th dc, then crochet both dcs together, rep from *, ending with 1 dc in the dc, 1 dc in the last ch, crochet both dcs together, ch 4, turn.

Row 3: 1 dc in the top of the 1st V-st, * 1 dc in the next 5 dc, 1 dc in the top of the V, ch 3, 1 more dc in top of the same V-st as the 1st dc, rep from *, ending with (1 dc, 1 ch, 1 dc) in the last ch, ch 3, turn.

Row 4: 2 dc in the 1-ch, * ch 2, begin 1 dc in 1st of the 5 dc, begin

1 dc in 2nd dc in 4th dc, then crochet the 2 dc together, rep from *, end with 3 dc in last ch, ch 3, turn.

Chapter V

Treble Crochet

1. Multiples of any number.

Row 1: Trc in the 6th ch and in each ch across the row, ch 4, turn.
Repeat row for pattern.

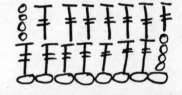

2. Multiples of any number.

Row 1: Sk 6 ch, * 1 trc in next ch, ch 1, sk 1 ch, rep from *, 1 trc, ch 6, turn.
Row 2: Sk 1st trc of the prev row, * 1 trc in next trc, ch 1, rep from *, 1 trc in 3rd ch at beg of prev row, ch 6.
Repeat row 2 for pattern.

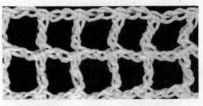

3. Multiples of 3 plus 1.

Row 1: Ch 4 * 1 trc in 1st st, ch 1, 1 trc in next st, sk 1 st, repeat from * across row.

Row 2: Ch 4 * 1 trc, ch 1, 1 trc in each ch 1 space of prev row, repeat from * across row.
Repeat row 2 for pattern.

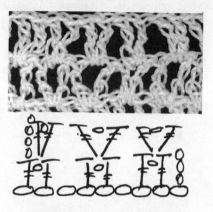

4. Multiples of 2.

Row 1: Ch 1, 1 sc in 2nd ch from hk, * 1 sc in next ch and rep from * across row, ch 1, turn.

Row 2: * 1 sc in next sc, rep from * across row, ch 1 turn.

Row 3: * 1 sc in next sc, rep from * across row, ch 1, turn.

Row 4: Sk 1st sc, * 1 trc in next sc, sk 1 sc, ch 1, rep from * across row, ending with 1 trc in last sc, ch 1, turn.

Row 5: * Sk 1 trc, 2 sc in next ch-1 sp, rep from * across row, ending with 2 sc in the last ch of prev row.
Repeat rows 2-5 for pattern.

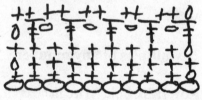

5. Multiples 4 plus 5.

Row 1: 1 dc in the 6th ch, 1 dc in the next ch, * 1 trc in the next ch and the one after, 1 dc in each of the next 2 chs, repeat from *,

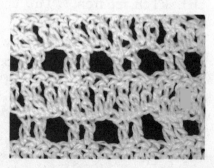

after the last 2 dc work 1 trc in last ch, ch 4, turn.

Row 2: * 1 dc in each of the 2 trc, ch 2, repeat from *, ending row with 2 chs, 1 dc in the last ch, ch 4, turn.

Row 3: Same as row 1, except the trc are worked in the dc and the dc worked in the chs.

Repeat rows 1-2 for pattern.

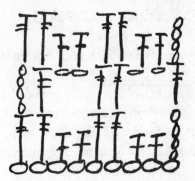

6. Multiples of 6 plus 4.

Row 1: * Sk 6 ch, 2 trc, ch 3, 2 trc in next ch, rep from * , sk 3 ch, 1 trc in last ch, ch 4, turn.

Row 2: * 2 trc, ch 3, 2 trc in 3-ch sp, rep from * across row, 1 trc in top of last ch, ch 4, turn.

Repeat row 2 for pattern.

7. Multiples of 6 plus 6.

Row 1: 1 trc in the 6th ch, * 1 trc in the next ch, 1 trc in the next ch, ch 3, trc in the ch after the last trc, 1 trc in the 3rd ch, repeat from *, ending row with 1 trc after the last group of sts in the 2nd and last ch, ch 4, turn.

Row 2: * make 3 trc in the 3-ch, ch 3, 1 trc in the same 3-ch, repeat from *, ending row with 1 trc in the last ch, ch 4, turn.

Repeat rows 1-2 for pattern.

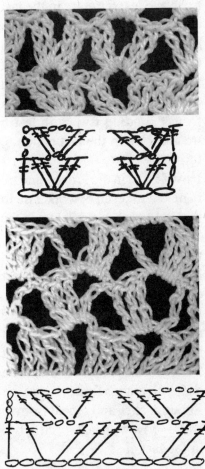

8. Multiples of 12 plus 11.

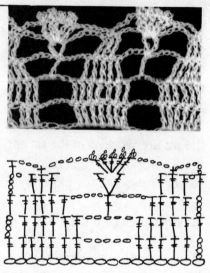

Row 1: Trc in the 6th ch, trc in each of the next 5 chs, * ch 5, trc in the 6th ch, trc in the next 6 chs, repeat from *, ending row with 1 trc in the last 7 chs, ch 4, turn.

Row 2: Sk 1 trc, trc in the next 6 trc, * ch 5 and trc in the next 7 trc, repeat from *, ending row with trc in the last 6 trc, trc in the last ch, ch 4, turn.

Row 3: Sk 1 trc, trc in the next 5 trc, * ch 5 and trc in the middle of the next 5 ch, ch 5, trc in the 2nd trc, trc in the next 4 trc, repeat from *, ending row with last 5 trc and 1 trc in the last ch, ch 5, turn.

Row 4: Trc in the 3rd trc, and trc in next 2 trc, * ch 6, work 2 trc in the 2nd trc, ch 6, work 1 trc in the 2nd trc, trc in the next 2 trc, repeat from *, ending row with last 3 trc, ch 1, and 1 trc in the last ch, ch 6, turn.

Row 5: Sk 1 trc, * sc in the middle of the 3 trc, ch 5, sk next trc, work 1 dc in between the next 2 trc, work 3-ch picot, work 1 dc and 3-ch picot 3 times, 1 dc in the same sp, ch 5, and repeat from *, ending row with last sc, ch 3, 1 dc in the last ch.

9. Multiples of 9 plus 8.

Row l: Ch 4, 1 trc in 5th ch from hk, * ch 4, sk 1 ch, 1 dc in the next 3 ch, ch 4, sk 1 ch, 1 trc in the next 4 ch, repeat from * across row, ending with 1 trc in each of last 2 ch, ch 1, turn.

Row 2: 1 sc in each of 1st 2 trc, * ch 4, sk ch-4, 1 dc in the next 3 dc, ch 4, sk ch-4, 1 sc in the next 4 trc, repeat from * across row, ending with 1 sc in the last trc, 1 sc in last ch of the prev row, ch 1, turn.

Row 3: 1 sc in each of 1st 2 sc, * ch 4, sk ch-4, 1 dc in each of the next 3 dc, ch 4, sk ch-4, 1 sc in the next 4 sc, repeat from * across row, ending with 1 sc in each last 2 sc, ch 1, turn.

Row 4: Repeat row 3.

Row 5: Ch 4, sk 1 sc, 1 trc in next sc, * ch 1, sk ch-4, 1 dc in the next 3 dc, sk ch-4, (ch 1, 1 trc in next sc) 4 times, repeat from * across row, ending with (ch 1, 1 trc in next sc) 2 times, ch 3, turn.

Row 6: Sk 1 trc, 1 dc in next ch-1 sp, 1 dc in next trc, *1 dc in next ch-1 sp, 1 dc in next 3 dc, (1 dc in next ch-1 sp, 1 dc in next trc) 4 times, repeat from * across row, ending with 1 dc in last trc, 1 dc in last ch of prev row, ch 4, turn.

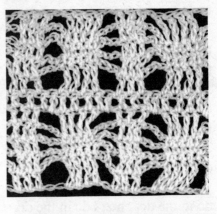

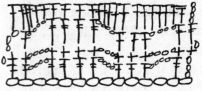

Row 7: Sk 1 dc, 1 trc in next dc, * ch 4, sk 1 dc, 1 dc in the next 3 dc, ch 4, (sk 1 dc, 1 trc in next dc) 4 times, repeat from * across row, ending with sk 1 dc, 1 trc in next dc, sk last dc, 1 trc in last ch of prev row, ch 1, turn.

Repeat rows 2-7 for pattern.

10. Multiples of 18 plus 4.

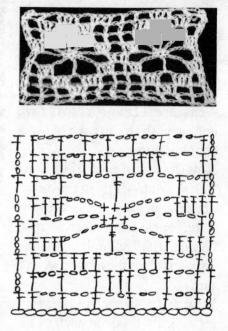

Row 1: Dc in the 5th ch, * ch 2, 1 dc in the 3rd ch, repeat from *, ending row with dc, 1 dc in the last ch, ch 3, turn.

Row 2: 1 dc in the 2nd dc, * ch 2, 1 dc in the dc, ch 2, 1 dc in the dc, 1 dc in the next 2 chs, 1 dc in the dc, ch 2, dc in the dc, ch 2, 1 dc in the dc, ch 2, 1 dc in the dc, repeat from *, ending row with 1 dc extra after the last dc, ch 3, turn.

Row 3: 1 dc in the 2nd dc, ch 2, * 1 dc in the dc, 1 dc in the next 2 chs, 1 dc in the dc, ch 2, 1 dc in the 3rd dc, 1 dc in next 2 chs, 1 dc in the dc, ch 2, 1 dc in the dc, ch 2, 1 dc in the dc, ch 2, repeat from *, ending row with 1 dc extra after the last dc, ch 3, turn.

Row 4: Sk 1 dc, * dc in the next dc, 1 dc in the 2-chs, 1 dc in the next dc, ch 5, 1 trc in the middle of the 2-ch, ch 5, 1 dc in the 4th dc, 1 dc in next 2-chs, 1 dc in the dc, ch 2, repeat from *, ending row with 1 dc extra after the last dc, ch 3, turn.

Row 5: 1 dc in the 2nd dc, * ch 5, 1 sc in the last of the 5-ch, 1 dc in the trc, 1 sc in the 1st of the 5-ch, ch 5, 1 dc in the 4th dc, 1 dc in the next 2 chs, 1 dc in the next dc, repeat from *, ending row with 1 dc extra after the last dc, ch 3, turn.

Row 6: Sk 1 dc, * dc in the next dc, 1 dc around each of the 3 chs, ch 5, 1 sc in each of the 3 sc, ch 5, 1 dc around the next 3 chs, 1 dc in the next dc, ch 2, repeat from *, ending row with 1 dc extra in the last ch, ch 3, turn.

Row 7: 1 dc in the 2nd dc, ch 2, * 1 dc in the 3rd dc, ch 5, 1 trc in the 2nd sc, ch 5, 1 dc in the dc, ch 2, 1 dc in the 3rd dc, ch 2, 1 dc in the next dc, ch 2, repeat from *, ending row with 1 dc extra in the last ch, ch 3, turn.

Row 8: 1 dc in the 2nd dc, * ch 2, 1 dc in the next dc, 3 dc in the next 4-ch, dc in the next dc, ch 2, 3 dc in the next 4-ch, dc in the next dc, ch 2, 3 dc in the next 4-ch, dc in the next dc, ch 2, dc in the next dc, ch 2, dc in the next dc, repeat from *, ending row with 1 dc extra in the last ch, ch 3, turn.

Row 9: 1 dc in the 2nd dc, ch 2, * 1 dc in the next dc, ch 2, 1 dc in the 3rd dc, 1 dc in the next 2 chs, 1 dc in the next dc, ch 2, 1 dc in the 3rd dc, ch 2, dc in the dc, ch 2, dc in the dc, ch 2, repeat from *, ending row with 1 dc extra in the last ch, ch 3, turn.

Repeat rows 1-9 for pattern.

11. Multiples of 9 plus 5.

Row 1: Ch 4, 1 trc in 5th ch from hk, * ch 3, sk 3 ch, 1 sc in next ch, ch 3, 1 sc in next ch, ch 3, sk 3 ch, 4 trc in the next ch, repeat from *, ending with 2 trc in last ch, ch 1, turn.

Row 2: 1 sc in 1st trc, * ch 3, sk 1 trc, ch-3 sp, 1 sc, 4 trc in next ch-3 sp, ch 3, sk 1 sc, ch 3 sp, 1 tr, 1 sc in next tr, ch 3, 1 sc in next trc, repeat from * across row, ending with 1 sc in last ch of prev row, ch 4, turn.

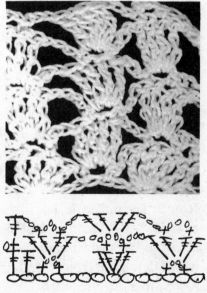

55

Row 3: 1 trc in 1st sc, ch 3, sk ch-3 sp, 1 trc, * 1 sc in next trc, ch 3, 1 sc in next trc, ch 3, sk 1 trc, ch-3 sp, 1 sc, 4 tr in next ch-3 sp, ch 3, sk 1 sc, ch 3-sp, 1 trc, repeat from * across row, ending with 2 trc in last sc, ch 1, turn.

Repeat rows 2-3 for pattern.

12. Multiples of 11 plus 4.

Row 1: 1 dc in 5th ch and across the row, ch 3, turn.

Row 2: 1 dc in 2nd dc, 1 dc in 3rd dc, * ch 3, 1 trc in the 3rd dc and the next 3 dc, ch 3, 1 dc in the 3rd dc, 1 dc in the next 2 dc, repeat from *, ending with 3 dc in the 2 last dc and in the last ch, ch 3, turn.

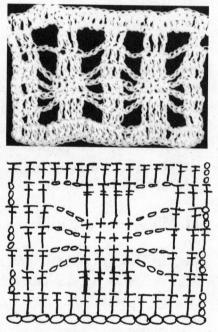

Row 3: 1 dc in 2nd dc and the 3rd, * ch 3, 1 sc in the next 4 trc, ch 3, 3 dc in the 3 dc, repeat from *, ending row with 3 dc, ch 3, turn.

Row 4: 1 dc in 2nd dc and the next, * ch 3, 1 sc in each of the 4 sc, ch 3, 1 dc in each of the 3 dc, repeat from *, ending row with 3 dc, ch 3, turn.

Row 5: 1 dc in 2nd dc, 1 dc in the next dc, * ch 3, 1 sc in each of the next 4 sc, ch 3, 1 dc in each of the next 3 dc, repeat from *, ending row with 3 dc, ch 3, turn.

Row 6: 1 dc in 2nd dc, 1 dc in the next, * ch 3, 1 trc in each of the next 4 sc, ch 3, 1 dc in the next 3 dc, repeat from *, ending row with 3 dc, ch 3, turn.

Row 7: Repeat row 1, dc across row in each st.

Repeat rows 1-6 for pattern.

13. Multiples 16 plus 6.

Row 1: Ch 3, 3 trc in 1st st, * sk 5 sts, 4 trc in next st, ch 5, sk 4 sts, 1 dc, ch 5, sk 4 sts, 4 trc in next st, rep from * across row, sk 4 sts, 1 trc in last st.

Row 2: Ch 3, 4 trc in 4th trc, * ch 5, 1 dc in dc, ch 5, 4 trc in 1st trc and 4 trc in the 8th trc, rep from * across row, ch 5, turn.

Row 3: Ch 3, 3 trc in 1st trc, * 4 trc in 8th trc, ch 5, 1 dc, ch 5, 4 trc in 1st trc, rep from *, 1 trc at end.

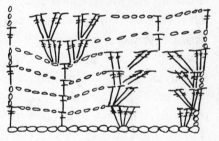

Row 4: Ch 1, 1 dc, * ch 5, 4 trc in 3rd of 1st 5-chs, 4 trc in 3rd of the 2nd 5-ch, 1 dc in 4th trc, rep from *, ch 3, 1 trc at end.

Row 5: Ch 6, * 1 dc in dc, ch 5, 4 trc in 1st trc, 4 trc in 8th trc, ch 5, rep from *, 1 dc.

Row 6: Ch 1, 1 dc, * ch 5, 4 trc in 1st trc, 4 trc in 8th trc, ch 5, 1 dc, rep from *, ch 3, 1 trc at end.

Repeat rows 1-6 for pattern.

14. Multiples of 3 plus 1.

Row 1: Ch 1, * 1 dc, ch 2, sk 2, rep from * across row, 1 dc, turn.
Row 2: Ch 3, 1 trc in 1st dc, then 3 trc in each dc across row, 2 trc in last dc, turn.
Row 3: Ch 1, 1 dc in 1st trc, * ch 2, 1 dc in center of trc group, rep from *, ch 2, 1 dc in 3 ch.
Repeat row 2 for pattern.

15. Multiples of 2.

Row 1: Ch 1, 1 dc in each ch across row, turn.
Row 2: Same as row 1.
Row 3: Ch 3, 1 trc in 1st 2 sts, * ch 1, sk 1, 1 trc in next 2 sts, rep from * across row, turn.
Row 4: Ch 4, * 1 trc in 2nd trc, 1 trc in ch-1 sp, ch 1, 1 trc, rep from *, turn.
Row 5: Ch 1, * 1 dc in each trc, 1 dc in each ch-1 sp, rep from *.
Repeat row from 2 for pattern.

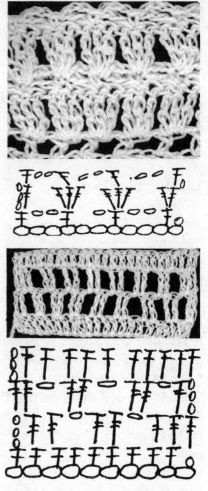

Chapter VI

V-Stitch and Shell

1. Multiples of any number plus 3.

Row 1: 2 dc in the 4th ch, * make 2 dc in the 2nd ch, repeat from *, ending row with 1 dc in the last ch, ch 3, turn.
Row 2: * work 2 dc in the middle of the 2nd dc in the prev row, repeat from *, ending with 1 dc in the last ch, ch 3, turn.
Repeat for pattern.

2. Multiples of 2 plus 1.

Row 1: 1 sc in 2nd ch and across the row, ch 3, turn.
Row 2: 1 dc in 1st sc, * 1 dc in 2nd dc, 1 dc in the same sc, repeat from *, ending row with last set, 1 dc in the last sc, ch 1, turn.
Repeat for pattern.

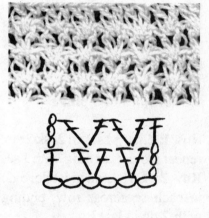

3. Multiples of 4 plus 4.

Row 1: 4 dc in the 6th ch, * 4 dc in the 4th ch, repeat from *, ending with 3 dc in the last ch, ch 1, turn.

Row 2: 1 sc in the 1st dc and each dc across the row, 2 dc in the last ch, ch 3, turn.

Row 3: 2 dc in the 2nd sc, * 4 dc in the 4th sc, repeat from *, ending with 1 dc in the last st, ch 1, turn.

Row 4: 1 sc in every dc across the row.

Repeat for pattern.

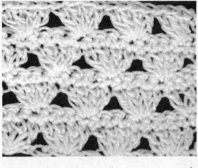

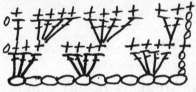

4. Multiples of 3 plus 1.

Row 1: Ch 1, * 1 sc, ch 2, sk 2 sts, repeat from *, ending with 1 sc.

Row 2: Ch 3, 1 dc in 1st dc, 3 dc in each sc across row, ending with 2 dc in last sc.

Row 3: Ch 1, 1 sc in 1st dc, * ch 2, 1 sc in middle of the set, repeat from *, ending with ch 2, 1 sc in ch 3 of prev row.

Repeat rows 2-3 for pattern.

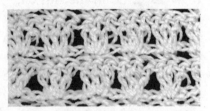

5. Multiples of any number.

Row 1: Ch 3, (1 dc, ch 2, 1 sc), in 1st ch, * sk 2 sts, (2 dc, ch 2, 1 sc) in next ch *, repeat from * to

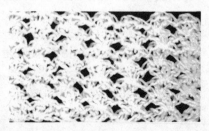

end.

Row 2: Ch 2, * (2 dc, ch 2, 1 sc) in 2nd ch sp, repeat from * to end of row.

Repeat row 2 for pattern.

6. Multiples of 6 plus 2.

Row 1: 1 dc in 3rd ch from hk, 1 dc in next ch, * ch 2, sk 1 ch, 1 sc in the next 2 chs, ch 2, sk 1 ch, 1 dc in the next 2 chs, repeat from * across row, ch 1, turn.

Row 2: 1 sc in both of the 1st 2 dc, * ch 2, sk ch-2, 1 dc in the next 2 sc, ch 2, sk ch-2, 1 sc in the next 2 dc, repeat from * across row, ch 2, turn.

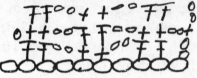

Row 3: 1 dc in both of 1st 2 sc, ch 2, sk ch-2, 1 sc in the next 2 dc, ch 2, sk ch-2, 1 dc in both of the next 2 sc, repeat from * across row, ch 1 turn.

Repeat rows 2-3 for pattern.

7. Multiples of 6 plus 5.

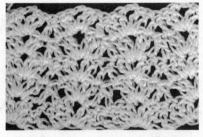

Row 1: 1 dc in the 4 ch, * (2 dc, ch, 2 dc) in next ch, yo, insert hk in next ch, pull up a loop, yo pull yarn through 2 loops, sk 3 sts, yo, insert hk in next ch, pull up a loop, yo, pull through 2 loops, 3 times *, 1 dc, ch 3, turn.

Row 2: 1 dc in 1st dc before ch

sp, * (2 dc, ch 1, 2 dc) in ch sp, yo, insert hk in next dc, pull up a loop, yo, pull through 2 loops, sk 3 sts, yo, insert hk in next dc, pull up loop, yo, pull through 2 loops, 3 times, rep from *, make last st in top of last st, ch 3, turn. Repeat row 2 for pattern.

8. Multiples of 6 plus 3.

Row 1: * (2 dc, ch 1, 2 dc) in 1st ch, sk 2 sts, (1 dc, ch 1, 1 dc) in next st, sk 2 sts, repeat from * across row, ending with (2 dc, ch 1, 2 dc) in next to last ch, 1 dc in last ch, ch 3, turn.

Row 2: Repeat row 1, inserting hk in ch 1 spaces of prev row. Repeat row 2 for pattern.

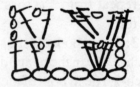

9. Multiples of 8 plus 4.

Row 1: 1 sc in 2nd dc from hk, * 1 sc in next ch, repeat from * across row, ch 6, turn.

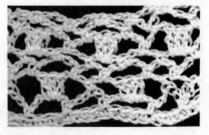

Row 2: Sk 3 sc, 1 sc in next sc, * ch 5, sk 3 sc, 1 sc in next sc, repeat from * across row, ch 4, turn.

Row 3: 1 sc in 1st ch-5 sp, * ch 3, 3 dc in next ch-5 sp, ch 3, 1 sc in next 5-ch sp, repeat from * across row, ending with ch 6, turn.

Row 4: 1 sc in 1st ch-3 sp, * ch 5, 1 sc in next ch-3 sp, repeat from * across row, ending with ch 5, 1 sc in last ch of prev row, ch 4, turn.

Row 5: 2 dc in 1st ch-5 sp, * ch 3, 1 sc in next ch-5 sp, ch 3, 3 dc in next ch-5 sp, repeat from * across row, ch 6, turn.

Row 6: 1 sc in 1st ch-3 sp, * ch 5, 1 sc in next ch-3 sp, repeat from * across row, ending with 1 sc in last ch of prev row, ch 4, turn.

Repeat rows 3-6 for pattern.

10. Multiples of 6 plus 1.

Row 1: 2 dc in 4th ch, sk 2 ch, 1 sc, * sk 2 ch, 4 dc in next ch, sk 2 ch, 1 sc *, ch 3, turn.

Row 2: 2 dc in 1st sc, * 1 sc between 2nd and 3rd dc of next 4-dc set, 4 dc in next sc, rep from *, 1 sc in 3-ch sp at start of row, ch 3, turn.

Repeat row 2 for pattern.

11. Multiples of any number.

Row 1: (dc, ch 3, 1 dc) in 4th ch, * ch 3, sk 3 sts, 1 sc in the next 3 sts, ch 3, sk 3 sts, (1 dc, ch 3, 1 dc) in next ch, repeat from *.

Row 2: Ch 3, * 7 dc in ch 3 sp between dc of prev row, ch 3, 1 sc

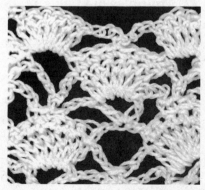

in 2nd sc, ch 3, rep from * across row, ending with 7 dc.

Row 3: * 1 sc in each dc of set, ch 5 *, rep from * across row, ending row with 7 sc.

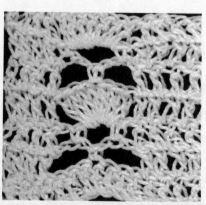

Row 4: Ch 5, * 3 sc in the 3 center set of dc, ch 3, (1 dc, ch 3, 1 dc) in 3rd of ch 5, ch 3, rep from * across row, ending row with 3 sc.

Row 5: Ch 5, * 1 sc in 2nd sc, ch 3, 7 dc in ch 3 sp between dc of prev row, ch 3, rep from * across row, ending row 1 sc, ch 3, 1 sc in ch 5 loop.

Row 6: Ch 5, * 7 dc of set, ch 5, repeat from * across row, ending with 1 sc in ch 5 loop.

Row 7: Ch 3, * (1 dc, ch 3, 1 dc) in 3rd of the 5th ch, ch 3, 3 sc in middle of set, ch 3, rep from * across row, ending with (1 dc, ch 3, 1 dc) in last loop.

Repeat rows 2-7 for pattern.

12. Multiples of 13 plus 1.

Row 1: Ch 3, dc in every ch to end of row, ch 3, turn.

Row 2: 3 dc, * ch 3, sk 3 dc, 1 sc in next dc, ch 3, sk 3 dc, 6 dc, repeat from * across row, ending with 4 dc, ch 3, turn.

Row 3: 3 dc, * ch 1, 1 sc in 1st ch-3 sp, 1 sc in 2nd ch-3 sp, ch 1, 6 dc, rep from * across row, ending with 4 dc, ch 3, turn.

Row 4: 3 dc, * 7 dc in ch-3 sp, 6 dc, rep from *, ending with 4 dc, ch 3, turn.

Repeat rows 2-4 for pattern.

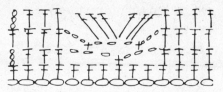

13. Multiples of 6 plus 4.

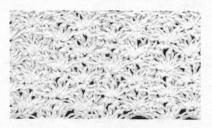

Row 1: 2 dc in 3rd ch from hk, skip 2 sts, 1 sc, * skip 2 sts, 4 dc in next st, skip 2 sts, 1 sc, repeat from * to end of row, ch 3, turn.

Row 2: 2 dc in sc, *1 sc between the 2nd and 3rd dc, 4 dc in the next sc, repeat from * across row, ending with 1 sc in the ch-3 sp at beg of prev row, ch 3, turn.

Repeat row 2 for pattern.

14. Multiples of 7 plus 4.

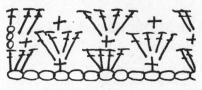

Row 1: Ch 3, 1 dc in same ch, sk 2 sts, * 5 dc in the next st, sk 2 sts, 2 dc, sk 2 sts, repeat from *, ending with 3 dc in last st, ch 3, turn.

Row 2: 2 dc between the 1st 2 dc, * 5 dc between the 1st, 2nd dc, 2 dc in the 3rd dc, rep from *, ending with 3 dc in ch-3 sp, ch 3, turn.

Repeat row 2 for pattern.

15. Multiples of 3 plus 1.

Row 1: Sk 2 ch, 2 dc in next ch
* (1 sc, 2 dc) in next ch, sk 2 ch,
rep from * across row, ending
with 1 sc in last ch, ch 2, turn.

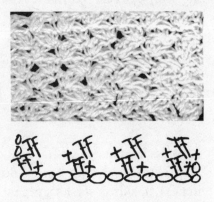

Row 2: 2 dc in 1st sc * (sc, 2 dc)
in every sc of prev row, rep from
* across row, ending with 1 sc in
last ch, ch 2, turn.

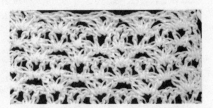

Repeat row 2 for pattern.

16. Multiples of 3 plus 4.

Row 1: 1 dc in 6th ch, * ch 1, 1
dc in same ch, 1 dc in the 3rd ch,
rep from *, ending row with 1 dc
and 2 chs after the last group, ch
3, turn.

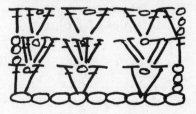

Row 2: 2 dc in 1st ch, ch 1, 2 dc
in same st, * ch 1, 2 dc in the 2nd
1-ch, ch 1, 2 dc in same 1-ch,
repeat from *, ending with 2 dc
in last ch, ch 3, turn.

Row 3: Same as row 1, except
sets are worked in each 1-ch sp.
Repeat rows 1-2 for pattern.

17. Multiples of 6 plus 1.

Row 1: Ch 1, 1 sc in 2nd ch from
hk, * sk 2 ch, 5 dc in the next ch,
sk 2 ch, 1 sc in next ch, repeat

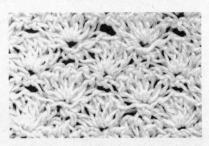

from * across row, ch 3, turn.

Row 2: 2 dc in lst sc, * sk 2 dc, 1 sc through back loop only of next dc, sk 2 dc, 5 dc through back loop only of next sc, repeat from *, ending with 3 dc in last sc, ch 1, turn.

Row 3: 1 sc in lst dc, * sk 2 dc, 5 dc through back loop only of next sc, sk 2 dc, 1 sc through back loop only of next dc, repeat from * across row, ending with 1 sc in last ch of prev row, ch 3, turn.

Repeat rows 2-3 for pattern.

18. Multiples of 7 plus 4.

Row 1: Ch 1, 1 sc in 2nd ch from hk, sk 2 ch, 3 dc in next ch, * ch 3, sk 3 ch, 1 sc in next ch, sk 2 ch, 3 dc in next ch, repeat from * across row, ch 1, turn.

Row 2: 1 sc in lst dc, sk 2 dc, 3 dc in next sc, * ch 3, 1 sc in next ch-3 sp, sk 3 dc, 3 dc in next sc, repeat from * across row, ch 1, turn.

Repeat row 2 for pattern.

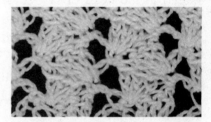

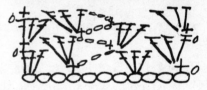

19. Multiples of 6 plus 4.

Row 1: Ch 3, 2 dc in lst st, * sk 2 sts, 1 dc, sk 2 sts, 5 dc in next st, repeat from * across row, ending with sk 2 sts, 1 dc in last st, ch 3,

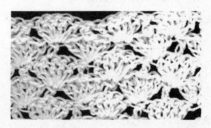

turn.

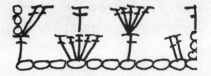

Row 2: 2 dc in lst st, * 1 dc in center dc, 5 dc in dc, repeat from * across row, ending with 1 dc in last ch, ch 3, turn.

Repeat row for pattern.

20. Multiples of any number

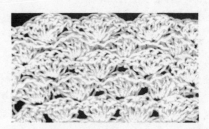

Row 1: Ch 3, 3 dc in lst st, sk 2 sts, 1 sc, * sk 2 sts, 5 dc in next st, sk 1 st, 1 sc, repeat from * across row, ch 3, turn.

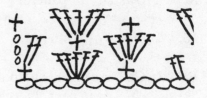

Row 2: 3 dc (insert hk in back thread at the head of last sc of prev row), * 1 sc (insert hk in back thread at the head of 3rd dc), 5 dc (insert hk in back thread at the head of sc), repeat from * across row, ending with 1 sc, ch 3, turn.

21. Multiples of 7 plus 1.

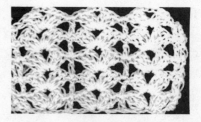

Row 1: Ch 3, * 1 dc, sk 2 sts, 3 dc in lst, ch 2, 3 dc in same st, sk 2 sts, repeat from * ending row with 2 dc, ch 3, turn.

Row 2: 1 dc in 2nd dc, * (3 dc, ch 2, 3 dc) in ch 2 sp, 1 dc in single dc, repeat from * across row, ending with 1 dc in last ch, ch 3, turn.

Repeat row 2 for pattern.

22. Multiples of any number.

Row 1: Ch 3, 1 dc, * sk 3 sts, (1 dc, ch 1, 1 dc) in next st, sk 3 sts, (1 dc, ch 1, 1 dc) in next st, repeat from * across row, ch 3, turn.
Row 2: 1 dc in ch-1 sp, * 6 dc in ch 3 sp, (1 dc, ch 1, 1 dc) in ch-1 sp, repeat from * across row, ch 3, turn.
Row 3: 1 dc in ch-1 sp, * (1 dc, ch 3, 1 dc) between 2 center dc (1 dc, ch 1, 1 dc) in ch-1 sp, repeat from * across row, ch 3, turn.
Repeat row 2-3 for pattern.

23. Multiples of 6 plus 1.

Row 1: Ch 1, 1 sc in 2nd ch from hk, ch 5, 1 sc in same ch, * sk 2 ch, 5 dc in next ch, sk 2 ch, (1 sc, ch 5, 1 sc) in next ch, repeat from * across row, ending with (1 sc, ch 2, 1 dc) in last ch, ch 1, turn.
Row 2: 1 (1 sc, ch 5, 1 sc) in 1st ch-2 sp, * 5 dc in center dc of next shell, 1 (1 sc, ch 2, 1 dc) in next ch-5 sp, repeat from * across row, ending row with (1 sc, ch 2, 1 dc) in last ch, ch 1, turn.

24. Multiples of 6 plus 1.

Row 1: Ch 1, 2 sc, * ch 3, sk 3 sts, 3 sc, repeat from * across row, ending row with sk 3 sts, 2 sc, ch 1, turn.

Row 2: 1 sc, * 5, dc in ch-3 sp, 1 sc in 2nd sc, repeat from * across row, ch 3, turn.

Row 3: * 1 sc in each of 3 center dc, repeat from * across row, ending with ch 2, 1 sc, ch 3, turn.

Row 4: 2 dc in ch-2 sp, * 1 sc in 2nd sc, 5 dc in ch-3 sp, repeat from *, ending with 1 sc in 2nd sc, 2 dc in ch-3 sp, ch 1, turn.

Row 5: 1 sc in each of 1st 2 dc, * ch 3, 1 sc in each 3 center dc, repeat from *, ending row with ch 3, 1 sc in last dc, 1 sc in last ch, ch 2, turn.

Repeat rows 2-5 for pattern.

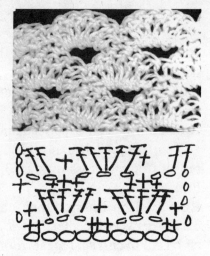

25. Multiples of 8 plus 3.

Row 1: Sk 2 ch, * 1 dc, ch 3, sk 3 ch, 1 sc, ch 3, sk 3 ch, repeat from * across row, ending with 1 dc, ch 3, turn.

Row 2: * 1 sc in 2nd ch of 3-ch group, ch 3, 1 sc in 2nd ch of next 3-ch group, ch 1, 1 dc in the dc, ch 1, repeat from * across row, ending with 1 dc in last ch, ch 3, turn.

Row 3: * 7 dc in 3-ch sp, 1 dc in the dc, repeat from * across row, ending with 1 dc in the last ch, ch 3, turn.

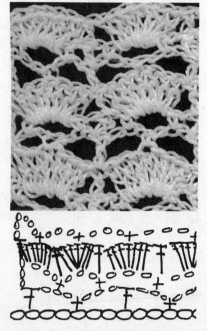

Row 4: * ch 3, 1 sc in the center of 7 dc shell, ch 3, 1 dc in the dc, repeat from * across row, ending with 1 dc in the last ch, ch 3, turn. Repeat rows 2-4 for pattern.

26. Multiples of 12 plus 4.

Row 1: 1 dc in 7th ch, * 5 dc in 3rd ch, 1 dc in 3rd ch, ch 1, 1 dc in 2nd ch, ch 1, 1 dc in 2nd ch, ch 1, 1 dc in 2nd ch, repeat from * across row, ending with last set, 1 ch, 1 dc, ch 5, turn.

Row 2: sk 1st dc, * dc in next dc, 1 dc in the next 5 dc, 1 dc in the next dc, ch 1, 1 dc, ch 1 and 1 dc, ch 1, repeat from * across row, ending with 1 ch, 1 dc, ch 5, turn.

Row 3: sk 1st dc, * dc in 2nd dc, and in the 4 next dc, ch 2, 1 dc in the 2nd dc, 1 ch, and 1 dc in the next dc, ch 2, repeat from *, ending row with 2 ch and 1 dc in last ch, ch 5, turn.

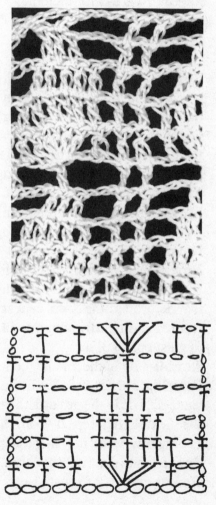

Row 4: Sk 1st dc, * dc in 2nd dc, 1 dc in each of the next 2 dc, ch 3, 1 dc in 2nd dc, ch 1, 1 dc in next dc, ch 3, repeat from *, ending with 3 chs and 1 dc in the last ch, ch 6, turn.

Row 5: Sk 1st dc, * dc in 2nd dc, ch 4, 1 dc in the next dc, ch 1, 1 dc in next dc, ch 4, repeat from *, ending with 4 chs and 1 dc in the

71

last ch, ch 4, turn.

Row 6: Repeat row 1, except single dcs are worked in the ch, the 5 dc are worked in the single dc.

Repeat rows 2-5 for pattern.

27. Multiples of 10 plus 5.

Row 1: 7 dc in the 10th ch, * ch 1, 1 dc in the 5th ch, ch 1, 7 dc in the 5th ch, repeat from *, ending with 1 ch and 1 dc, ch 4, turn.

Row 2: 1 dc in the 1st dc, * ch 1, 1 dc in the 3rd dc and in the next 2 dc, ch 1, 1 dc in the 3rd dc, ch 3, 1 dc in the dc just used, rep from * ending row with 1 dc, 1 ch and 1 dc in the last ch, ch 3, turn.

Row 3: 3 dc in the 1st 1-ch, * ch 1, 1 dc in the center of the 3 dc, ch 1, 7 dc around the 3-ch, repeat from *, ending row with 4 dc in the last ch, ch 3, turn.

Row 4: 1 dc in the 2nd dc, ch 1, 1 dc in the 3rd dc, ch 3, 1 dc in the same dc, 1 dc in the 3rd dc and in the next 2 dc, repeat from * ending row with 2 dc, 1 in the last dc and 1 in the last ch, ch 4, turn.

Repeat rows 1-4 for pattern.

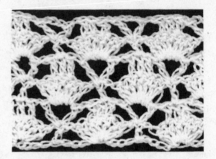

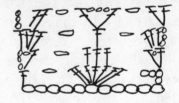

28. Multiples of 3.

Row l: Ch 2, in 1st st * yo, insert hk, yo, pull through a loop, yo, pull through 2 loops on hook *, repeat * to *, in next st, yo and pull through 3 loops on hook, * ch 1, repeat * to * in next 2 sts, yo and pull through 3 loops on hook, repeat from * to *, ending row with 1 dc in the last st, ch 2, turn.

Row 2: 1 dc in closing st of 3 loops, * sk ch 1 of prev row, work 5 dc in closing st of next group, 1 dc in next group, repeat from * to *, ending row with 1 dc, ch 2, turn.

Row 3: 1 dc in 1st of 5 dc, * repeat * to * as in 1 in 2nd dc group of 5, then 4th dc, yo and pull through 3 loops on hk, ch 1, repeat * to * in 5th dc, then * to * in 1st dc of next group, yo and pull yarn through 3 loops, * repeat * to *.

Repeat rows 1-3 for pattern, working sk 1 st after * ch 1 on all repeats of row 1 only.

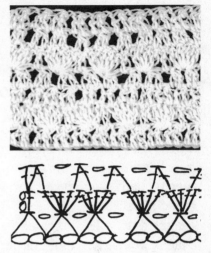

29. Multiples of 14 plus 2.

Row 1: Sk 1 ch, 1 sc, * sk 6 ch, 1 elongated dc [yo, insert hk, pull up a loop 1/2" long, yo, pull

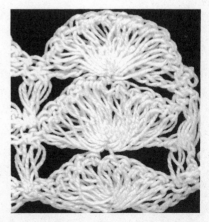

73

through 2 loops, yo, pull through 2 loops], 12 more elongated dc in the same ch, sk 6 ch, 1 sc, repeat from *, ch 3, turn.

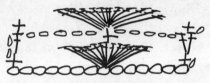

Row 2: 1 elongated dc in 1st sc, * ch 5, 1 sc in the 7th of 13 elongated dc, ch 5, 2 elongated dc in sc between the fans, repeat from *, ending row with 2 elongated dc in the last sc, ch 1, turn.

Row 3: 1 sc between the 1st 2 elongated dc, * 13 elongated dc in the sc worked at center of fan in prev row, 1 sc between the 2 long dc of prev row, repeat from *, ch 3, turn.

Repeat row 2 for pattern.

30. Multiples of 10 plus 4.

Row 1: 1 dc in 5th ch, 1 sc in next ch, * ch 3, 1 dc in 3rd ch, 1 dc in 2nd ch, ch 1, 1 dc in the prev ch, 1 dc in 2nd ch, 5 dc in 3rd ch, repeat from *, ending with last group and 1 dc in the last ch, ch 5, turn.

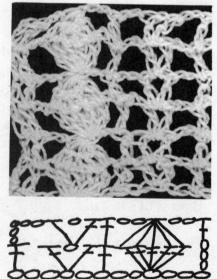

Row 2: Sk 1 dc, * work 5 dc together in the next 5 dc, ch 2, 1 dc in the dc, (1 dc, 1 ch, 1 dc), in the ch-1 sp, dc in the dc, ch 2, repeat from *, ending with 1 dc in the last ch, ch 3, turn.

Repeat rows 1-2 for pattern.

31. Multiples of 4 plus 2.

Row 1: (2 dc, ch 1, 1 dc) in 3rd ch, * sk 3 sts, (3 dc, ch 1, 1 dc) in next ch, repeat from *, ending with sk 2 chs, 1 dc in last ch, ch 3, turn.
Row 2: (2 dc, ch 1, 1 dc) in 1st ch 1 sp, * (3 dc, ch 1, 1 dc) in next ch 1 sp, repeat from *, ending with 1 dc in 3 ch, ch 3, turn.
Repeat row 2 for pattern.

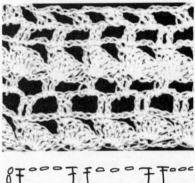

32. Multiples of 5 plus 4.

Row 1: 1 sc in the 2nd ch, * ch 3, work 5 dc in prev ch, 1 sc in the 5th ch, repeat from *, ending with sc after the last group, ch 5, turn.
Row 2: * 1 sc in the 5th dc, 1 sc in the top of the 3-ch, ch 3, repeat from *, ending with 1 sc in the last dc, 2 sc in last ch, ch 3, turn.
Row 3: 1 dc in the 2nd sc and the next, * ch 3, 1 dc in each sc, repeat from *, ending with 2 chs and 1 dc in last ch, ch 3, turn.
Row 4: 1 dc in the 2-ch, * ch 3, 2 dc in the 3-ch, repeat from *, ending with 3 chs, 1 dc in the last ch, ch 1, turn.
Row 5: 1 sc in the 1st dc, * ch 3, 5 dc in the prev st, 1 sc in the 2nd dc, repeat from *, ending with

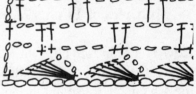

last group, 1 sc in last ch, ch 5, turn.
Repeat rows 1-4 for pattern.

33. Multiples of 10 plus 5.

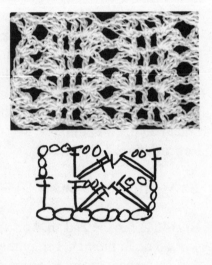

Row 1: * 2 dc in the 6th ch, ch 2, 1 dc in the prev ch, ch 1, 1 dc in the 2nd ch, ch 1, 1 dc in the 2nd ch, ch 2, 2 dc in the prev ch, repeat from *, ending with (2 dc, 2 ch, 1 dc) in last ch, ch 5, turn.
Row 2: 2 dc in the 1st dc, * 2 dc in the 3rd dc of the next group, ch 2, 1 dc in the dc just used, ch 1, dc in the next dc, ch 1, dc in the next dc, ch 2, 2 dc in the prev dc, repeat from *, ending with (2 dc, 2 chs, 1 dc) in the last ch, ch 5, turn.
Repeat rows 1-2 for pattern.

34. Multiples of 14 plus 7.

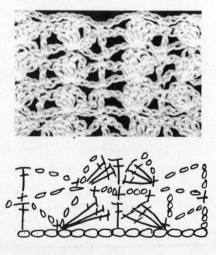

Row 1: 1 sc in 10th ch, * ch 3, 3 dc in 10th ch, 1 dc, sk 4 ch, 3 dc in the 4th ch, ch 3, 1 sc in the same ch, ch 3, 1 dc in the 3rd ch, 1 sc in the 3rd ch, repeat from *, ending with 1 dc in the 4th ch after the set, ch 1, turn.
Row 2: 1 sc in the dc, ch 3, 1 sc in the top of the 3-ch, * ch 3, 1 sc in the dc, ch 3, 1 sc in the top of the 3-ch, repeat from *, ending

with 1 sc in the last ch, ch 6, turn.
Repeat rows 1-2 for pattern.

35. Multiples of 6 plus 1.

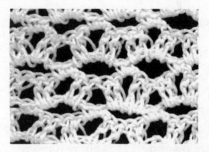

Row 1: 1 sc in the 2nd ch and the 3rd ch, * ch 4, 1 sc in the 5th ch, 1 sc in the next ch, repeat from *, ending with 2 sc, ch 3, turn.
Row 2: 2 dc around the 4-ch, ch 2, 2 dc around the same 4-ch, repeat from *, ending with 1 dc in last ch, ch 5, turn.

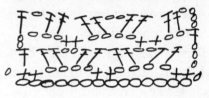

Row 3: 1 sc in the 1st ch, 1 sc in the next ch, ch 4, repeat from *, ending with 2 chs, 1 dc in the last ch, ch 4, turn.
Row 4: 2 dc around the 2-ch, * 2 dc around the 4-ch, ch 2, 2 dc around the same 4-ch, repeat from *, ending row with (2 dc, 1 ch, 1 dc), ch 1, turn.
Repeat rows 1-4 for pattern.

36. Multiples of 7 plus 5.

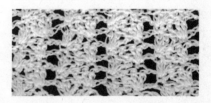

Row 1: 2 dc in 5th ch, * ch 2, 1 sc in 4th ch, ch 2, 1 trc, 2 dc in 3rd ch, repeat from *, ending with 2 chs, 1 sc, ch 4, turn.

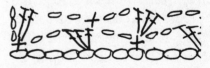

Row 2: 2 dc in sc, * ch 2, 1 sc in top of 2-ch, ch 2, 1 trc, 2 dc in sc, repeat from *, ending with 2 chs, 1 sc in the last ch, ch 4, turn.
Repeat rows 1-2 for pattern.

37. Multiples of 16 plus 6.

Row 1: 1 sc in 8th ch, * ch 5, 1 sc in 4th ch, rep from * across row, ending with last sc, 2 chs, 1 dc in 2nd ch, ch 1, turn.

Row 2: 1 sc in the dc, * ch 5, 1 sc around middle of 5-ch, ch 5, 1 sc around middle of next ch-5, 8 dc around middle of next 5-ch, 1 sc around next 5-ch, rep from * across row, ending with 1 sc in last ch, ch 5, turn.

Row 3: 1 sc around 5-ch, * ch 4, 1 dc in 2nd dc, 1 dc in next 5 dc, ch 4, 1 sc around 5-ch, ch 5, 1 sc around 5-ch, rep from * across row, ending with last sc, 2 chs, 1 dc in sc, ch 1 turn.

Row 4: 1 sc in 1st dc, * ch 5, 1 sc around 5-ch, ch 5, 1 sc around middle of 4-ch, ch 3, 1 dc in 2nd dc, 1 dc in next 3 dc, ch 3, 1 sc around 4-ch, rep from * across row, ending with last sc in last ch, ch 5, turn.

Row 5: * 1 sc around 5-ch, ch 5, 1 sc in 3-ch, ch 3, 1 dc in 2nd dc, 1 dc in 3rd dc, ch 3, 1 sc in 3-ch, ch 5, 1 sc in 5-ch, ch 5, rep from * across row, ending with last sc, 2 chs, 1 dc in the sc, ch 1, turn.

Row 6: 1 sc in dc, * 8 dc in 5-ch, 1 sc around 5-ch, ch 5, 1 sc in last ch, ch 5, 1 sc in 5-ch, rep

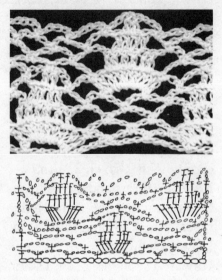

from * across row, ending with 4 dc in the last ch, ch 3, turn.

Row 7: 1 dc in 2nd dc, 1 dc in 3rd dc, * ch 4, 1 sc in 5-ch, ch 5, 1 sc in 5 ch, ch 4, 1 dc in 2nd dc, 1 dc in next 5 dc, rep from * across row, ending with last group, 1 ch, 1 dc in sc, ch 5, turn.

Row 8: 1 sc in 1-ch, * ch 3, 1 dc in 2nd, 1 dc in 3rd dc, ch 3, 1 sc in 4-ch, ch 5, 1 sc in 5-ch, ch 5, 1 sc in 4-ch, rep from * across row, ending with 1 dc in last dc, 1 dc in the last ch, ch 6, turn.

Row 9: *1 sc in 3-ch, ch 5, 1 sc in 5-ch, ch 5, 1 sc in 3-ch, ch 3, 1 dc in 2nd, 1 dc in 3rd dc, ch 3, rep from * across row, ending with last group, 2 chs, 1 dc, ch 1,

78

turn.

Repeat rows 1-9 for pattern.

38. Multiples of 7 plus 4.

Row 1: 1 dc in the 5th ch, * ch 2, 1 dc in the 7th ch, ch 3, 1 dc in the 7th ch, rep from * across row, ending with 1 dc in 7th ch, ch 1, 1 dc in the 7th ch, ch 3, turn.

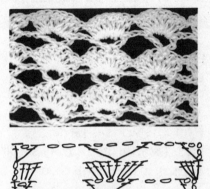

Row 2: 3 dc in the 1st ch, * 8 dc around 3-ch, rep from * across row, with 5 dc in last ch, ch 4, turn.

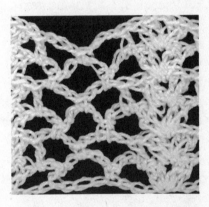

39. Multiples of 12 plus 4.

Row 1: 2 dc in 4th ch, * ch 3, 1 sc in 4th ch, ch 5, 1 sc in 4th ch, ch 3, 2 dc in 4th ch, (ch 1, 2 dc, ch 1, 2 dc) in 4th ch, rep from * across row, ending with 3 dc in last ch, ch 3, turn.

Row 2: 2 dc in 1st dc, *1 dc around 1st 3-ch, 1 sc around next 5-ch, ch 3, 1 dc around 3-ch, (2dc, 1 ch, 2 dc) around 1-ch between the 2 dc of the prev row, rep from * across row, ending with 3 dc in last ch, ch 3, turn.

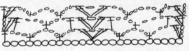

Row 3: Repeat row 1, make sc just after the dc, ch 5, make next sc before the db ch.

Repeat rows 1-2 for pattern.

40. Multiples of 14 plus 4.

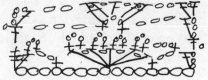

Row 1: 1 dc in the 4th ch, * ch 2, 1 sc in the 3rd ch, make 5 dc with ch 1 in between each 5 dc, ch 2, rep from * across row, ending with 3 dc with ch 1 between each dc, 2 chs in last ch, ch 1, turn.

Row 2: 1 sc in the 1st dc, * (1 sc, ch 3, 1 sc), in the 1-ch, (1 sc, ch 3, 1 sc), in the next 1-ch, ch 3, (1 sc, ch 3, 1 sc), in the 1-ch between the 2 sides of the V-st, ch 3, (1 sc, ch 3, 1 sc) in the next 1-ch, ch 3, (1 sc, ch 3, 1 sc) in the next 1-ch, rep from * across row, ending with (1 sc, ch 1, 1 hdc), in last ch, ch 3, turn.

Row 3: 1 dc in the hdc, * ch 3, (1 sc, ch 3, 1 sc) in 3rd 3-ch, ch 3, (1 dc, ch 1, 1 dc) in the 3rd 3-ch, rep from * across row, ending with 1 sc, 1 ch, 1 hdc in last sc, ch 1, turn.

Row 4: Repeat row 1, except work (1 sc, 3 ch, 1 sc) in 1-ch, and the 5 dc, ch 1 are worked in the middle of the 3-ch.

Repeat rows 1-3 for pattern.

Chapter VII

Relief Stitch

1. Multiples of 4 plus 2.

Row 1: 1 sc in the 2nd ch and across row, ch 3, turn.

Row 2: 1 dc in the 2nd sc, * ch 1, 1 other dc in the same sc, 1 dc in the 2nd sc, 1 dc in the 2nd sc, repeat from * across row, ending with 1 dc in the last sc, ch 3, turn.

Row 3: * 1 dc in the 1-ch, ch 1, 1 other dc in the same ch-1 sp, work from the front, 1 relief dc around the base of the single standing dc, repeat from *, ending with 1 dc in the last ch, ch 3, turn.

Row 4: Repeat row 3, except work the relief st from the back. Repeat rows 3-4 for pattern.

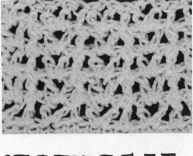

2. Multiples of 2.

Row 1: 1 dc in 3rd ch and each ch across row, ch 2, turn.
Row 2: * Yo, insert hk horizontally from right to left under next dc, yo and pull through, yo and pull through 2 lps on hk, yo and pull through last 2 lps, repeat from * across row, ch 2, turn.
Repeat row 2 for pattern.

3. Multiples of 4 plus 3.

Row 1: 1 dc in the 4th ch and across the row, ch 3, turn.
Row 2: 1 dc in the 2nd and 3rd dc, * from the front, work 1 relief dc around the base of the next dc, 1 dc in the next 3 dc, repeat from *, ending with 1 dc in the last dc, ch 3, turn.
Row 3: 1 dc in the 2nd dc and across the row, ch 3, turn.
Row 4: Work 1 front relief dc around the base of the 2nd dc, * dc in the next 3 dc, work 1 front relief dc around the base of the next dc, repeat from * ending with a dc in the last ch, ch 3, turn. Make sure to stagger the relief stitches.
Repeat rows 1-4 for pattern.

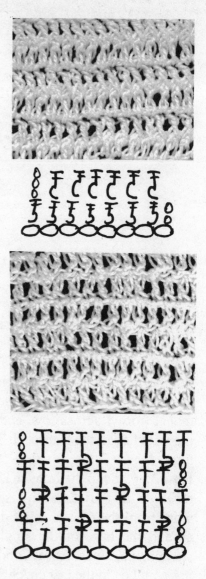

4. Multiples of 2.

Row 1: Sk 3 ch, 1 dc in each ch across row, ch 1, turn.

Row 2: 1 sc in each dc across row, ch 2, turn.

Row 3: * 1 relief hdc around the front of 1 dc of row 1, 1 dc in next sc, repeat from * across row, ch 1, turn.

Row 4: * 1 sc in top of relief hdc, 1 sc between relief hdc and the dc, repeat from *across row, ch 2, turn.

Row 5: * 1 relief hdc around the front of 1 relief hdc of 2 rows below, 1 dc in next sc, repeat from * across row, ch 1, turn. Repeat row 4-5 for pattern.

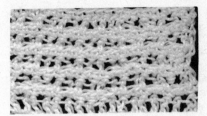

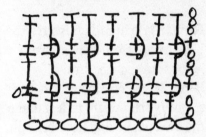

5. Multiples of 4 plus 4.

Row 1: 1 dc in the 4th ch and across the row, ch 1, turn.

Row 2: 1 sc in the 1st dc and across the row, ch 3, turn.

Row 3: Work 2 front relief dc around the base of the 2nd dc and the next 2nd dc, with the 2 sts finishing together, * ch 1, 1 dc in the 2nd sc, ch 1, work 2 front relief dc around the base of the 2nd and 4th dc, making these sts finish together, repeat from *, ending with 1 dc in the last sc, ch

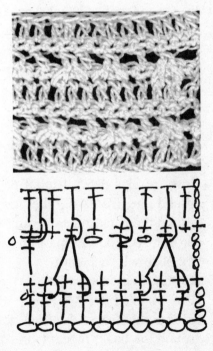

1, turn.
Row 4: 1 sc in each st and ch across the row, ch 3, turn.
Repeat rows 1-4 for pattern.

6. Multiples of 4.

Row l: 1 dc in 3rd ch from hk, * 1 dc in next ch, repeat from * across row, ch 2, turn.

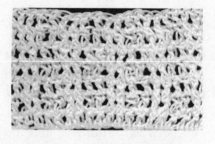

Row 2: * (Yo, insert hk horizontally from right to left under the next dc, yo and pull through, yo and pull through 2 lps on hk, yo and pull through last 2 lps) 2 times, (yo, insert hk from back to front, over and around next dc, yo and pull through last 2 lps) 2 times, repeat from * across row, ch 2, turn.
Repeat row 2 for pattern.

7. Multiples of 8 plus 3.

Row l: 1 dc in 3rd dc from hk, and across the row, ch 2, turn.

Row 2: Sk 1 dc, * 4 relief dc around the front, 4 relief dc around the back, repeat from * across row, 1 dc in top of ch at beg of row 1, ch 2, turn.
Row 3: Same as row 2.
Row 4: Sk 1 dc, * 4 relief dc around the front, 4 relief dc around the back, repeat from *

across row, 1 dc in last ch, ch 2, turn.

Row 5: Sk 1 dc, * 4 relief dc around the front, 4 relief dc around the back, repeat from * across row, 1 dc in last ch, ch 2, turn.

Repeat row 4-5 for pattern.

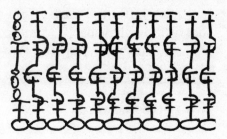

8. Multiples of 6 plus 1.

Row 1: 1 dc in 3rd ch from hk, * sk 2 ch, (2 dc, ch 1, 2 dc) in next ch, sk 2 ch, 1 dc in next ch, repeat from * across row, ch 2, turn.

Row 2: Sk 3 dc, * (2 dc, ch 1, 2 dc) in next ch-1 sp, sk 2 dc, yo, insert hk horizontally from right to left under next dc, yo and pull through, yo and pull through 2 lps on hk, yo and pull through last 2 lps on hk, sk 2 dc, repeat from * across row, ch 3, turn.

Row 3: Sk 3 dc, * (2 dc, ch 1, 2 dc) in next ch-1 sp, sk 2 dc, 1 dc around post of next dc, sk 2 dc, repeat from * across row, ending with 1 dc in last ch, ch 3, turn.

Repeat row 3 for pattern.

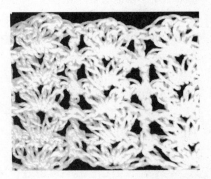

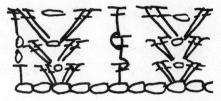

9. Multiples of 6.

Row 1: 1 dc in 3rd ch and each ch across row, ch 2, turn.

Row 2: Sk 1 dc * (1 relief dc

around the front) 3 times, (1 relief dc around the back) 3 times, * (1 relief dc around the front) 3 times, 1 dc in the top of the last ch, ch 3, turn.

Row 3: Same as row 2.

Row 4: Sk 1 dc, * (1 relief dc around the back) 3 times, (1 relief dc around the front) 3 times, (1 relief dc around the front) 3 times, 1 dc in top of the last ch, ch 2, turn.

Row 5: Same as row 4.

Repeat rows 3-5 for pattern.

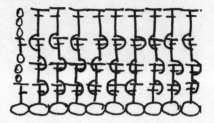

10. Multiples of 10 plus 4.

Row 1: 1 dc in the 5th ch and 6th ch, * work 2 dc in the 3rd ch, ch 2, 2 dc in same ch, 1 dc in the 3rd ch and the 4th ch, repeat from * across row, ending row with 3 dc, ch 3, turn.

Row 2: Work 1 front relief dc around the base of the 2nd dc, work another relief dc in the next dc, * 2 dc in the 2-ch, ch 2, 2 dc in the same 2-ch, work 1 front relief dc around the base of the 3rd dc, work another front relief dc in the 4th dc, repeat from * across row, ending with 2 front relief dc around the base of the last 2 dc and 1 dc in the last ch, ch 3, turn.

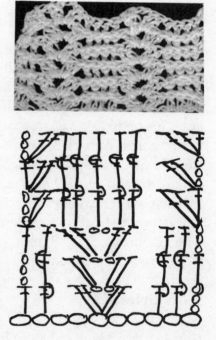

86

Row 3: 1 back relief dc around the base of the relief dc, 1 back relief dc around the next dc, * 2 dc in the 2-ch, ch 2, 2 dc in the same 2-ch, work 1 back relief dc around the base of the relief dc, repeat in the next 4 sts, repeat from * across row, ending row with 2 back relief dc around the last 2 relief dc, 1 dc in the last ch, ch 3, turn.

Repeat rows 1-3 for pattern.

Chapter VIII

Puff Stitch

1. Multiples of 2 plus 3.

Row 1: Work 4-lp puff st in the 4th ch,* ch 1, work 4-lp puff st in 2nd ch, repeat from * across row, ending with 1 dc in the last ch, ch 3, turn.

Row 2: Work 4-lp puff st in the 1-ch * ch 1, work 4-lp puff st in the 1-ch, repeat from * across row, ending with 1 ch and 1 dc in the last ch, ch 3, turn.

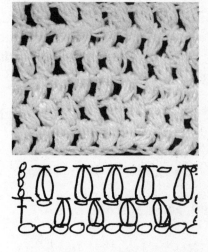

2. Multiples of 8 plus 4.

Row 1: 1 dc in the 4th ch and the next 2 chs, * ch 1, 1 dc in the 2nd ch and the next 6 chs, repeat from * across row, ending with 4 dc, ch 3, turn.

Row 2: 1 dc in the 2nd dc and the next 2 dc, * work a 4-lp puff around the 1-ch, 1 dc in the next 7 dc, repeat from * across row,

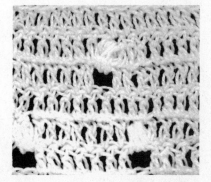

ending with 4 dc, ch 3, turn.

Row 3: 1 dc in each dc, 1 dc in each puff across row, ch 3, turn.

Row 4: Same as row 3.

Row 5: 1 dc in the 2nd dc and the next 6 dc, * ch 1, 1 dc in the 2nd dc and the next 6 dc, repeat from * across row, ending with 7 dc and 1 dc in the last ch, ch 3, turn.

Row 6: 1 dc in the 2nd dc and the next 6 dc, * work a 4-lp puff st around the 1-ch, 1 dc in the next dc, 1 dc in the next 6 dc, repeat from * across row, ending with 7 dc and 1 dc in the last ch, ch 3, turn.

Row 7: Work 1 dc in each st and in the last ch, ch 3, turn.

Row 8: Same as row 7.

Repeat rows 1-8 for pattern.

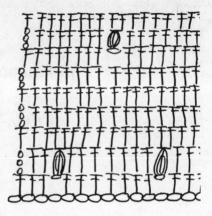

3. Multiples of 6 plus 4.

Row 1: 1 sc in the 4th ch, * ch 3, 1 sc in the 3rd ch, repeat from * across row, ending row with, 1 ch, 1 hdc in the 2nd ch, ch 1, turn.

Row 2: 1 sc in the hdc, * 7 dc around the 1st 3-ch, 1 sc around the 2nd 3-ch, rep from * across row, ending row with sc in the last ch, ch 6, turn.

Row 3: * 1 sc in the 4th dc, ch 3, make a 4-lp puff st in the sc, ch 3, repeat from * across row,

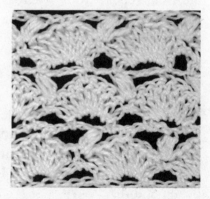

ending with ch 3, 1 dc in the sc, ch 4, turn.

Row 4: *1 sc around the middle of the 3-ch, ch 3, repeat from * across row, ending with ch 1, 1 hdc in the last ch, ch 3, turn.

Row 5: 3 dc in the 1-ch, *1 sc in the 3-ch , 7 dc in the next 3-ch, repeat from * across row, ending with 4 dc in the last ch, ch 1, turn.

Row 6: 1 sc in the 1st dc, * ch 2, make a 4-lp puff st in the sc, ch 2, 1 sc in the 4th dc, repeat from * across row, ending with 2 chs, 1 sc in the last ch, ch 3, turn. Repeat rows 1-6 for pattern.

4. Multiples of 14 plus 4.

Row 1: 1 dc in the 4th ch and the next 3, * ch 1, 1 dc in the 2nd ch, 5 times, 1 dc in the next 4 chs, repeat from * across row, ending with 5 dc, ch 3, turn.

Row 2: Same as row 1.

Row 3: 1 dc in the 2nd dc and the next 3, * ch 1, 1 dc in the next dc, ch 1, 1 dc in the next dc, make a 4-lp puff st in next ch, 1 dc in the next dc, ch 1, 1 dc in the next dc, 1 dc in the next 4 dc, repeat from * across row, ending with 5 dc, ch 3, turn.

Row 4: 1 dc in the 2nd dc and the

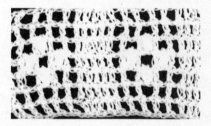

next 3, * ch 1, 1 dc in the next dc, make a 4-lp puff st in the next 1-ch, 1 dc in the next dc, ch 1, 1 dc in the next dc, make a 4-lp puff st in the next ch, 1 dc in the next dc, ch 1, 1 dc in the next dc and the next 4 dc, repeat from * across row, ending with 5 dc, ch 3, turn.

Row 5: 1 dc in the 2nd dc and the next 3, * ch 1, 1 dc in the next dc, ch 1, 1 dc in the next dc, make a 4-lp puff st in the next 1-ch, 1 dc in the next dc, ch 1, 1 dc in the next dc, ch 1, 1 dc in the next dc, 1 dc in the next 4 dc, repeat from * across row, ending with 5 dc, ch 3, turn.

5. Multiples of 10 plus 4.

Row 1: 1 dc in the 4th ch, * ch 2, 5 dc in the 4th ch, ch 2, 1 dc in the 4th ch and in the next 2 chs, repeat from * across row, ending with 2 dc, ch 5, turn.

Row 2: Sk 1st 2 dc, * 1 dc in the 1st dc, 2 dc in the next dc, 1 dc in the next dc, 2 dc in the next dc, 1 dc in the next dc, ch 2, 1 dc in the 2nd dc, ch 2, repeat from * across row, ending with 1 dc in the last ch, ch 3, turn.

Row 3: Sk 1 dc, make a 4-lp puff st in the next dc, * ch 2, make a

4-lp puff st in the 2nd dc, ch 2, make a 4-lp puff st in the 2nd dc, repeat from * across row, ending with 1 dc in the last ch, ch 5, turn.

Row 4: 1 dc in the 2-ch after the 1st puff st, * ch 2, 1 dc in the 2-ch after the 2nd puff st, ch 2, 1 dc in the ch just used, ch 2, 1 dc after the 3rd puff st, ch 3, repeat from * across row, ending with 2 chs, 1 dc in the last ch, ch 3, turn.

Row 5: Repeat row 1, except the 5 dc are worked in the 2-ch between the sides of the v-st and the 3 dc are worked in the 3-chs between the sets.

Repeat rows 1-4 for pattern.

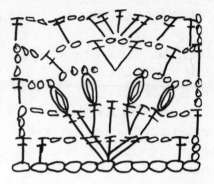

6. Multiples of 6 plus 1.

Row 1: 1 sc in 2nd ch, * ch 3, make a 4-lp puff st in the 3rd ch, ch 3, 1 sc in the 3rd ch, repeat from * across row, ch 7, turn.

Row 2: 1 sc in the 3-ch, ch 3,* make a 4-lp puff st around the next 3-ch, ch 3, 1 sc in the next 3-ch, ch 3, repeat from * across row, ending with 1 trc in the last sc, ch 1, turn.

Repeat rows 1-2 for pattern.

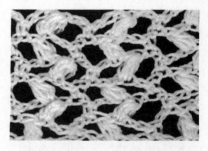

7. Multiples of 8 plus 4.

Row 1: 1 dc in the 4th ch, * 1 dc in the next 2 chs, make a 3-lp puff st in the next ch, 1 dc in the next 3 chs, ch 1, 1 dc in the 2nd ch, repeat from * across row, ending with 1 extra dc, ch 4, turn.

Row 2: * 1 dc in the 3rd dc, and the next dc, 1 dc in the puff st and the next 2 dc, ch 1, 1 dc in the 1-ch, ch 1, repeat from * across row, ending with 5 dc, 1 ch, 1 dc in the last ch, ch 3, turn.

Row 3: * 1 dc in the 1-ch, ch 1, 1 dc in the 2nd dc and the next 2 dc, ch 1, 1 dc in the 1-ch, 1 dc in the dc, repeat from * across row, ending with 1 dc in the 1-ch, 1 dc in the last ch, ch 3, turn.

Row 4: 1 dc in the 2nd dc, * 1 dc in the 1-ch, ch 1, 1 dc in the 2nd dc, ch 1, 1 dc in the next 3 dc, repeat from * across row, ending with 3 dc, ch 3, turn.

Row 5: 1 dc in the 2nd dc, 1 dc in the next dc, 1 dc in the 1-ch, * ch 1, 1 dc in the 1-ch, 1 dc in the next 2 dc, make a 3-lp puff in the next dc, 1 dc in the next 2 dc, 1 dc in the 1-ch, repeat from * across row, ending with 4 dc, ch 3, turn.

Row 6: 1 dc in the 2nd dc, 1 dc in the 3rd dc, * ch 1, 1 dc in the 1-ch, ch 1, 1 dc in the 2nd dc, and the

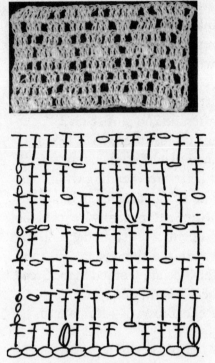

next dc, 1 dc in the puff st and the next 2 dc, repeat from * across row, ending with 3 dc, ch 3, turn.

Row 7: 1 dc in the 2nd dc, * ch 1, 1 dc in the 1-ch, 1 dc in the dc, 1 dc in the 1-ch, ch 1, 1 dc in the 2nd dc and the next 2 dc, repeat from * across row, ending with 2 dc, ch 4, turn.

Row 8: * 1 dc in the 1-ch, 1 dc in the next 3 dc, 1 dc in the 1-ch, ch 1, 1 dc in the 2nd dc, ch 1, repeat from *, ending row with 1 ch, 1 dc in the last ch, ch 3, turn.

Repeat rows 1-8 for pattern.

8. Multiples of 6 plus 4.

Row 1: Sk 3 ch, * (1 dc, ch 2, 1 dc) in next ch, sk 2 ch, 1 4-lp puff, ch 1, sk 2, repeat from * across row, ending with (1 dc, ch 2, 1 dc) in last ch, ch 3, turn.

Row 2: * 1 puff in 2-ch sp between 2 dc of prev row, ch 1, (1 dc, ch 2, 1 dc) under lp that closes the puff in prev row, repeat from * across row, ending with 1 puff, 1 dc in 3-ch sp at beg of prev row, ch 3, turn.

Row 3: (1 dc, ch 2, 1 dc) in top of puff, * 1 puff in 2-ch sp, ch 1, (1 dc, ch 2, 1 dc) in top of puff, repeat from * across row, ending with 1 dc in 3-ch sp at beg of prev row, ch 3, turn.

Repeat rows 2-3 for pattern.

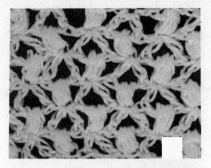

9. Multiples of 10 plus 5.

Row 1: 1 dc in the 5th ch, * ch 1, 1 dc in the 2nd ch, repeat from * across row, ch 4, turn.

Row 2: Repeat row 1.

Row 3: 1 dc in the 2nd dc, * ch 2, make 3-lp puff in the next dc, make 2nd 3-lp puff st in the 2nd dc, crochet both puff sts together, ch 4, 1 dc in the next dc, ch 1, 1 dc in the next dc, repeat from * across row, ending with 1

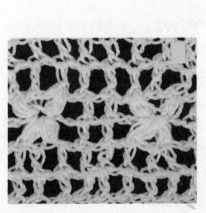

dc in the last ch, ch 4, turn.

Row 4: 1 dc in the 2nd dc, * make 3-lp puff st in the top of the 2 puff sts, ch 3, make another 3-lp st in the same place as the lst puff st, ch 2, 1 dc in the dc, ch 1, 1 dc in the dc, repeat from * across row, ending with 1 dc in the last ch, ch 4, turn.

Repeat rows 1-4 for pattern.

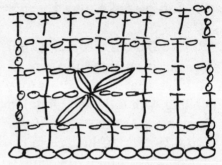

10. Multiples of 4 plus 4.

Row 1: 1 hdc in the 5th ch, * ch 1, 1 hdc in the 2nd ch, repeat from * across row, ch 3, turn.

Row 2: * 1 hdc in the 1-ch, ch 1, make a 4-lp puff st in the next 1-ch, ch 1, repeat from * across row, ending with 1 hdc in the last ch, ch 4, turn.

Row 3: 1 hdc in the 1-ch, ch 1, repeat from * across row, ending with 1 hdc in the last ch, ch 3, turn.

Row 4: * Make a 4-lp puff st in the next 1-ch, ch 1, 1 hdc in the next 1-ch, ch 1, repeat from * across row, ending with 1 ch, 1 hdc in the last ch, ch 4, turn.

Repeat rows 1-4 for pattern.

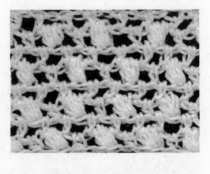

Chapter IX

Popcorn Stitch

l. Multiples of 4 plus 3.

Row l: l sc in 2nd ch, * 3 trc in next ch, (keeping last lp of each trc on hk, yo and pull through 4 lps on hk), (popcorn made), l sc in the next 3 chs, repeat from * across row, ending with l sc in last ch, ch l, turn.

Row 2: * l sc in next st, repeat from * across row, ch l, turn.

Row 3: * l sc in the next 3 sc, l popcorn st in next sc, repeat from * across row, ending with l sc in the last 3 sc, ch l, turn.

Row 4: Same as row 2.

Row 5: l sc in lst sc, * l popcorn in next sc, l sc in the next 3 sc, repeat from * across row, ending with l sc in the last sc, ch l, turn.

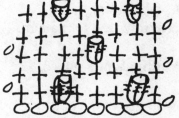

97

2. Multiples of 6 plus l.

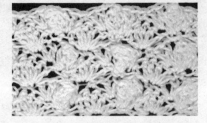

Row l: 2 dc in 4th ch, * sk 2 ch, l sc in next ch, sk 2 ch, 5 dc in last ch, repeat from * across row, ending with 3 dc in last ch, ch 1, turn.

Row 2: l sc in lst dc, * sk l dc, 2 dc in next dc, 4 dc in next sc, (take lp of hk, insert hk in lst dc of 4-dc group, yo and pull lp of 4th dc through, ch l), (popcorn st made), 2 dc in next dc, sk l dc, l sc in next dc, repeat from * across row, ending with l sc in last ch of prev row, ch 3, turn.

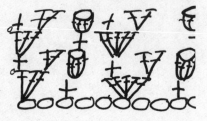

Row 3: 2 dc in lst sc,* sk 2 dc, l sc in top of next popcorn st, sk 2 dc, 5 dc in next sc, repeat from * across row, ending with 3 dc in last sc, ch l, turn.

Repeat rows 2-3 for pattern.

3. Multiples of 6 plus 3.

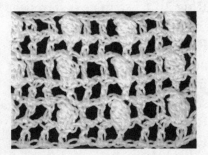

Row l: l dc in 6th ch, * ch 1, sk l ch, l dc in next ch, repeat from * across row, ch 4, turn.

Row 2: Sk (l dc, ch l), * 4 dc in next dc, (take lp off hk, insert hk through lst dc of 4-dc group, pull lp of 4th through), (l popcorn st made) (ch l, sk ch-l, l dc next dc) twice, ch 1, sk ch-l sp, repeat from * across row, ending with l popcorn st in next dc, (ch 1, sk 1 ch, 1 dc), in last ch of prev row, ch 4, turn.

Row 3: Sk 1 dc, ch-1, * 1 dc in next popcorn st, (ch 1, sk ch-1, 1 dc) twice in next dc, ch 1, sk ch-1, repeat from * across row, ending with 1 dc in next popcorn st, ch 1, sk 1 ch, 1 dc in last ch of prev row, ch 4, turn.

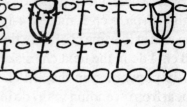

4. Multiples of 12 plus 1.

Row 1: 1 sc in 2nd ch, * ch 3, make a 4-lp popcorn st in the 3rd ch, ch 3, sc in the 3rd ch, repeat from *, ending with sc, ch 1, turn.

Row 2: 1 sc in the 1st sc, * make 1 sc around each of the 3-chs, make 1 sc around each of the next 3-chs, repeat from *, ending with 1 extra sc in the last sc, ch 2, turn.

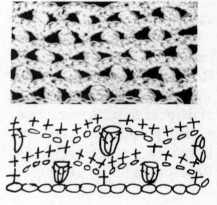

Row 3: Make 1 dc in the 1st sc, * ch 3, 1 sc over the popcorn st, ch 3, make a 4-lp popcorn st between the 2 sc over the sc of the prev row, repeat from * across row, ending with 2-lp popcorn st in the last sc, ch 1, turn.

Row 4: 1 sc in the popcorn st, * make 1 sc in each of the 3-chs, repeat from *, ending with 1 extra sc in the last dc, ch 1, turn. Repeat rows 1-4 for pattern.

5. Multiples of 14 plus 4.

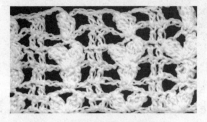

Row 1: Make a 4-lp popcorn st in the 7th ch, * ch 3, make a 4-lp popcorn st in same ch, 1 dc in the 3rd ch, 1 dc in the next ch, make a 4-lp popcorn st in the 3rd ch, repeat from *, ending with 1 dc in the 3rd ch after the last set, ch 6, turn.

Row 2: * 1 sc around the 3-ch, ch 3, 1 dc in the dc, dc in the next dc, ch 3, repeat from *, ending with 3 chs, 1 dc in the last ch, ch 5, turn.

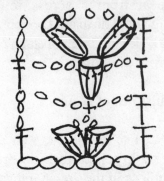

Row 3: * Make a 4-lp popcorn st in the sc, ch 2, 1 dc in the dc, dc in the next dc, ch 3, repeat from *, ending with 2 chs, 1 dc in the last ch, ch 3, turn.

Repeat rows 1-3 for pattern.

6. Multiples of 24 plus 4.

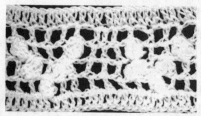

Row 1: 1 dc in the 4th ch and across the row.

Row 2: 1 dc in the 2nd dc, and the next dc, * ch 1, 1 dc in the 2nd dc, 6 times, 1 dc in each of the next 2 dc, repeat from *, ending with 2 dc in the dc, 1 dc in the last ch, ch 3, turn.

Row 3: 1 dc in the 2nd dc and the next dc, * ch 1, make a 5-lp popcorn st in the next dc, ch 1, (dc in

100

the next dc, ch 1), 3 times, make a 5-lp popcorn st in the next dc, ch 1, dc in the next dc, and the next 2 dc, repeat from *, ending with 2 dc in the last 2 dc, 1 dc in the last ch, ch 4, turn.

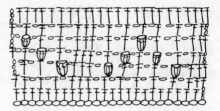

Row 4: 1 dc in the 2nd dc, 1 dc in the next dc, * ch 1, dc in the top of the 5-lp popcorn st, ch 1, 5-lp popcorn st in the next dc, ch 1, dc in the dc, ch 1, 5 lp popcorn st in the next dc, ch 1, dc in the top of the popcorn st, ch 1, 1 dc in each of the next 3 dc, repeat from *, ending with 1 dc in each of the last 2 dc, 1 dc in the last ch, ch 3, turn.

Row 5: 1 dc in the 2nd dc and the next, * ch 1, dc in the next dc, ch 1, 5-lp popcorn st in next dc, ch 1, dc in the dc, ch 1, dc in the dc, ch 1, 1 dc in each of the next 3 dc, repeat from *, ending with 2 dc in dc, 1 dc in the last ch, ch 3, turn.

Row 6: 1 dc in the 2nd and 3rd dc, * ch 1, dc in the dc, ch 1, dc in the dc, ch 1, dc in the popcorn st, ch 1, dc in the dc, ch 1, dc in the dc, ch 1, dc in the dc, 1 dc in the next 2 dc, repeat from * across row, ending with 2 dc in the last 2 dcs, 1 dc in last ch, ch 3, turn.

Row 7: Repeat row 1, except 1 dc in each ch and dc across row. Repeat rows 1-6 for pattern.

7. Multiples of 12 plus 7.

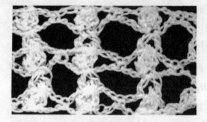

Row 1: 1 sc in the 10th ch, * ch 3, 4-lp popcorn st in 3rd ch, ch 3, 1 sc in the 3rd ch, repeat from * ending with 3 chs and 1 dc in last ch, ch 3, turn.

Row 2: 1 dc in the 1st dc, * ch 5, 1 more dc in the same st, repeat from *, ending with 2 dc in the last ch, ch 6, turn.

Row 3: Repeat row 1, except make sc in the middle of the 5-ch, popcorn st made in the middle of the V-st.

Repeat rows 1-2 for pattern.

8. Multiples of 8 plus 4.

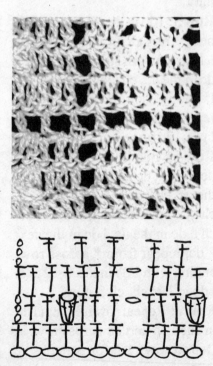

Row 1: 1 dc in the 4th ch and the next 5 chs, * 1 dc in the 2nd ch and the next 6 chs, repeat from *, ending with 7 dc, ch 3, turn.

Row 2: 1 dc in the 2nd dc, 1 dc in the next dc, * make a 4-lp popcorn st in the next dc, 1 dc in the next 3 dc, ch 1, 1 dc in the next dc and the next 2 dc, repeat from *, ending with last set, ch 3, turn.

Row 3: 1 dc in the 2nd dc, 1 dc in the 3rd dc, 1 dc in the popcorn st and the next 3 dc, * ch 1, 1 dc in the next 3 dc, the popcorn st, the next 3 dc, repeat from *, ending with the last set in the last ch, ch

4, turn.

Row 4: 1 dc in the 3rd dc, ch 1, 1 dc in the 2nd dc, ch 1, 1 dc in the 2nd dc, * (ch 1, 1 dc in the 1st dc, 1 dc in the 2nd dc, ch 1), 3 times, repeat from *, ending with 1 sc in the last ch, ch 4, turn.

Repeat rows 1-4 for pattern.

9. Multiples of 16 plus 4.

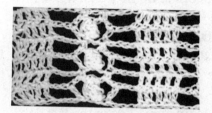

Row 1: 1 dc in the 4th ch and in the next 3 chs, * ch 5, 1 sc in the 5th ch, ch 3, 1 sc in the 2nd ch, ch 5, 1 dc in the 5th ch and in the next 4 chs, repeat from * ending with 5 dc, ch 3, turn.

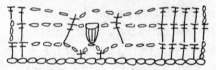

Row 2: Make 1 dc in the 2nd dc, and the next 4 dc, 1 dc in the middle of the 5-ch, ch 1, make a 4-lp popcorn st in the 3-ch, ch 1, make 1 dc in the middle of the next 5-ch, ch 5, 1 dc in each of the next 5 dc, repeat from *, ending with 1 extra dc in the last ch, ch 3, turn.

Row 3: Repeat row 1.

Repeat rows 1-2 for pattern.

10. Multiples of 16 plus 5.

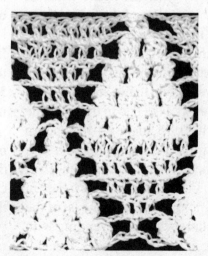

Row 1: 1 dc in the 4th ch, * ch 3, make a 4-lp popcorn st in the 4th ch, ch 1, 4-lp in the 2nd ch, ch 1, 4-lp popcorn st in the 2nd ch, ch

103

1, 4-lp popcorn in the 2nd ch, ch 1, 4-lp popcorn in the 2nd ch, ch 1, 4-lp popcorn in the 2nd ch, ch 3, 1 dc in the 4th ch, repeat from *, ending with 1 dc in the next 2 chs, ch 3, turn.

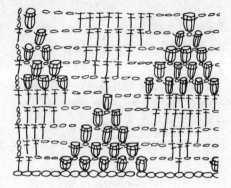

Row 2: 1 dc in the 2nd dc, 1 dc in the 1st ch, * ch 3, make a 4-lp popcorn st in the 1-ch, ch 1, 4-lp popcorn st in the next 1-ch, ch 1, make a 4-lp popcorn st in the next 1-ch, ch 3, 1 dc in the last of the 3-ch, dc in the dc, 1 dc in the 1st of the next 3-ch, repeat from *, ending with 1 dc in the last dc, 1 dc in the last ch, ch 3, turn.

Row 3: 1 dc in the 2nd dc and the 3rd dc, 1 dc in the 1st ch of the 3-ch, * ch 3, make a 4-lp popcorn st in the 1-ch, ch 1, 4-lp popcorn st in the next 1-ch, ch 1, make a 4-lp popcorn st in the next 1-ch, ch 3, 1 dc in the last of the 3-ch, 1 dc in the next 3 dc, 1 dc in the 1st of the 3-ch, repeat from *, ending with 1 extra dc in the last ch, ch 1, turn.

Row 4: 1 dc in the 2nd dc, 1 dc in the next 2 dc, 1 dc in the 1st of the 3-ch, * ch 3, make a 4-lp popcorn st in the 1-ch, ch 1, make a 4-lp popcorn st in the next 1-ch, ch 3, 1 dc in the last of the 3-ch, 1 dc in the next 5 dc, 1 dc in the 1st of the 3-ch, repeat from *, ending with 1 dc in the last ch, ch 3, turn.

Row 5: 1 dc in the 2nd dc, 1 dc in the next 3 dc, 1 dc in the 1st of the 3-ch, * ch 3, make a 4-lp popcorn st in the 1-ch, ch 3, 1 dc in the last of the 3-ch, 1 dc in the next 7 dc, 1 dc in the 1st of the 3-ch, repeat from * ending with 1 extra dc in the last ch, ch 3, turn.

Row 6: Make a 4-lp popcorn st in the 2nd dc, ch 1, make a 4-lp popcorn in the 2nd dc, ch 1, make a 4-lp popcorn st in the 2nd dc, * ch 3, 1 dc in the popcorn st, ch 3, make a 4-lp popcorn st in the next dc, ch 1, make a 4-lp popcorn st in the 2nd dc, ch 1, make a 4-lp popcorn st in the 2nd dc, ch 1, 4-lp popcorn st in the 2nd dc, ch 1, make another 4-lp popcorn st in the 2nd dc, repeat from *, ending with 1 dc in the last ch, ch 3, turn.

Row 7: Make a 4-lp popcorn st in the 1-ch, ch 1, make a 4-lp popcorn st in next 1-ch, * ch 3, 1 dc in last of the 3-ch, dc in the dc, dc in 1st of the 3-ch, ch 3, make a 4-lp popcorn st in first 1-ch, ch 1, make a 4-lp popcorn st in next 1-ch, ch 1, make a 4-lp popcorn st in next 1-ch, rep from * across row, ending with 1 dc in the last ch, ch 3, turn.

Row 8: Make a 4-lp popcorn st in the 1-ch, ch 1, make a 4-lp popcorn st in the next 1-ch, * ch 3, 1 dc in the last of the 3-ch, ch 3, dc in the dc, dc in the 1st of the 3-ch, ch 3, make a 4-lp popcorn st in the 1-ch, ch 1, make a 4-lp popcorn st in the next 1-ch, ch 1, make a 4-lp popcorn st in the next 1-ch, ch 1, make a 4-lp popcorn st in the next 1-ch, repeat from *, ending with 1 dc in the last ch, ch 3, turn.

Row 9: Make a 4-lp popcorn st in the 1-ch, * ch 3, 1 dc in the last of the 3-ch, 1 dc in the next 5 dc, 1 dc in the 1st of the 3-ch, ch 3, make a 4-lp popcorn st in the 1-ch, ch 1, make a 4-lp popcorn st in the next 1-ch, repeat from *, ending with 1 dc in the last ch, ch 3, turn.

Row 10: Make a 4-lp popcorn st in the 1-ch, * ch 3, 1 dc in the last of the 3-ch, 1 dc in the next 7 dc, and 1 dc in the 1st of the next 3-ch, ch 3, make a 4-lp popcorn st in the 1-ch, repeat from *, ending with 1 dc in the last ch.

Repeat rows 1-10 for pattern.

Chapter X

Cluster Stitch

1. Multiples of any number.

Row 1: * (yo hk, insert hk, yo, pull through a lp, yo, pull through 2 lps) twice in 1st ch, (sk 1 ch), repeat from * across row, ch 2, turn.
Row 2: Repeat row across, working 1 st in each st of prev row across.
Repeat row 1 for pattern.

2. Multiples of 2.

Row 1: * (Yo, insert hk in 1st ch, yo, pull yarn through a loop, yo, pull through 2 lps on hk) 3 times, ch 1, sk 1 ch, repeat from * across row, ch 2, turn.
Row 2: Sk 1st ch, repeat prev row (inserting hk in each ch of prev row.
Repeat row 2 for pattern.

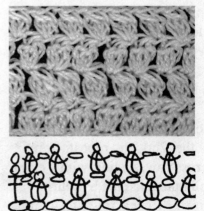

3. Multiples of any even number.

Row 1: * (yo, insert hk, yo, pull through 1 lp, yo, pull through 2 lps) 3 times in 2nd st, yo, pull through all lps, ch 1, sk 1, repeat from * across row, ending with 1 dc in last ch, ch 1, turn.

Row 2: * 1 sc in sp, 1 sc in cluster st, repeat from *, ending with 1 sc in last ch.

Repeat rows 1-2 for pattern.

4. Multiples of 8 plus 1.

Row 1: 1 sc in the 2nd ch, * ch 3, 1 sc in the 3rd ch, repeat from * across row, ending with 1 sc, ch 3, turn.

Row 2: * Make a 3-lp cluster in the next 3-ch, ch 5, 1 sc in the next 3-ch, ch 4, make a 3-lp cluster in the next 3-ch, repeat from *, across row, ending with 1 dc in the sc, ch 1, turn.

Repeat rows 1-2 for pattern.

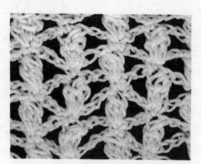

5. Multiples of 4 plus 4.

Row 1: 2 dc in the 4th ch, * 2 dc in the 2nd ch, repeat from * across row, ending with 1 extra dc in the 2nd ch, ch 3, turn.

Row 2: Repeat row 1, ch 4, turn.

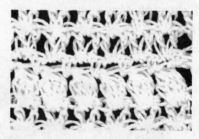

Row 3: Make a 4-lp cluster in the middle of the 2 dc, ch 1, repeat from * across row, ending row after last cluster with 1 extra dc in the last ch, ch 2, turn.

Row 4: * 1 sc in the 1-ch, ch 2, repeat from * across row, ending row with sc in last ch-1, 1 sc in the last ch, ch 3, turn.

Repeat rows 1-4 for pattern.

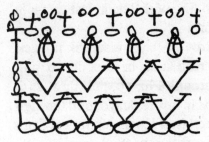

6. Multiples of 5 plus 1.

Row 1: 1 sc in 2nd ch, * ch 4, 4 trc in same ch, sk 4 chs, 1 sc in next ch, repeat from * across row, ending with 1 sc in last ch, ch 1, turn.

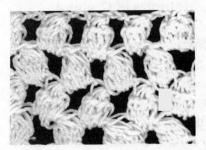

Row 2: * (1 sc, ch 4, 4 trc) through the back lp of next sc, sk (4 trc, ch-4), repeat from * across row, ending with 1 sc through back lp in last sc, ch 1, turn.

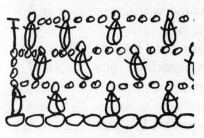

Row 3: * (1 sc, ch 4, 4 trc) through front lp of next sc, sk (4 trc, ch-4) repeat from * across row, ending with 1 sc in front lp of last sc, ch 1, turn.

Repeat rows 2-3 for pattern.

7. Multiples of any number.

Row 1: * 3 dc in 3rd ch, sk 2 sts, ch 2, repeat from * across row,

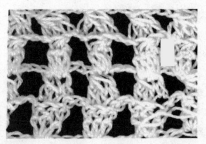

ending with 3 dc in last ch, ch 3, turn.

Row 2: * yo, insert hk in back thread at the head of dc, yo, pull through 1 lp, yo, pull through 2 lps in next 2 dc, yo, pull through the last 4 lps on hk, repeat from * across row, ch 2, turn.

Repeat rows 1-2 for pattern.

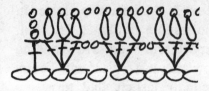

8. Multiples of 12 plus 4.

Row 1: 3 dc in 4th ch, * (3 dc, ch 2, 3 dc) in the 6 ch, repeat from * across row, ending with 4 dc in last ch, ch 3, turn.

Row 2: 1 dc in 2nd dc, * ch 5, 4-lp cluster in 2-ch, repeat from *, ending with 2-lp cluster in last ch, ch 3, turn.

Row 3: * (3 dc, ch 2, 3 dc) in 3rd ch, working group in middle of each 5-ch, repeat from *, ending with 1 dc in last ch, ch 5, turn.

Row 4: 4-lp cluster in 2-ch, * ch 5, 4-lp cluster in 2-ch, repeat from *, ending with 2 chs, 1 dc in last ch, ch 3, turn.

Repeat rows 1-4 for pattern.

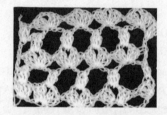

9. Multiples of 4 plus 3.

Row 1: 1 dc in 4th ch, * ch 1, sk 1 ch, 1 dc in next ch, repeat from * across row, ch 4, turn.

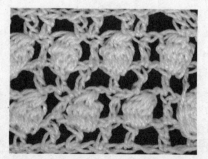

Row 2: Sk (1 dc, ch-1), make a 4-lp cluster in next dc, repeat from * across row, ending with ch 1, 1 dc in last ch of prev row, ch 4, turn.

Row 3: Sk (1 dc, ch-1), * 1 dc in next st, ch 1, sk ch-1, repeat from * across row, ending with 1 dc in 3rd ch of last turning ch of prev row, ch 2, turn.

Row 4: Make a 4-lp cluster st in 1st dc, * ch 1, sk ch-1, 1 dc in next dc, ch 1, sk ch-1, make a 4-lp cluster st in next dc, repeat from * across row, ending with 1 dc in last cluster st, ch 4, turn.

Repeat rows 2-5 for pattern.

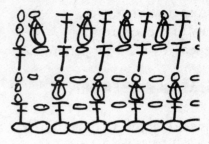

10. Multiples of 4 plus 1.

Row 1: 1 sc in 5th ch, * ch 3, sk 3 ch, 1 sc in next ch, repeat from * across row, ch 5, turn.

Row 2: 1 sc in 1st ch-3 sp, * ch 3, 4-lp cluster in next ch-3 sp, ch 3, 1 sc in next ch-3 sp, repeat from * across row, ending with 1 sc in last ch of prev row, ch 5, turn.

Row 3: 1 sc in 1st ch-3 sp, * ch 3, 1 sc in next ch-3 sp, repeat from * across row, ending with 1 sc in last ch of prev row, ch 5, turn.

Row 4: Make a 4-lp cluster st in 1st ch-3 sp, ch 3, 4-lp cluster st in the next ch-3 sp, repeat from *

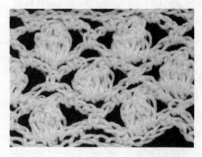

across row, ch 5, turn.

Row 5: Repeat row 3.

Repeat rows 1-5 for pattern.

11. Multiples of 4 plus 3.

Row l: (1 dc, ch 3, 1 dc) in 4th ch, * sk 3 ch, (1 dc, ch 3, 1 dc), in next ch, rep from * across row, ending with sk 1 ch, 1 dc in last ch, ch 1, turn.

Row 2: 1 sc in 1st dc, * sk 1 dc, 3 sc in next ch-3 sp, sk 1 dc, make a 3-lp cluster st in next ch, rep from * across row, ending with 3 sc in last ch-3 sp, 1 sc in last ch of prev row, ch 1, turn.

Row 3: 1 sc in each sc and in top of each cluster st across row, ch 3, turn.

Row 4: Sk 1st 2 sc, *(1 dc, ch 3, 1 dc) in next sc, sk 3 sc, rep from * across row, ending with sk 1 sc, 1 dc in last sc, ch 1, turn.

Row 5: 1 sc in 1st dc, * sk 1 dc, 3 sc in next ch-3 sp, sk 1 dc, 1 sc in next sp, rep from * across row, ending with 1 sc in last ch of prev row, ch 1, turn.

Row 6: 1 sc in each of 1st 4 sc, * make a 3-lp cluster st in next sc, 1 sc in each of the next 3 sc, rep from * across row, ending with 1 sc in each of the last 4 sc, ch 1, turn.

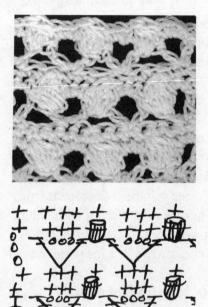

12. Multiples of 12 plus 5.

Row 1: 1 dc in 7th ch, * ch 1, dc in the 2nd ch, rep from * across row, ending with 1 dc in the last ch, ch 3, turn.

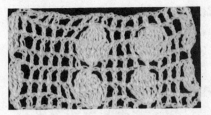

Row 2: 3 trc in the 1st dc, * 1 dc in the 2nd dc, ch 1, dc in the next dc, ch 1, dc in the next dc, make 7 trc in the 2nd dc, rep from * across row, ending with 4 trc in the last ch, ch 3, turn.

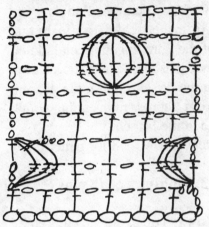

Row 3: Crochet 3 trc together in the 1st ch, * ch 3, dc in the dc, ch 1, dc in the dc, ch 1, dc in the dc, ch 3, crochet all 7 trc together, rep from * across row, ending with 1 dc in the last ch, ch 4, turn.

Row 4: * 1 dc in the 3-ch, ch 1, 1 dc in the dc, ch 1, 1 dc in the dc, ch 1, 1 dc in the dc, ch 1, 1 dc in the 3-ch, ch 1, 1 dc in the top of the 7 trc crochet together, ch 1, rep from * across row, ending with 1 dc in the last ch, ch 4, turn.

Row 5: Sk 1st dc, * dc in the dc, ch 1, rep from * across row, ending with 1 dc in the last ch, ch 4, turn.

Row 6: 1 dc in the 2nd dc, * 7 trc in the 2nd dc, 1 dc in the 2nd dc, ch 1, 1 dc in the 2nd dc, ch 1, 1 dc in the next dc, rep from * across row, ending with 1 dc in the last ch, ch 4, turn.

Row 7: 1 dc in the 2nd sc, * ch 3, crochet 7 trc together in the next 7 trc, ch 3, 1 dc in the next dc, ch 1, dc in the dc, ch 1, dc in the dc, rep from * across row, ending with dc in the last ch, ch 4, turn.

Row 8: 1 dc in the 2nd dc, * ch 1, dc in the 3-ch, ch 1, dc in the top of the 7 trc together, ch 1, dc in the 3-ch, ch 1, dc in the dc, ch 1, dc in the dc, ch 1, dc in the dc, rep from * across row, ending with 1 dc in the last ch.

Repeat rows 1-8 for pattern.

13. Multiples of 18 plus 6.

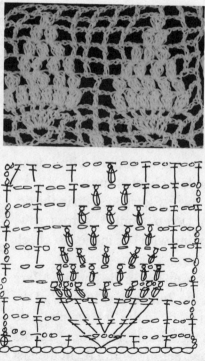

Row 1: 1 dc in the 9th ch, * ch 2, 1 dc in 3rd ch, (1 dc, ch 3, 1 dc) in the 3rd ch, 1 dc in the 3rd ch, ch 2, 1 dc in the 3rd ch, ch 2, rep from * across row, ending with 2 chs, 1 dc in the 3rd ch, ch 5, turn.

Row 2: 1 dc in the 2nd dc, * ch 2, 6 dc around the 3-ch, ch 2, 1 dc in the dc, ch 2, 1 dc in the cluster, ch 2, 1 dc in the dc, rep from * across row, ending with 2 chs, 1 dc in the last ch, ch 5, turn.

Row 3: 1 dc in the dc, * (1 dc in dc, ch 1) 5 times, 1 dc in the last dc of the group, 1 dc in the next dc, ch 2, 1 dc in the dc, ch 2, 1 dc in the dc, rep from * across row, ending with 2 chs, 1 dc in the last ch, ch 5, turn.

Row 4: Make a 3-lp cluster in the 1st dc, ch 1, make 7 clusters, ch 2, 1 dc in the 2 dc, ch 2, rep from * across row, ending with 2 chs, 1 dc in the last ch, ch 5, turn.

Row 5: * Make a 3-lp cluster in the next 1-ch, ch 1, make 6 clusters, ch 2, 1 dc in the dc, ch 2, rep from * across row, ending with 1 dc in the last ch, ch 5, turn.

Row 6: * 1 dc in the cluster, ch 1, make a 3-lp cluster in the 1 ch, ch 1, make 5 clusters, ch 1, 1 dc in the last cluster, ch 2, 1 dc in the dc, ch 2, rep from * across row, ending with 2 chs, 1 dc in the last ch, ch 5, turn.

Row 7: * 1 dc in the dc, ch 2, make a 3-lped cluster in the 1-ch, ch 1, make 4 clusters, ch 2, 1 dc in the dc, ch 2, 1 dc in the dc, ch 2, rep from * across row, ending with 2 chs, 1 dc in the last ch, ch 5, turn.

Row 8: Sk 1 dc, * 1 dc in the dc, ch 2, make a 3-lped cluster in each 1-ch, ch 1, make 3 clusters, ch 2, 1 dc in the dc, ch 2, 1 dc in the dc, ch 2, rep from * across row, ending with 2 chs, 1 dc in the last ch, ch 5, turn.

Row 9: * 1 dc in the dc, ch 2, 1 dc in the 1st cluster, ch 1, make a 3-lped cluster in the 1st 1-ch, ch 1, make a 3-lped cluster in the 1-ch, ch 1, 1 dc in the last cluster, ch 2, 1 dc in the dc, ch 2, 1 dc in the dc, ch 2, dc in the next dc, rep from * across row, ending with 1 dc in the last ch, ch 4, turn.

Row 10: Repeat row 1 except form the pattern in the middle of the space by the 1st set.

Repeat rows 1-9 for pattern.

14. Multiples of 36 plus 4.

Row 1: 1 dc in the 5th ch, and across the row, ch 7, turn.

Row 2: Make 4-lp cluster in the 3rd dc, * ch 1, 4-lp cluster in the 4th dc, ch 1, 4-lp cluster in the 4th dc, ch 4, 1 dc in the 2nd dc, 1 ch 6 times, dc in the 2nd dc, ch 4, 4-lp cluster in the 2nd dc, rep from * across row, ending with 1 dc in the last ch, ch 7, turn.

Row 3: * 1 sc in the top of the 1st cluster, 1 sc in the top of the 2nd cluster, 1 sc in the next cluster, ch 4, 1 dc in every dc 6 times, dc in the last dc, ch 4, rep from * across row, ending with 4 chs, 1 dc in the last ch, ch 4, turn.

Row 4: * Make a 4-lp cluster in the 1st sc, ch 3, a 4-lped cluster in the next sc, ch 3, a 4-lp cluster in the next sc, ch 1, 1 dc in each dc with a ch in between, ch 1, rep from * across row, ending with dc in the last ch, ch 3, turn.

Row 5: * 1 dc in the 1-ch, 1 in the cluster, 3 dc in the 3-ch, 1 in the cluster, 3 in the 3-ch, 1 in the cluster, 1 in the 1-ch, 1 in each dc, 1 in each ch, rep from * across row, ending with 2 dc in the last ch, ch 4, turn.

Row 6: 1 dc in the 3rd dc, * ch 1, 1 dc in the 2nd dc 5 times, ch 4,

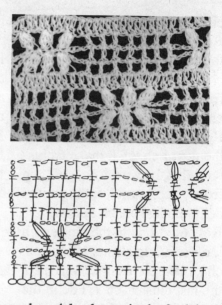

make a 4-lp cluster in the 2nd dc, ch 1, make a 4-lp cluster in the 4th dc, ch 1, a 4-lp cluster in the 4th dc, ch 4, 1 dc in the 2nd dc, ch 1, dc in the 2nd dc, rep from * across row, ending with 1 dc in the last ch, ch 4, turn.

Row 7: * 1 dc in each dc, ch 1 in between, ch 4, 1 sc in each of the next 4-lp cluster, ch 4, rep from * across row, ending with 1 dc in the last ch, ch 4, turn.

Row 8: * 1 dc in each dc, respace with a ch, ch 1, make a 4-lp cluster in the 1st sc, ch 3, a 4-lp cluster in the 2nd sc, ch 3, a 4-lp cluster in the next sc, ch 1, rep from * across row, ending with 1 dc in the last ch, ch 3, turn.

Repeat rows 1-8 for pattern.

15. Multiples of 36 plus 4.

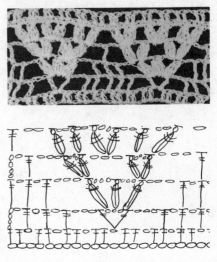

Row 1: 1 dc in the 5th ch, * ch 1, 1 dc in the 2nd ch, 1 dc in the next ch, rep from * across row, ending with 2 dc, ch 5, turn.

Row 2: * 1 trc in the 1st 1-ch, ch 1, 1 trc in the 2nd dc, ch 1, 1 trc in next dc, ch 3, 1 trc in next dc, ch 1, (1 trc, ch 3, 1 trc) in 2nd ch-2 sp, ch 3, rep from * across row, ending with 1 extra trc in the last ch, ch 5, turn.

Row 3: 1 trc in the 2nd trc, ch 1, 1 trc in the next trc, * ch 3, make a (3-lp cluster, ch 3, 3-lp cluster) between the 2 sides of the V-st, ch 3, 1 trc in the next trc, rep from * across row, ch 6, turn.

Row 4: 1 trc in the 2nd trc, * ch 3, make a 3-lp cluster in the 3-ch between the 1st 2 clusters, ch 3, make another 3-lp cluster in same st, ch 3, sc in top of 2nd cluster of prev row, ch 3, make a 3-lp cluster st in next ch, ch 3, make another 3-lp cluster, ch 3, 1 trc in the next trc, rep from * across row, ending with 1 trc in the 2nd trc, ch 1, 1 trc in last ch, ch 6, turn.

Row 5: * Make a 3-lp cluster in the 2nd 3-ch, ch 2, make 2nd 3-lp cluster in the same 3-ch, ch 2, make a 3-lp cluster in the next 3-ch, ch 2, make a 3-lp cluster in the same 3-ch, ch 2, rep from * across row, ending with 1 trc in the last ch, ch 1, turn.

Row 6: * 1 sc in the trc, 1 in each of the 2-chs, 1 in the cluster, 3 in the 2-ch, 1 in the cluster, 1 in each of the 2 ch, 1 in the cluster, 1 in the 2-ch, 1 in the cluster, 1 in each of the chs, 1 in the cluster, 3 in the 2-ch, 1 in the cluster, 1 in the ch, rep from * across row, ending with 1 sc in each of the last 3-chs, ch 3, turn.

117

Chapter XI

Dropped Stitch

1. Multiples of 14 plus 1.

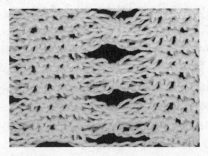

Row 1: 1 sc in the 2nd ch, the next 3 chs, * ch 6, 1 sc in the 6th ch, and the next 4 chs, rep from * across row, ending with 4 sc, ch 1, turn.
Row 2: Repeat row 1.
Row 3: Repeat row 1.

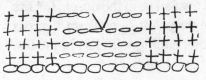

Row 4: 1 sc in each of the 1st 4 sc, * ch 3, make 1 sl st around the 3 chs below, crochet all 3 together, ch 3, 1 sc in each of the next 7 sc, rep from * across row, ending with 4 sc, ch 1, turn.
Repeat rows 1-4 for pattern.

2. Multiple of 6 plus 1.

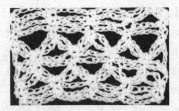

Row 1: 1 sc in the 2nd ch, * ch 5, 1 sc in the 6th ch, rep from * across row, ending with sc, ch 1, turn.
Row 2: Repeat row 1.

Row 3: 1 sc in the 1st sc, * ch 7, 1 sc in the next sc, rep from * across row, ending with sc after the last group, ch 1, turn.

Row 4: Repeat row 3, ch 5, turn.

Row 5: * Make 1 sc around the middle of the chs in the 2 prev rows, ch 5, rep from * across row, ending with 1 sc around the 2 rows, ch 2, 1 dc in the sc, ch 1, turn.

Row 6: Sc in 1st dc, ch 2, * sc in sc, ch 5, rep from * across row, ending with 1 sc in the last ch, ch 1, turn.

Row 7: * 1 sc in the sc, ch 7, rep from * across row, ending after the last group with sc, ch 3, 1 dc in the sc, ch 1, turn.

Row 8: 1 sc in the dc, ch 3, * 1 sc in the sc, ch 7, rep from * across row, ending with 1 sc in the last ch, ch 1, turn.

Repeat rows 1-8 for pattern.

3. Multiples of 14 plus 1.

Row 1: 1 sc in the 2nd ch, ch 2, 1 sc in the 3rd ch, * sc in the next 4 chs, ch 5, 1 sc in the 6th ch, rep from * across row, ending with 2 chs, 1 sc in the 3rd ch, ch 1, turn.

Row 2: Repeat row 1.

Row 3: 1 sc in the 1st sc, 1 sc in the next 2 chs, * ch 5, 1 sc in the

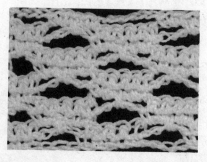

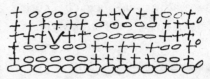

next 2 chs, make 1 sl st around the 2 prev rows of chs, 1 sc in the last 2 chs, rep from * across row, ending with 2 sc in the 2 chs, 1 sc in the last sc, ch 1, turn.

Row 4: 1 sc in lst 3 sc, * ch 5, 1 sc in the next 2 sc, 1 sc in the sl st, and the next 2 sc, rep from * across row, ending with sc in the 3rd sc, ch 1, turn.

Repeat rows 1-4 for pattern.

4. Multiples of 8 plus 4.

Row 1: 1 dc in the 4th ch and the next ch, * ch 3, make 1 dc in the 4th ch and the next 4 chs, rep from * across row, ending with 3 dc, ch 3, turn.

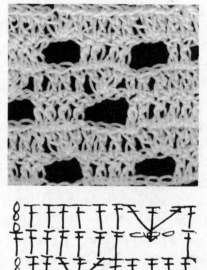

Row 2: 1 dc in the 2nd dc, 1 dc in the 3rd dc, * make 3 dc through the next 3-ch and around the chs of the prev row, 1 dc in the next 5 dc, rep from * across row, ending with 3 dc, ch 3, turn.

Row 3: 1 dc in the 2nd dc and the next 5 dc* ch 3, 1 dc in the 4th dc and the next 4 dc, rep from * across row, ending with 1 dc in each dc, 1 dc in the last ch, ch 3, turn.

Row 4: 1 dc in the 2nd dc and the next 5 dc, * make 3 dc through 2 prev rows, make 1 dc in each of the next dc, rep from * across

121

row, ending with 7 dc, ch 3, turn.
Repeat rows 1-4 for pattern

5. Multiples of 14 plus 1.

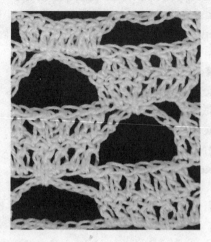

Row 1: 1 dc in the 4th ch and the
next 6 chs, * ch 7, 1 dc in the 8th
ch and the next 6 chs, rep from *
across row, ending after the 7
chs with 1 dc in the 8th and last
ch, ch 10, turn.

Row 2: * dc in each dc, ch 7, rep
from * across row, ending with 1
extra dc in the last ch, ch 10, turn.

Row 3: * 1 dc in each of the 1st 3-
chs, 1 dc around the next ch, also
the middle of the 2 prev 2 chs, 1
dc in each of the next 3-chs, ch 7,
rep from * across row, ending
with 8 dc, ch 3, turn.

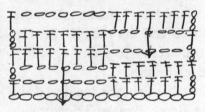

Row 4: * 1 dc in each dc, ch 7,
rep from * across row, ending
with 7 chs, 1 dc in the last ch, ch
3, turn.

Row 5: Repeat row 1 except
work the middle of the 7 dc as a
dropped dc.
Repeat rows 1-5 for pattern.

6. Multiples of 6 plus 4.

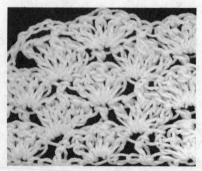

Row 1: 5 dc in the 7th ch, * 1 dc
in the 3rd ch, 5 dc in the 3rd ch,
rep from * across row, ending
after last group with 1 dc, ch 3,

turn.

Row 2: 2 dc in the 1st dc, * make 1 relief dc around the base of the middle 3 dc from the back, 5 dc in the next dc, rep from * across row, ending with 3 dc in last ch, ch 3, turn.

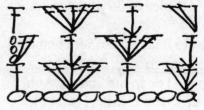

Row 3: * 5 dc in the relief dc, make 1 relief dc around the middle of the 3 dc from the front, rep from * across row, ending with 1 dc after the last group in the last ch, ch 3, turn.

Repeat rows 2-3 for pattern.

7. Multiples of 7 plus 4.

Row 1: 3 dc in the 5th ch, ch 2, * 3 dc in the 7th ch, ch 1, 3 dc in the same ch, ch 2, rep from * across row, ending with 2 chs, 3 dc in the 7th ch, 1 dc in the next ch, ch 3, turn.

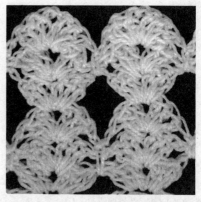

Row 2: Repeat row 1.

Row 3: 3 dc in the 2nd dc, * ch 1, sl st around the 2 prev rows, ch 1, 3 dc in the next 1-ch, ch 1, 3 dc in the 1-ch just used, rep from * across row, ending with 1 dc in the last ch, ch 3, turn.

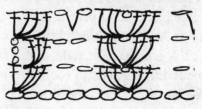

Repeat rows 1-3 for pattern.

8. Multiples of 30 plus 6.

Row 1: 1 dc in the 5th ch and across the row, ch 3, turn.

Row 2: 1 dc in the 2nd dc, * ch 10, 1 dc in the 11th dc, 1 dc in the 9th dc, rep from * across row, ending with 1 dc in the last dc, 1 dc in the last ch, ch 3, turn.

Row 3: 1 dc in the 2nd dc, * ch 10, 1 dc in the 1st, 1 dc in the 2nd dc, ch 2, 1 dc in the 3rd dc, and the next dc, ch 2, 1 dc in the 3rd dc and the next dc, rep from * across row, ending with 1 dc in the last dc and 1 dc in the last ch, ch 3, turn.

Row 4: 1 dc in the 2nd dc, * ch 10, 1 dc in each of the next 2 dc, 1 dc in each of the 2-chs, ch 2, 1 dc in each of the 2-chs, 1 dc in each of the 2 dc, rep from * across row, ending with 1 dc in the dc, 1 dc in the last ch, ch 3, turn.

Row 5: 1 dc in the 2nd dc, * ch 4, make 1 sc around prev 3-chs, make another sc around prev 3-chs, ch 4, 1 dc in the next dc, and the next dc, ch 2, 1 dc in each of the 2-chs, ch 2, 1 dc in the 3rd dc and the next dc, rep from * across row, ending with 1 dc in the last dc and 1 dc in the last ch, 1 ch 3, turn.

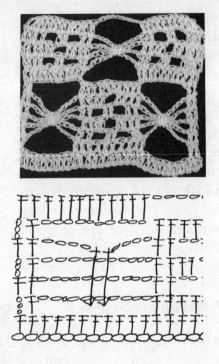

Row 6: 1 dc in the 2nd dc, * ch 10, 1 dc in the next 2 dc, 1 dc in the 2-chs, 1 dc in the next 2 dc, rep from * across row, ending with 1 dc in the last dc, 1 dc in the last ch, ch 3, turn.

Row 7: 1 dc in 2nd dc, * 10 dc around the 10-ch, ch 10, rep from * across row, ending with 1 dc in the last dc, 1 dc in the last ch, ch 3, turn.

Rows 8-10: Alternate pattern. Repeat rows 1-10 for pattern.

Chapter XII

X-Stitch

1. Multiples of 9 plus 4.

Row 1: 1 dc in 7th ch, * ch 1, 1 dc backwards in 2 chs, 1 dc in 3rd ch, rep from * across row, ending with 1 dc in ch after last goup, ch 2, turn.

Row 2: 1 dc in 1-ch, * ch 2, crochet 2 dc tog in 1-ch already used and next 1-ch, rep from * across row, ending with 2 dc crocheted tog in last 1-ch, and last ch, ch 2, turn.

Row 3: 1 dc in 2-ch, ch 1, 1 dc backwards in 2 dc crocheted tog, * 1 dc in next 2-ch, ch 1, 1 dc backwards in last 2-ch, rep from * across row, ending with 2 dc crocheted tog, 1 dc in last 2-ch, 1 dc in last ch, ch 3, turn.

Row 4: Crochet 2 dc tog in 1st dc, and 1-ch sp, * ch 2, begin 2 dc crocheted tog in the 1-ch and next 1-ch, rep from * across row,

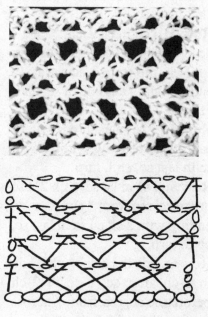

ending with 2 dc crocheted tog in last 1-ch and last ch, ch 3, ch 3, turn.

2. Multiples of 12 plus 1.

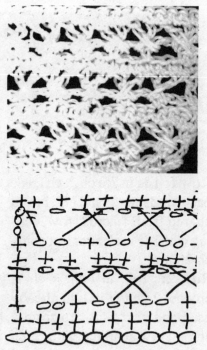

Row 1: 1 sc in 2nd ch and across the row, ch 1, turn.

Row 2: 1 sc in 1st sc, * ch 2, 1 sc in 3rd sc, rep from * across row, ending with 2 chs, 1 sc in last sc, ch 3, turn.

Row 3: 1 dc in 1st 2-ch, * ch 1, 1 dc in 2nd 2-ch, 1 dc backwards in 1st 2-ch, rep from * across row, ending with 1 ch, 1 dc in sc, ch 1, turn.

Row 4: 1 sc in each dc, 1 dc in each ch across row, ending with sc in last sc, ch 1, turn.

Row 5: 1 sc in 1st sc, * ch 2, 1 sc in 3rd sc, rep from * across row, ending with 2 chs, 1 sc in last sc, ch 3, turn.

Row 6: 1 dc in 1st ch, * ch 1, 1 dc in 2-ch after sc, 1 dc in 2-ch before the sc, rep from * across row, ending with 1 ch, 1 dc in sc, ch 1, turn.

Row 7: 1 sc in each ch, 1 sc in each dc.

Repeat rows 1-7 for pattern.

3. Multiples of 14 plus 4.

Row 1: 1 dc in 5th ch, 1 dc in next ch, * ch 2, 1 dc in 3rd ch, 1 dc in 4 chs, rep from * across row, ending with 3 dc in last 3 chs, ch 4, turn.

Row 2: 1 dc in 3rd dc, * ch 2, 1 dc in 1st dc, ch 1, 1 dc in 2nd dc, ch 1, 1 dc in 2nd dc, rep from * across row, ending with 1 dc, 1 ch, 1 dc in last ch, ch 3, turn.

Row 3: 1 dc in 1st ch, 1 dc in 2nd dc, * ch 2, 1 dc in 1st dc, 1 dc in ch, 1 dc in next dc, 1 dc in ch, (made 5 dcs), rep from * across row, ending with 1 dc in last dc, 2 dc in last ch, ch 4, turn.

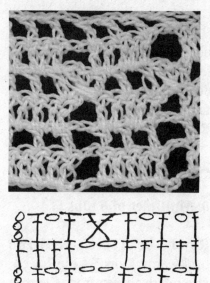

Row 4: 1 dc in 3rd dc, * 1 dc in 2nd ch, 1 dc back in 1st ch, (making X), 1 dc in next dc, 1 dc in 2nd dc, ch 1, dc in 2nd dc, rep from * across row, ending with 1 dc, 1 ch and 1 dc in last ch, ch 3, turn.

Repeat rows 1-4 for pattern.

4. Multiples of 4 plus 6.

Row 1: Make 1 trc in 6th ch, 1 trc in the 3rd ch, with 2 chs between, * make 1 trc in next ch, and 3rd ch, with 2 chs between, rep from * across row, ending with last group, 1 trc in last ch, ch

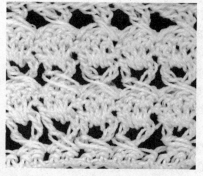

127

1, turn.

Row 2: 1 sc in 1st trc, * (1 hdc, 1 dc, 1 hdc) in 2-ch, 1 sc between 2 trc X-st, rep from * across row, ending with 1 sc in last ch, ch 5, turn.

Row 3: Repeat row 1, except sides of X-st ar formed in sc. Repeat rows 1-2 for pattern.

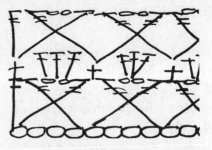

5. Multiples of 6 plus 5.

Row 1: 1 trc in 8th ch, * ch 1, 1 trc backwards, 2 chs, 3 trc in 2nd ch, 1 trc in 4th ch, rep from * across row, ending with 1 trc in last ch, ch 4, turn.

Row 2: Sk 1st trc, * 1 trc in 3rd trc, ch 1, 1 trc backwards, 2 trc, 3 trc in 1-ch between 2 sides of X, rep from * across row, ending with 1 trc in last ch, ch 4, turn. Repeat rows 1-2 for pattern.

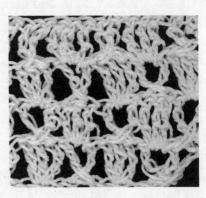

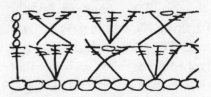

6. Multiples of 2 plus 4.

Row 1: 1 dc in 5th ch, and in each ch across row, ch 3, turn.

Row 2: 1 dc in 3rd dc, 1 dc backwards 1 dc making an X, * 1 dc in 2nd dc, 1 dc in 1st dc, rep from * across row, ending with 1 dc in last ch, ch 3, turn.

Row 3: * 1 dc between 2 sides of X, ch 1, rep from * across row,

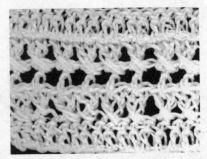

ending with 1 ch, 1 dc in last ch, ch 3, turn.

Row 4: Sk 1 dc * 1 dc in ch after the next dc, 1 dc in ch before same dc, rep from * across row, ending with 1 dc in last ch. Repeat rows 1-4 for pattern.

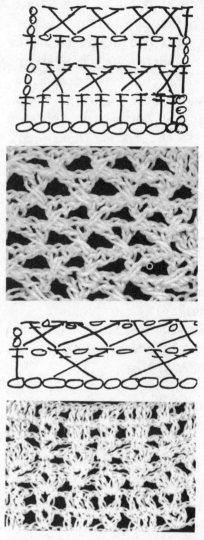

7. Multiples of 4 plus 5.

Row 1: 1 dc in 9th ch * ch 1, 1 dc backwards 2 chs, ch 1, 1 dc in 4th ch, rep from * across row, ending with 1 ch, 1 dc in next ch after finished group, ch 2, turn.

Row 2: Sk 1 dc, * 1 dc in next dc, ch 1, 1 dc backwards in dc, ch 1, rep from * across row, ending with 1 dc finished tog in last ch. Repeat rows 1-2 for pattern.

8. Multiples of 16 plus 4.

Row 1: 1 dc in 5th ch, * ch 1, 1 dc in 3rd ch, ch 1, 1 dc in next ch, ch 1, 1 dc in 3rd ch, and next 2 chs, rep from * across row, ending with 2 dc, ch 3, turn.

Row 2: Repeat row 1.

Row 3: 1 sc in the 1st dc, * ch 1, 2 dc in 1-ch between 2 sides of V-st, ch 1, rep 2 dc in same ch, ch 1, 1 sc in middle of 3 dc, rep from * across row, ending with 1 sc in last ch, ch 3, turn.

129

Row 4: 1 dc in sc, * ch 2, 1 sc in 1-ch between 2 groups of dc, ch 2, make 1 dc in 3rd dc in 2 prev rows, ch 1, make 1 dc backwards in 1st dc, rep from * across row, ending with 2 dc in sc, ch 3, turn.

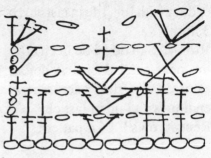

Row 5: 2 dc in 1st dc, * ch 1, 1 sc in sc, ch 1, 2 dc in 1-ch between 2 sides of X-st, ch 1, 2 dc in same 1-ch, rep from * across row, ending with 3 dc in last ch, ch 1, turn.

Row 6: 1 sc in 1st dc, * ch 2, 1 dc in 1-ch after sc, ch 1, 1 dc backwards in 1-ch before sc, ch 2, 1 sc in 1-ch, rep from * across row, ending with 1 sc in last ch, ch 3, turn.

Row 7: Repeat row 1, except make the V-st in 1-ch between sides of X-st.

9. Multiples of 10 plus 4.

Row 1: 1 dc in 5th ch and across row, ch 5, turn.

Row 2: Make 1 trc-X-st in 2nd dc, 1 trc-X-st in 3rd dc, leaving 2 chs in between, ch 1, * ch 1, make 1 trc-X-st in 2nd, then 3rd dc, leaving 2 chs in between, rep from * across row, ending with last group, 1 extra trc in last ch, ch 3, turn.

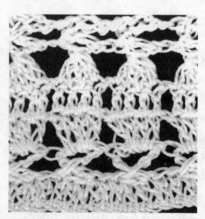

Row 3: * Make 4 dc around 2-ch, ch 1, rep from * across row,

ending with 1 extra dc in last ch, ch 3, turn.

Row 4: 1 dc in 2nd dc and in next 3 dc, * ch 1, 1 dc in next 4 dc, rep from * across row, ending with 1 extra dc in last ch after last group, ch 5, turn.

Row 5: Sk 1st dc, * crochet 4 dc tog in next 4 dc, ch 5, rep from * across row, ending row with last group, 2 chs, 1 dc in last ch, ch 5, turn.

Row 6: * Make 1 trc X-st in 2nd ch before group and 2nd ch after group, with 2 chs between 2 sides of X, ch 1, rep from * across row, ending after last group with 1 extra trc in last ch, ch 3, turn.

Row 7: Repeat rows 1-4 for pattern.

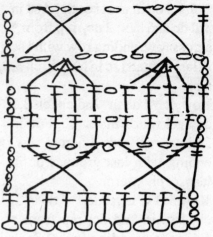

10. Multiples of 12 plus 4.

Row 1: 1 dc in 5th ch, 1 dc in 3rd ch, * 1 dc in 4th ch, ch 3, 1 dc backwards in 2nd ch, 1 dc in 2nd ch, rep from * across row, ending with 1 dc, 1 ch and 1 dc in 3rd ch, ch 3, turn.

Row 2: 3 dc in 1st ch, 1 sc in 3rd dc, * 7 dc around 3-ch, 1 sc in 2nd dc, rep from * across row, ending with 4 dc in last ch, ch 1, turn.

Row 3: 1 sc in 1st dc and 2nd dc,

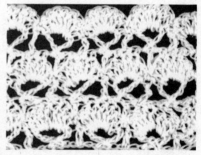

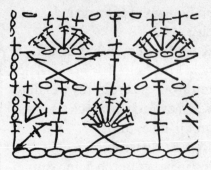

* ch 1, 1 dc in next sc, ch 1, 1 sc in 3rd dc and next 2 dc, rep from * across row, ending row with 1 sc in last dc, and 1 sc in last ch, ch 3, turn.

Row 4: * 1 dc in 2nd ch, ch 3, 1 dc backwards in 1st ch, 1 dc in 2nd sc, rep from * across row, ending with last group, 1 dc in last sc, ch 1, turn.

Row 5: 1 sc in 1st dc, * 7 dc in 3-ch, 1 sc in 2nd dc, rep from * across row, ending with 7 dc in last 3 chs, 1 sc in last ch, ch 4, turn.

Row 6: * 1 sc in 3rd dc, 1 sc in next 2 dc, ch 1, 1 dc in next sc, ch 1, rep from * across row, ending with 1 ch, 1 dc, ch 4, turn.

Repeat rows 1-6 for pattern.

Chapter XIII

Wraparound Stitch

1. Multiples of 6 plus 4.

Row 1: 1 dc in 5th ch, 1 dc in next ch, make 1 dc back around middle of 1st dc, * 1 dc in 2nd ch, 1 dc in next ch, make 1 dc back around 1st dc of group, rep from * across row, ending with 1 extra dc in last ch, ch 3, turn.

Row 2: * 1 dc in top of dcs worked across 1st 2 dc, 1 dc in each of next 2 dc, rep from * across row, ending with 1 dc in last ch, ch 3, turn.

Repeat rows 1-2 for pattern.

2. Multiples of 6 plus 4.

Row 1: 2 dc in 5th ch, * 3 dc in 3rd ch, rep from * across row, ending with 2 dc in last ch, ch 3, turn.

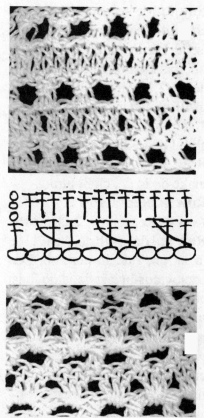

Row 2: 1 dc in 2nd dc, 1 dc in next dc, * 1 dc worked from back around middle of lst dc, 1 dc in 2nd dc and next dc, rep from * across row, ending after last group with 1 dc, ch 3, turn.

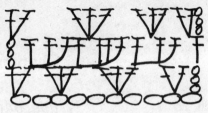

Row 3: Repeat row 1, except work 3 dc between groups of dcs.

Repeat rows 1-2 for pattern.

3. Multiples of 11 plus 4.

Row 1: 1 dc in 6th ch, 1 dc in next ch, * 1 dc backwards in ch before lst dc, 1 dc in 2nd ch and next ch, 1 dc backwards in ch before lst dc, ch 2, 1 dc in 3rd ch, ch 2, 1 dc in 4th ch and in next ch, rep from * across row, ending with 1 dc, ch 1, 1 dc in 2nd ch, ch 4, turn.

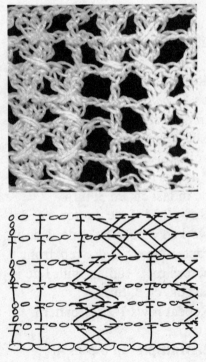

Row 2: Repeat row 1, except make dc in dc, ch 3, turn.

Row 3: Repeat row 2.

Row 4: Repeat row 2, ch 5, turn.

Row 5: 1 dc in 4th dc, * ch 2, 1 dc in lst ch, 1 dc in next ch, 1 dc backwards in last dc, 1 dc in lst ch, 1 dc in next ch, 1 dc backwards in dc, ch 2, 1 dc in 3rd dc, rep from * across row, ending with last group and 1 extra dc, crocheted tog with last group in the last 1 ch, ch 2, turn.

4. Multiples of 6 plus 4.

Row 1: 1 dc in 5th, and next ch, * make 2 dc crocheted tog around the middle of 1st dc, 1 dc in 3rd ch, ch 1, 1 dc in ch just used, 1 dc in 2nd ch, and next ch, rep from * across row ending with 1 dc in 2nd ch after group, ch 3, turn.

Row 2: 1 dc in 2 dc crocheted tog, 1 dc in next 2 dc , * 1 dc in 1-ch, ch 1, 1 dc in 1-ch just used, 1 dc in top of 2 dc crocheted together, 1 dc in next 2 dc, rep from * across row ending with 1 extra dc in last ch, ch 3, turn.
Repeat rows 1-2 for pattern.

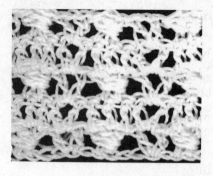

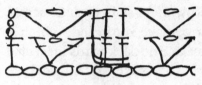

5. Multiples of 6 plus 4.

Row 1: 1 dc in 5th ch, * ch 3, crochet all 3 dc tog, work around middle of 1st dc, 1 dc in the 3rd ch, rep from * across row, ending with last group, ch 4, turn.

Row 2: * 1 dc around middle of 3-ch, ch 3, work 3 dc around middle of dc just made, crochet tog with 1 dc in 3-ch, rep from * across row, ending after last group with 1 dc in last ch.
Repeat rows 1-2 for pattern.

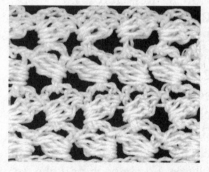

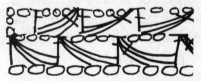

6. Multiple of 24 plus 4.

Row 1: 1 dc in 5th ch, 1 dc in next 11 chs, * ch 3, 1 sc in the 3rd ch, ch 3, 1 dc in 3rd ch, ch 3, 1 sc in 3rd ch, ch 3, 1 dc in 3rd ch, 1 dc in next 12 chs, rep from * across row, ending with last dc, ch 1, turn.

Row 2: * 1 sc in each dc across row, make 3 dc in 2nd 3-ch, ch 3, make 3 dc backwards in 1st ch, 1 sc in dc, make 3 dc in 2nd 3-ch, ch 3, make 3 dc backwards in 1st 3-ch, rep from * across row, ending with sc over dc, 1 sc in last ch, ch 3, turn.

Row 3: Repeat row 1.

Row 4: Repeat row 2.

Row 5: * dc in each sc, ch 2, 1 sc in top of 3-ch, ch 2, 1 dc in sc, ch 2, 1 sc in 3-ch, ch 2 rep from * across row, ending with dc in sc, ch 6, turn.

Row 6: Sk 1 dc, * 1 sc in 3rd dc, ch 3, 1 dc in 3rd dc, ch 3, 1 dc in last dc, 1 dc in each of 2 chs, sc, 2-ch, dc, 2-ch, sc, 2-ch, 1st dc, rep from * across row, ending with 3 chs and 1 dc in last ch.

Rows 7-10: Repeat rows 2-5, alternate pattern like checkerboard.

Repeat rows 1-10 for pattern.

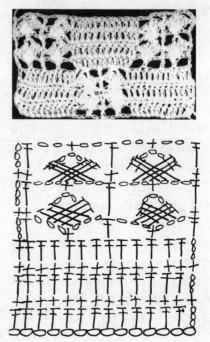

136

Chapter XIV

Y-Stitch

1. Multiples of 12 plus 5.

Row l: * l trc, l ch, l dc through the middle of the trc (making l Y-st) repeat in every 3rd ch, rep from * across row, ending with trc in the last ch, ch 4, turn.

Row 2: Repeat row 1, except make the Y-st in between the 2 lps in the ch of the Y-st in the lst row.

Repeat rows 1-2. for pattern.

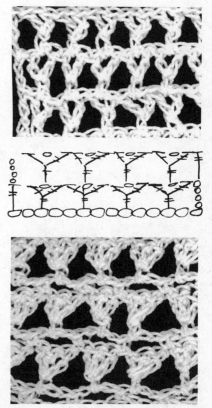

2. Multiples of 12 plus 1.

Row 1: l sc in the 2nd ch, * ch 3, l sc in the 4th ch, repeat from * across row, ending with 3 chs, and l sc, ch 4, turn.

Row 2: Make l Y-st around the middle of the 3-ch (l trc, 2 dc), ch 1, repeat from * across row, ending with 1 trc in the last sc, ch 1, turn.

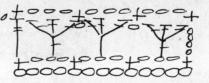

Row 3: Repeat row 1, except work sc in the 1-ch across row.

Repeat rows 1-3 for pattern.

Chapter XV

Motifs

l. Eyelet Square

Ch 8 and join with sl st to form a ring.

Round l: 16 sc in ring.

Round 2: (1 sc, ch 10, sk 3 sc) 4 times, sl st in 1st sc.

Round 3: (11 sc in 10-ch sp, 1 sc in next sc) 4 times, sl st in 1st sc.

Round 4: * sc in each of 6 sts, 2 sc in next st to form corner, 1 sc in each of 5 sts *, rep from * 3 times, sl st in 1st sc.

Round 5: 1 sc in each st and 2 sc at each corner, sl st in 1st sc.

Repeat rnd 5 for desired size.

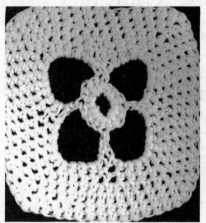

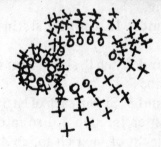

2. Puff Stitch Square

Ch 8 and join with sl st to make ring.

Round 1: * 1 4-lped puff st in

ring, ch 2, rep from *, sl st in lst st.

Round 2: 1 4-lped puff st in ch sp before sl st, * ch 2, 1 puff st in next sp, ch 2, (1 dc, ch 2, 1 dc) in next puff st to form corners, ch 2, 1 puff st in next sp, rep from * after dc group at end of rnd, ch 2, sl st in lst puff st.

Round 3: 1 puff st in sp before sl st, * (ch 2, 1 puff st) in each sp up to corner, ch 2, (1 dc, ch 2, 1 dc) between dc groups at corner, ch 2, rep from *, 1 sl st in lst st.

Repeat from rnd 3, working 1 more puff st on each side for each rnd, until the desired size.

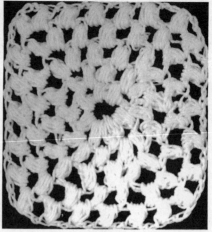

3. Flower Square

Ch 5 and join with sl st to make a ring.

Round 1: 12 sc in ring, sl st in lst sc.

Round 2: (ch 11, sl st in next sc) 12 times .

Round 3: Sl st in each of lst 6 ch of lst ch lp. * ch 4, 1 sc in the center st of next ch lp, ch 4, 1 cluster in next ch lp, 1 more cluster in the same st to form corner, ch 4, 1 sc in next lp, * rep from * 3 times.

Round 4: 2 sl sts in lst 4-ch sp,

140

ch 3, 1 cluster st in same st, ch 4,
1 sc in next 4-ch sp, * ch 4, 1 sc in
next 4-ch sp, ch 4, (1 cluster, ch
4, 1 cluster) in corner sp, ch 4, 1 sc
in next 4-ch sp, ch 4, 1 cluster in
next 4-ch sp , rep from * 3 times,
ch 4, sl st in top of 1st cluster.

4. Old American Square

Ch 6 and join with sl st to form a
ring.
Round 1: Ch 3, 2 dc in ring, ch
2 (3 dc, ch 2) 3 times, sl st in top
of beg st.
Round 2: Sl st in 1st ch sp, ch 3,
(2 dc, ch 2, 3 dc) in same sp to
form corner, (ch 1, 3 dc, ch 2, 3 dc
in next 2-ch sp) 3 times for 3
more corners, sl st in top of beg
ch.
Round 3: Sl st in 1st ch sp, ch 3,
(2 dc, ch 2, 3 dc) in same sp, * (ch
1, 3 dc) in each 1-ch sp, along the
side, (ch 1, 3 dc, ch 2, 3 dc) in
each 2-ch sp to form corner, rep
from *, sl st in top of beg ch.
Repeat rnd 3 for desired size.

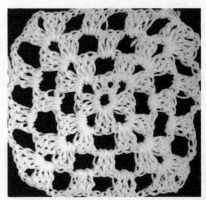

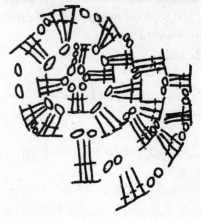

5. Double-Eyelet Square

Ch 8, join with sl st to form a
ring.
Round 1: Ch 3, * make 1 cluster
st in ring, ch 5, make 1 cluster st

141

in ring, ch 2, rep from * to end of rnd until 8 cluster stitches in ring rnd, ch 3.

Round 2: 2 cluster stitches in ch-5 sp, ch 2, 3 dc in ch-2 sp, ch 2, continue pattern, making (1 cluster, ch 2, 1 cluster) in ch-5 sp and (ch 2, 3 dc, ch 2) in ch-2 sp to end of rnd, join with sl st into 3rd ch of ch 3.

Round 3: 1 sl st, ch 3, * make (1 cluster, ch 2, 1 cluster) into corner chain, ch 2, 2 dc into ch-2 sp, 3 dc on 3 dc of previous rnd, 2 dc into ch 2-sp, ch 2, rep from *, join with a sl st.

Round 4: Make as for rnd 3, except make dc on dc of prev rnd with 2 dc on either side of ch 2 sp, join with sl st.

Rounds 5 & 6: Repeat.

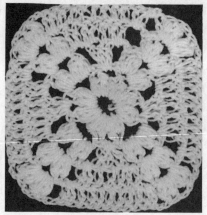

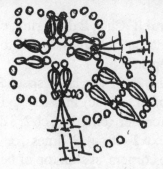

6. Spoked-Wheel Eyelet Square

Ch 8, join with sl st to form a ring.

Round 1: Ch 2, 15 dc in ring, join with a sl st in the 2nd ch of beg ch 2.

Round 2: Ch 4, (1 dc, ch 2) 15 times, join with sl st in 2nd of beg ch 4 (16 spokes).

Round 3: Ch 2, make 2 dc in the 1st sp, ch 1 (3 dc, ch 1) in each sp,

142

sl st in the 1st sp.

Round 4: * (ch 3, 1 sc in next ch 1-sp) 3 times, ch 6, 1 sc in next sp, rep from *, sl st in 1st sp to join.

Round 5: Ch 2, 2 dc in 1st ch-3 sp, 3 dc in next 2 ch-3 sp, * (5 dc, ch 2, 5 dc) in corner sp, 3 dc in each ch-3 sp, * continue to end of rnd, sl st.

Round 6: Ch 2, make 1 dc in each st and (1 dc, 1 tr, 1 dc) in each ch-2 sp at the corners, sl st.

Round 7: Repeat rnd 6.

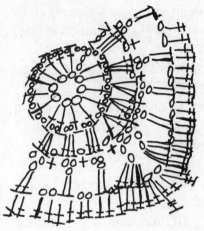

7. Framed Circle

Ch 6, join with sl st to form ring.

Round 1: Ch 3, make 15 dc in ring, join with sl st in ch-3 of beg ch 3.

Round 2: Ch 5, 1 dc, ch 2 (15 times), join with a sl st in 3rd ch of beg ch 3 (16 spokes).

Round 3: Ch 3, make (1 dc, ch 3, 2 dc) in last ch 3 of ch 5 (ch 2, 1 sc in ch-2 sp 3 times), ch 2, (2 dc, ch 3, 2 dc) in ch 2 sp (3 times), ch 2, 1 sc in ch-2 sp (3 times) ch 2, join with a sl st in 3rd ch of beg ch 3.

Round 4: 1 sl st, ch 2, (1 dc, ch 3, 2 dc) in next ch-2 sp, ch 2, 1 sc in ch 2 sp (4 times), ch 2, (2 dc, ch 3, 2 dc) in ch 2 sp (3 times), ch 2,

1 sc in ch-2 sp (4 times), ch 2, join with sl st in 2nd ch of beg, ch 2.

Round 5: 1 sl st, ch 2, (2 dc, ch 2, 3 dc) in ch 3 sp, ch 1, 2 dc (5 times), ch 1 (3dc, ch 2, 3 dc) in ch-3 sp (3 times), ch 1, 2 dc (5 times), ch 1.

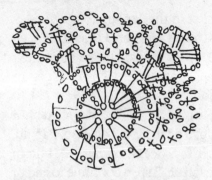

8. Four-Leaf Square

Ch 10, join with sl st to form a ring.

Round 1: Ch 10, * 4 trc in center of ring, ch 7, rep from * twice in 3 trc in center of ring with sl st to 3rd ch of starting ch 10.

Round 2: Ch 3, * 1 trc in each of the next 3 ch, ch 7, sk 1 ch, 1 trc in each of next 3 ch, 1 trc in each of next 4 trc, rep from * twice and end with 1 trc in each of next 3 ch, ch 7, sk 1 ch, 1 trc in each of next 3 ch, 1 trc in each of next 3 trc, join with sl st to 3rd ch of starting ch 3.

Round 3: Ch 3, * 1 trc in each of next 3 trc, 1 trc in each of next 3 ch, ch 7, sk 1 ch, 1 trc in each of next 3 ch, 1 trc in each of next 7 trc, rep from * twice and end with 1 trc in each of next 3 trc, 1 trc in each of next 3 trc, ch 7, sk 1 ch, 1 trc in each of next 3 ch, 1

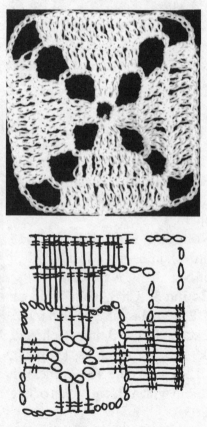

trc in each of next 6 trc, join with sl st to the 3rd ch of starting ch 3.

9. Granny-Square Wheel

Ch 8, join with sl st to form a ring.

Round 1: Ch 6 (counts as 1 dc and ch 3), * 1 dc in center of ring, ch 3, rep from * 6 times, join with sl st to 3rd ch of starting ch 6.

Round 2: Ch 2, 3 dc in next ch-3 sp, ch 2, * 4 dc in next ch-3 sp, ch 2, * rep from * around, join with sl st to 2nd ch of starting ch 2.

Round 3: 1 sl st in each of next 3 dc, ch 2, 5 dc in next ch 2 sp, ch 1, * 6 dc in next ch 2 sp, ch 3, 6 dc in next ch 2 sp, ch 1, rep from * twice and end 6 dc in next ch 2 sp, ch 3, join with sl st to 2nd ch of starting ch 2.

Round 4: Ch 5, sk 2 dc, * 1 sc in sp before next dc, ch 3, 1 sc in next ch 1 sp, ch 3, sk 3 dc, 1 sc in sp before next dc, ch 3, (2 dc, ch 3, 2 dc) in next ch 3 sp, ch 3, sk 3 dc, rep from * twice and end with 1 sc in sp before next dc, ch 3, 1 sc in next ch 1 sp, ch 3, sk 3 dc, 1 sc in sp before next dc, ch 3, (2 dc, ch 3, 1 dc) in next ch 3 sp, join with sl st to second ch of starting ch 5.

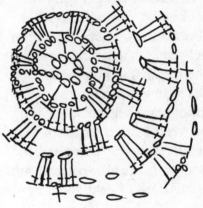

10. Scalloped Wheel

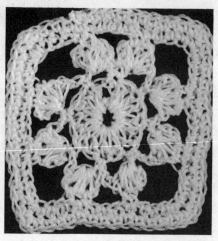

Ch 5, join with sl st to form a ring.

Round 1: Ch 3, 15 dc in center of ring, join with sl st to 3rd ch of starting ch 3.

Round 2: 1 sc in joining sp, * ch 8, make 1 shell in 2nd ch from hk, ch 1, sk 1 dc, 1 sc in next dc, rep from * 6 times, end with 1 shell, sk 1 dc, join with sl st to 1st sc. (8 shells made).

Round 3: Attach yarn in sp between 4th and 5th lps of any shell, ch 1, 1 sc in same sp, * ch 7, 1 sc in sp between 4th and 5th lps of next shell, ch 4, 1 sc in sp between 4th and 5th lps of next shell, rep from * twice and end with ch 7, 1 sc in sp between 4th and 5th lps of next shell, ch 4, join with sl st to 1st sc.

Round 4: Ch1, 1 sc in joining sp, * 1 sc in each of next 3 ch, 3 sc in next ch (to make corner), 1 sc in each of next 3 ch, 1 sc in next sc, 1 sc in each of next 4 ch, 1 sc in next sc, rep from * twice and end 1 sc in each of next 3 ch, 3 sc in next ch, 1 sc in each of next 3 ch, 1 sc in next sc, 1 sc in each of next 4 ch, join with sl st to 1st sc.

Round 5: 1 sc in each sc and 3

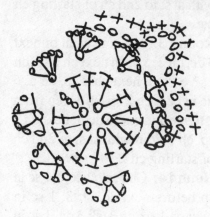

sc in each center corner sc around.

11. Double Square

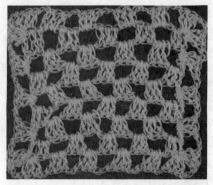

Chain any desired length.

Row 1: Ch 3, 1 dc in 3rd ch from hk, * ch 3, 1 dc in next 3 chs, rep from * across row, ch 6, turn.

Row 2: * Make 3 dc in between each of the group of dc of prev row, rep from * across row, ch 6, turn.

Repeat rows 1-2 for pattern.

Edges worked 3 dc in each sp around piece, except make 3 dc, 3 ch, 3 dc in each corner sp.

12. Framed Star

Ch 5, join with sl st to form a ring.

Round 1: Ch 6 (counts as 1 dc and ch 3), * 1 dc in ring, ch 3, rep from * 6 times, join with sl st to 3rd ch of starting ch 6 (8 dc).

Round 2: Ch 3 (counts as 1 dc), * 4 dc in next ch-3 sp, 1 dc in next dc, rep from * around, end with 4 dc in last ch-3 sp, join with sl st to 3rd ch of st ch-3 (40 dc made).

Round 3: * Ch 6, 1 sc in 2nd ch from hk, 1 hdc in next ch, 1 dc in next ch, 1 trc in next ch, 1 dtr in last ch, sk 5 dc, 1 long sc in dc 1 rnd below next dc, rep from * 7 times.

Round 4: Attach yarn to turning ch of any star point, ch 4 (1 trc, ch 3, 2 trc) in same ch * ch 6, 1 sc in turning ch of next star point, ch 6, (2 trc, ch 3, 2 trc) in turning ch of next star point (corner made), rep from * twice, end with ch 6, 1 sc in next star point, ch 6, join with sl st to 4th ch of starting ch 4.

Round 5: Ch 3 (counts as 1 dc), 1 dc in next trc, * 5 dc in ch-3 sp (corner made), 1 dc in next sc, 6 dc in next * twice, end with 5 dc in next ch-3 sp (corner made, 1 dc in next 2 trc, 6 dc in next 6-ch sp, join with sl st to 3rd ch of starting ch-3. (88 dc made).

Round 6: Ch 4, sk 1 dc, (1 dc, ch 3, 1 dc) in next dc (corner made), * (ch 1, sk 1 dc, 1 dc in next dc) 10 times, ch 1, sk 1 dc, (1 dc, ch 3, 1 dc) in next dc, rep from * twice, end with (ch 1, sk 1 dc, 1 dc in next dc) 8 times, ch 1, join with sl st to 3rd ch of starting ch-4.

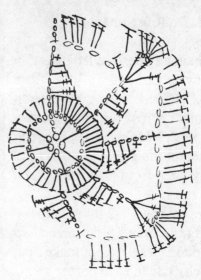

13. Grape Eyelet Square

Ch 10, join with sl st to form a ring.

Round 1: Ch 3, 4 dc in center of ring, take lp off hk, insert hk in 3rd ch of starting ch-3, pull lp of 4th dc through, * ch 3, 5 dc in

center of ring, take lp off hk, insert hk in 1st dc of 5-dc, pull lp of 5th dc through (popcorn st made), rep from * 6 times, ch 2, join with sl st to top of 1st popcorn (8 popcorns made).

Round 2: (1 sl st, ch 6, 1 dc) in next ch-3 sp, * ch 3, (1 dc, ch 3, 1 dc) in next ch-3 sp, rep from * around, ch 3, join with sl st to 3rd ch of starting ch-6.

Round 3: (1 sl st, ch 3, 4 dc) in next ch-3 sp, take lp off hk, insert hk in 3rd ch of starting ch-3, pull lp of 4th dc through, * ch 3, 1 popcorn in next ch-3 sp, rep from * around, ch 3, join with sl st to top of 1st popcorn.

Round 4: Repeat round 2.

Round 5: Repeat round 5.

Round 6: 1 sl st in next ch-3 sp, * ch 8, sk next ch-3 sp, 1 sc in next ch-3 sp, rep from * around, ch 8, join with sl st to starting sl st.

Round 7: Ch 3, * (1 popcorn, ch 2) 3 times in each of next 2 ch-8 sps, 8 trc in each of next 2 ch-8 sps, ch 2, rep from * around, join with sl st to top of 1st popcorn.

Round 8: (1 sl st, ch 3, 1 popcorn) in next ch-2 sp, * (ch 2, 1 popcorn in next ch-2 sp) 4 times, ch 5, sk 1 popcorn, 1 sc in next trc, (ch 5, sk 1 trc, 1 sc in next trc)

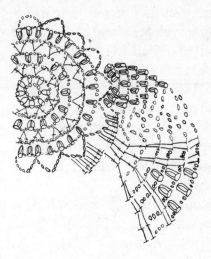

twice, ch 5, sk 1 trc, 1 trc in each of next 4 trc, (ch 5, sk 1 trc, 1 sc in next trc) 3 times, ch 5, sk 1 popcorn, 1 popcorn in next ch-2 sp, rep from * around and end with ch 5, join with sl st to top of 1st popcorn.

Round 9: (1 sl st, ch 3, 1 popcorn) in next ch-2 sp, * (ch 2, 1 popcorn in next ch-2 sp) 3 times, sk 1 popcorn, (ch 5, 1 sc in next ch-5 sp) 3 times, ch 5, sk next ch-5 sp, ch 5, 1 trc in next trc, (ch 2, 1 trc in next trc) 3 times, ch 5, sk next ch-5 sp, 1 sc in next 5-ch sp, (ch 2, 1 trc in next trc) 3 times, ch 5, sk next ch 5, 1 sc in next ch-5 sp, (ch 5, 1 sc in next ch-5 sp) twice, ch 5, sk 1 popcorn, 1 popcorn in next ch-2 sp, rep from * around and end with ch 5, join with sl st to top of 1st popcorn.

Round 10: (1 sl st, ch 3, 1 popcorn) in next ch-2 sp, * (ch 2, 1 popcorn in next ch-2 sp) twice, sk 1 popcorn in next ch-2 sp) twice, sk 1 popcorn, (ch 5, 1 sc in next ch-5 sp) 3 times, ch 5, sk next ch-5 sp, 2 dc in next trc, (ch 3, 2 dc in next trc) 3 times, ch 5, sk next ch-5 sp, 1 sc in next ch-5 sp, (ch 5, 1 sc in next ch-5 sp) twice, ch 5, sk 1 popcorn, 1 popcorn in next ch-2 sp, rep from * around and end with ch 5, join with sl st to top of 1st popcorn.

Round 11: (1 sl st, ch 3, 1 popcorn) in next ch-2 sp, * ch 2, 1 popcorn in next ch-2 sp, * ch 2, 1 popcorn in next ch-2 sp, sk 1 popcorn, (ch 5, 1 sc in next ch-5 sp) 3 times, ch 5, sk next ch-5 sp, (1 dc in each of next 2 dc, ch 4) twice, 1 popcorn in next ch-3 sp, (ch 4, 1 dc in each of next 2 dc) twice, ch 5, sk next ch-5 sp, 1 sc in next ch-5 sp, (ch 5, 1 sc in next ch-5 sp) twice, ch 5, sk 1 popcorn, 1 popcorn in next ch-2 sp, rep from * around and end with ch 5, join with sl st to top of 1st popcorn.

Round 12: (1 sl st, ch 3, 1 popcorn) in next ch-2 sp, * sk 1 popcorn, (ch 5, 1 sc in next ch-5 sp) 3 times, ch 5, sk next ch-5 sp, (1 dc in each of next 2 dc, ch 4) twice, 1 popcorn in next ch-4 sp, ch 2, sk 1 popcorn, 1 popcorn in next ch-4 sp, (ch 4, 1 dc in each of next 2 dc) twice, ch 5, sk next ch-5 sp, 1 sc in next ch-5 sp, (ch 5, 1 sc in next ch-5 sp) twice, ch 5, sk 1 popcorn, 1 popcorn in next ch-2 sp, rep from * around and end ch 5, join with sl st to top of 1st popcorn.

Round 13: (1 sl st, 1 sc) in next ch-5 sp, ch 5, 1 sc in next ch-5 sp, * ch 7, 1 sc in next ch-5 sp, ch 5, sk next ch-5 sp, (1 dc in each of next 2 dc, ch 4) twice, 1 popcorn in next ch-4 sp, ch 2, 1 popcorn in next ch-2 sp, ch 2, 1 popcorn in next ch-4 sp, (ch 4, 1 dc in each of next 2 dc) twice, ch 5, sk next ch-5 sp, 1 sc in next ch-5 sp, ch 7, 1 sc in next ch-5 sp, (ch 5, 1 sc in next ch-5 sp) 3 times, rep from * around and end with ch 5, join with sl st to 1st sc.

14. Squared Eyelet

Ch 6, join with sl st to form a ring.

Round 1: Ch 2, (yo, insert hk in center of ring, yo and pull through, yo and pull through 1 lp on hk, yo and pull through 2 lps on hk) twice, yo and pull through last 3 lps on hk, * ch 5, (yo, insert hk in center of ring, yo and pull through, yo and pull through 1 lp on hk, yo and pull through 2 lps on hk) 3 times, yo and pull through last 4 lps on hk (cluster made), ch 2, 1 cluster, rep from * twice, end with ch 5, 1 cluster, ch 2, join with sl st to 2nd ch of starting ch-2.

Round 2: 1 sl st in next st, 1 sl st in next ch-5 sp, ch 2, (yo, insert hk in same ch-5 sp, yo and pull through, yo and pull through 1 lp on hk, yo and pull through 2 lps on hk) twice, yo and pull through last 3 lps on hk, * ch 2, 1 cluster in same ch-5 sp, ch 2, 3 dc in next ch-2 sp, ch 2, 1 cluster in next ch-5 sp, rep from * twice, end with ch 2, 1 cluster in same ch-5 sp, ch 2, 3 dc in next ch-2 sp, ch 2, join with sl st to 2nd ch of starting ch-2.

Round 3: 1 sl st in next st, 1 sl st in next ch-2 sp, ch 2 (yo, insert

hk in same ch-5 sp, yo and pull through, yo and pull through 1 lp on hk, yo and pull through 2 lps on hk) twice, yo and pull through last 3 lps on hk, * ch 2, 1 cluster in same ch-2 sp, ch 2, 2 dc in next ch-2 sp, 1 dc in each dc of next dc-group, 2 dc in next ch-2 sp, ch 2, 1 cluster in next ch-2 sp, rep from * twice end with ch 2, 1 cluster in same ch-2 sp, ch 2, 2 dc in next ch-2 sp, 1 dc in each dc of next dc-group, 2 dc in next ch-2 sp, ch 2, join with sl st to 2nd ch of starting ch-2.

Rounds 4 and 5: Repeat Round 3.

15. Posey

Ch 6 and join with sl st to form ring.

Round 1: Ch 2, 23 sc in ring, sl st in 2nd ch at beg of rnd to close.

Round 2: Ch 4, 1 hdc in same ch as last sl st, ch 1, (sk 2 sts, 1 dc in next st, ch 2, 1 dc, ch 1) 7 times, sl st in 2nd ch at beg of rnd to close.

Round 3: Ch 2, (1 hdc, ch 2, 2 hdc) in last 2 ch at beg of Round 2, 1 sc in 1-ch sp, * (2 hdc, ch 2, 2 hdc) in 2-ch sp, 1 sc in the 1-ch sp, rep from * 6 times, sl st in 2nd ch at beg of rnd.

Round 4: * (3 dc, ch 1, 3 dc) in the 2-ch sp, 1 sc on each side of the sc, repeat from * 8 times.

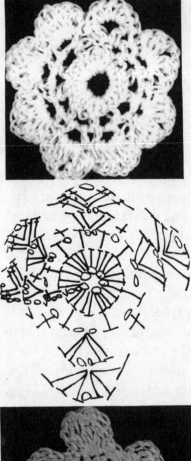

16. Four-Leaf Clover

Ch 5 and join with a sl st to form a ring.

Round 1: 14 sc in ring.

Round 2: 2 sc, 1 leaf [ch 4, (yo twice, insert hook in next st, pull up a loop, yo, pull through 2 loops, yo, pull through 2 lps) 3 times in same st, yo, pull through 4 lps, ch 3], 1 sc in each of next 2 sts, make 3 more leaves as above.

17. Star

Ch 2.

Round 1: 5 sc in 2nd ch from hook.

Round 2: 3 sc in each sc.

Round 3: (1 sc in next st, ch 6, sl st in 2nd ch from hook, 1 sc in next ch, 1 hdc in next ch, 1 dc in next ch, 1 trc in next ch, 1 tr in base of starting sc, sk 2 sc) 4 times, sl st in 1st sc to join.

18. Hexagon

Ch 6 and join with a sl st to form a ring.

Round 1: Ch 2, 2 dc in ring, ch 3, (3 dc in ring, ch 3) 5 times, sl st in top of beg ch to close.

Round 2: Ch 4, * (3 trc, ch 2, 3 trc) in each 3-ch sp, rep from *, sl st in top of beg ch to close.

Round 3: Ch 3, * 1 dc in each trc, (2 dc, ch 2, 2 dc) in each 2-ch sp, rep from *, sl st in top of beg ch to close.

Round 4: Ch 3, * sk 1 st, 1 dc in next st, 1 dc in the skipped st, rep from *, sl st in top of beg ch to close.

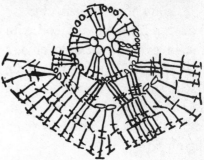

19. Granny Wheel Square

Ch 8 and join with a sl st to form a ring.

Round 1: Ch 6 (counts as 1 dc and ch 3), * 1 dc in center of ring, ch 3, rep from * 6 times, join with sl st to 3rd ch of starting ch-6.

Round 2: Ch 2, 3 dc in next ch-3 sp, ch 2, * 4 dc in next ch-3 sp, ch 2, rep from * around, join with sl st to 2nd ch of starting ch-2.

Round 3: 1 sl st in each of next 3 dc, ch 2, 5 dc in next ch-2 sp, ch 1, * 6 dc in next ch-2 sp, ch 3, 6 dc in next ch-2 sp, ch 1, rep from * twice and end 6 dc in next ch-2 sp, ch 3, join with sl st to 2nd ch of starting ch-2.

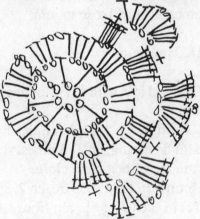

Round 4: Ch 5, sk 2 dc, * 1 sc in sp before next dc, ch 3, 1 sc in next ch-1 sp, ch 3, sk 3 dc, 1 sc in sp before next dc, ch 3, (2 dc, ch 3, 2 dc) in next ch-3 sp, ch 3, sk 3 dc, rep from * twice, end with 1 sc in sp before next dc, ch 3, 1 sc in next ch-1 sp, ch 3, sk 3 dc, 1 sc in sp before next dc, ch 3, (2 dc, ch 3, 1 dc) in next ch-3 sp, join with sl st to 2nd ch of starting ch-5.

20. Dogwood

Ch 2.

Round 1: Sk 1st ch, 8 sc in 2nd ch, sl st in 1st st, sc to close.

Round 2: Ch 5, sk 1 st, 1 sc in next st, (ch 4, sk 1 st, 1 sc in next st) twice, ch 4, sl st in 1st of 5 ch at beg of row.

Round 3: 1 sl st in next ch sp, ch 4, 6 dc in same sp as sl st, (ch 2, 7 dc) in each of next 3 ch sp, ch 2, sl st in top of 4 ch at beg of row.

Round 4: Ch 2, 1 sc in joining sp, (1 sc in each of next 2 sts, 2 sc in next st) twice, ch 3, * (2 sc in next st, 1 sc in each of next 2 sts) twice, 2 sc in next st, ch 3, rep from * twice, sl st in top of beg ch.

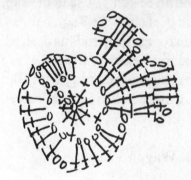

Round 5: Ch 4, 1 dc in joining st, 1 dc in next st, 2 dc in next st, 1 dc in next st, (2 dc in next st) twice, (1 dc in next st, 2 dc in next st) twice, ch 2, turn.

Round 6: (1 sc, 4 dc, 1 sc, ch 2, sk 2 sts) twice, sk 1 st, 1 sl st.

Repeat Rows 5 and 6 for 3 other petals, each time starting with right side facing you.

21. Paddle Wheel

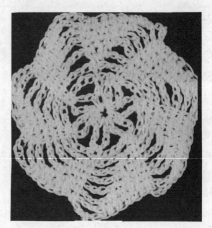

Ch 5 and join with a sl st to form
a ring.
Round 1: (ch 6, 1 sc in ring) 6
times, don't close row.
Round 2: (ch 4, 1 sc in next sp)
6 times.
Round 3: (ch 4, 1 sc in next sp,
1 sc in next sc), 6 times.
Round 4: (ch 4, 1 sc in next sp,
1 sc in next 2 sc), 6 times.
Round 5: (ch 4, 1 sc in next sp,
1 sc in each of the 3 sc), 6 times.
Rep for as many rnds as desired,
making 1 extra sc in each group
on each rnd, begining with 10th
rnd, make 5 ch in each sp instead
of 4.

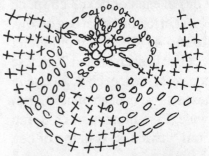

22. Wagon Wheel

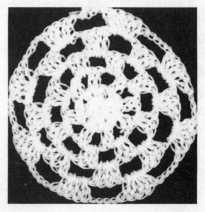

Ch 4 and join with sl st to form a
ring.
Round 1: Ch 3, 1 petal in ring
[(yo, insert hook, draw up a lp)
twice, yo, pull through 5 lps, ch
1], 7 more petals in ring, sl st in
top of beg ch.
Round 2: Ch 2, 1 dc in 1st ch sp,
ch 2, (2 dc, ch 2) in each of next
7 ch sps, sl st in 2nd ch at beg.
Round 3: Ch 2, (1 dc, ch 1, 2 dc,
ch 1) in 1st ch sp, (2 dc, ch 1, 2
dc, ch 1) in each of next 7 ch sp,

sl st in 2nd ch at beg.

Round 4: Ch 2, 2 dc in 1st ch sp, ch 1, (3 dc, ch 1) in each of next 15 ch sp, sl st in 2nd ch at beg. Repeat rnd 4 as many times as desired for size but after 5th round, ch 2 between dc groups.

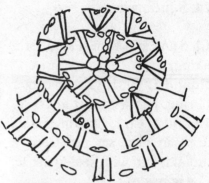

23. Geometric Circle

Ch 10 and join with sl st to form a ring.

Round 1: Ch 2, 30 dc in center of ring, join with sl st to 1st dc.

Round 2: Ch 5, * sk 2 dc, 1 dc in next dc, ch 3, rep from * 8 times, join with sl st to 2nd ch of starting ch-5.

Round 3: Ch 2, 2 dc in joining sp, * ch 3, 3 dc in next dc, rep from * around and end with ch 3, join with sl st to 2nd ch of starting ch-2.

Round 4: Ch 2, 1 dc in each of next 2 dc, * ch 4, 1 dc in each of next 3 dc, rep from * around and end with ch 4, join with sl st to 2nd ch of starting ch-2.

Round 5: Ch 2, 1 dc in each of next 2 dc, * ch 5, 1 dc in each of next 3 dc, rep from * around and end with ch 5, join with sl st to 2nd ch of starting ch-2.

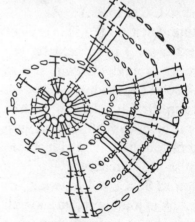

24. Sunflower

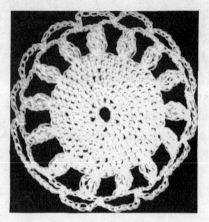

Ch 6 and join with sl st to form a ring.

Round 1: Ch 1, 12 sc in center of ring, join with sl st to 1st sc.

Round 2: Ch 1, * 1 sc in next sc, 2 sc in next sc, rep from * around, join with sl st to 1st sc, (18 sc made).

Round 3: Ch 1, * 1 sc in each of next 2 sc, 2 sc in next sc, rep from * around, join with sl st to 1st sc (24 sc made).

Round 4: Ch 1, * 1 sc in each of next 3 sc, 2 sc in next sc, rep from * around, join with sl st to 1st sc (30 sc made).

Round 5: Ch 1, * 1 sc in each of next 4 sc, 2 sc in next sc, rep from * around, join with sl st to 1st sc (36 sc made).

Round 6: Ch 1, * 1 sc in each of next 5 sc, 2 sc in next sc, rep from * around, join with sl st to 1st sc (42 sc made).

Round 7: Ch 1, * 1 sc in each of next 6 sc, 2 sc in next sc, rep from * around, join with sl st to 1st sc (48 sc made).

Round 8: Ch 4: [yo twice, insert hk in joining sp, yo and pull through, (yo and pull through 2 lps on hk) twice], yo and pull through last 3 lps on hk (2-trc

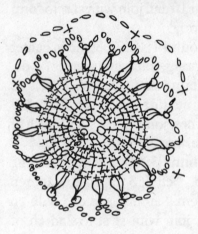

cluster made), * ch 5, sk 2 sc, [yo twice, insert hk in next sc, yo and pull through, (yo and pull through 2 lps on hk) 3 times], yo and pull through last 4 lps on hk (3-trc cluster made), rep from * around, end with ch 5, join with sl st to top of 1st cluster.

Round 9: Ch 7, * 1 sc in next ch-5 sp, ch 6, rep from * , end with 1 sc in last ch-5 sp, join with sl st to 1st ch of starting ch-7.

25. Six-Spoked Wheel

Ch 6 and join with sl st to form a ring.

Round 1: Ch 1, 12 sc in center of ring, join with sl st to 1st sc.

Round 2: Ch 4, 2 trc in joining sp, * ch 3, sk 1 sc, 3 trc in next sc, rep from * around and end with ch 3, join with sl st to 4th ch of starting ch-4.

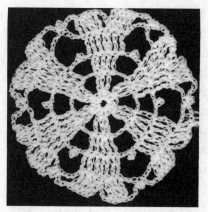

Round 3: Ch 4, 1 trc in joining sp, * 1 trc in next trc, 2 trc in next trc, ch 6, 1 sc in 4th ch from hk (picot made), ch 2, 2 trc in next trc, rep from * around, end with 1 trc in next trc, 2 trc in next trc, 1 picot, ch 2, join with sl st in 4th ch of starting ch-4.

Round 4: Ch 4, 1 trc in joining sp, * 1 trc in each of next 3 trc, 2 trc in next trc, ch 9 sk 1 picot, 2 trc in next trc, rep from * and end 1 trc in each of next 3 trc, 2 trc in next trc, ch 9, sk 1 picot, join with sl st to 4th ch of starting ch-4.

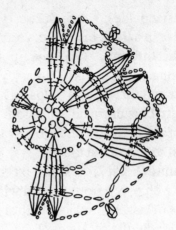

Round 5: Ch 4, yo twice, insert hk in joining sp, yo and pull through, (yo and pull through 2 lps on hk) twice, [yo twice, insert hk in next trc, yo and pull through, (yo and pull through 2 lps on hk) twice] twice, yo and pull through last 4 lps on hk, * ch 5, 1 sl st in next trc, ch 5, [yo twice, insert hk in next trc, yo and pull through, (yo and pull 2 lps on hk) twice] 3 times, yo twice, insert hk in same trc, yo and pull through, (yo and pull through 2 lps on hk) twice, yo and pull through last 5 lps on hk (left cluster made), ch 6, sk 4 ch, (1 sc, ch 4, 1 sc) in next ch, ch 6, sk 4 ch, yo twice, insert hk in next trc, yo and pull through, (yo and pull through 2 lps on hk) twice, yo twice, insert hk in same trc, yo and pull through, (yo and pull through 2 lps on hk) twice, [yo twice, insert hk in next trc, yo and pull through, (yo and pull through 2 lps on hk) twice] twice, yo and pull through last 5 lps on hk, rep from * 4 times, end with ch 5, 1 sl st in next trc, ch 5, 1 left cluster over next 3 trc, ch 6, sk 4 ch, (1 sc, ch 4, 1 sc) in next ch, ch 6, sk 4 ch, join with sl st to top of 1st cluster.

160

26. Lacy Hexagon

Ch 8, join with sl st to form a ring.

Round 1: Ch 4 (counts as 1 dc), * 1 dc in ring, ch 1, rep from * 10 times, join with sl st to 3rd ch of starting ch-4, (12 dc).

Round 2: 1 sc in 1st ch-1 sp, ch 4, * sk (1 dc, ch-1 sp, 1 dc), 1 sc in next ch-1 sp, ch 4, rep from * 4 times, join with sl st to 1st sc (6 ch-4 sps).

Round 3: 1 sc in same sc as joining, * ch 1, (1 dc, ch 1) 4 times in next ch-4 sp, 1 sc in next sc, rep from * 4 times, end with ch 1, (1 dc, ch 1) 4 times in next ch-4 sp, join with sl st to 1st sc.

Round 4: Ch 5, 1 trc in same sc as joining, ch 1, * sk (ch-1 sp, 1 dc) twice, 1 sc in next ch 1 sp, ch 1, sk (1 dc, ch-1 sp) twice, (1 trc, ch 1) 4 times in next sc, rep from * 4 times, end with sk (ch-1 sp, 1 dc) twice, 1 sc in next ch-1 sp, ch 1, (1 trc, ch 1) twice in same sc as joining, join with sl st to 4th ch of starting ch-5.

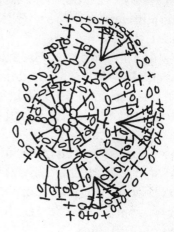

Round 5: Sl st in each of next 2 ch-1 sps, sl st in next sc, 1 sc in next ch-1 sp, ch 1, 1 sc in next ch-1 sp, * ch 1, (1 sc, ch 1, 1 sc) in next ch-1 sp, (ch 1, 1 sc in next ch-1 sp) 4 times, rep from * 4 times, end with ch 1, (1 sc, ch 1, 1 sc) in next ch-1 sp, (ch 1, 1 sc in next ch-1 sp) twice, join with sl st to 1st sc.

161

27. Grape

Ch 5.

Row l: 2 dc in 5th ch from hk, ch 3, 3 dc in same ch, turn.

Row 2: 1 sl st in each of lst 3 dc, (1 sl st, ch 3, 2 dc) in next ch-3 sp, (ch 2, 3 dc in same ch-3 sp) twice, turn.

Row 3: 1 sl st in each of lst 3 dc, (1 sl st, ch 3, 2 dc, ch 2, 3 dc) in next ch-2 sp, sk 3 dc, (3 dc, ch 2, 3 dc) in next ch-2 sp, (shell made), turn.

Row 4: 1 sl st in each of lst 3 dc, (1 sl st, ch 3, 2 dc, ch 2, 3 dc) in next ch-2 sp, sk 3 dc, 1 dc in sp before next dc, sk 3 dc, 1 shell in next ch-2 sp, turn.

Row 5: 1 sl st in each of lst 3 dc, (1 sl st, ch 3, 2 dc, ch 2, 3 dc) in next ch-2 sp, sk 3 dc, (1 dc, ch 3, 1 dc) in next dc, sk 3 dc, 1 shell in next ch-2 sp, turn.

Row 6: 1 sl st in each of lst 3 dc, (1 sl st, ch 3, 2 dc, ch 2, 3 dc) in next ch-2 sp, ch 1, sk 4 dc, 9 dc in next ch-3 sp, ch 1, sk 4 dc, 1 shell in next ch-2 sp, turn.

Row 7: 1 sl st in each of lst 3 dc, (1 sl st, ch 3, 2 dc, ch 2, 3 dc) in next ch-2 sp, ch 1, sk (3 dc, ch 1) 1 dc in each of the next 9 dc, ch 1, sk (ch-1, 3 dc) 1 shell in next ch-2 sp, turn.

Row 8: 1 sl st in each of lst 3 dc, (1 sl st, ch 3, 2 dc, ch 2, 3 dc) in next ch-2 sp, ch 1, sk (3 dc, ch-1), * insert hk in sp between next 2 dc, yo and pull through, (yo, insert hk in same sp, yo and pull through) twice, yo and pull through 6 lps on hk (puff st made), ch 2, rep from * 7 times, sk (ch-1, 3 dc), 1 shell in next ch-2 sp, turn.

Row 9: 1 sl st in each of lst 3 dc, (1 sl st, ch 3, 2 dc, ch 2, 3 dc) in next ch-2 sp, ch 1, sk (3 dc, ch-1), (1 puff st, ch 2) in each ch-2 sp between 2 puff sts of prev row, sk (last puff st ch-2, 3 dc), 1 shell in next ch-2 sp, turn, make 1 less puff st on each row.

Rows 10 - 15: Same as row 9.

Row 16: 1 sl st in each of lst 3 dc, (1 sl st, ch 3, 2 dc, ch 2, 3 dc) in next ch-2 sp, sk (3 dc, ch-1, 1 puff st, ch-2, 3 dc), 1 shell in next ch-2 sp, turn.

Row 17: 1 sl st in each of lst 3 dc, (1 sl st, ch 3, 2 dc) in next ch-2 sp, sk 6 dc, 3 dc in next ch-2 sp.

28. Rose

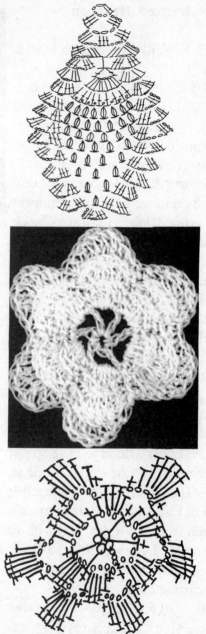

Ch 4, join with sl st to form a ring.

Round 1: Ch 6, (dc in ring, ch 3) 5 times, join to 3rd ch of beg ch-6.

Round 2: Ch 1 in each sp around, make (sc, hdc, 3 dc, hdc, and sc), join to lst sc (6 petals).

Round 3: Ch 1, sc in joining, ch 5, * sc in sp between last sc on next petal and lst sc on following petal, ch 5, rep from * around, join to lst sc. (Keep ch-5 sps behind petals).

Round 4: Ch 1 in each ch-5 lp around, make (sc, hdc, 5 dc, hdc, and sc), join to lst sc.

Round 5: Ch 1, sc in joining, ch 7, sc in sp between last sc on next petal and the lst on following petal, ch 7, rep from * around, join to lst sc.

Round 6: Ch 1 in each ch-7 lp around (sc, hdc, dc, 4 trc, dc, hdc and sc), join, F.O.

29. Spoked Hexagon

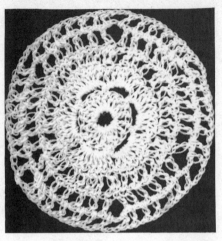

Ch 8, join with sl st to form a ring.

Round 1: Ch 3, (counts as 1 dc), 17 dc in ring, join with sl st to 3rd ch of starting ch-3.

Round 2: * Ch 5, sk 2 dc, 1 sc in next dc, rep from * 5 times.

Round 3: Ch 3 (counts as 1 dc), * 8 dc in next ch-5 sp, rep from * around, join with sl st to 3rd ch of starting ch-3 (49 dc).

Round 4: Working through back lps of sts only, ch 3 (counts as 1 sc), 1 dc in joining sp, * sk 1 dc, (ch 1, 1 dc in next dc) 5 times, ch 1, sk 1 dc, 2 dc in next dc, rep from * 4 times, end with sk 1 dc, (ch 1, 1 dc in next dc) 5 times, ch 1, join with sl st to 2nd ch of starting ch-3.

Round 5: Ch 6 (counts as 1 dc and ch 3), 1 dc in joining sp (1st corner), sk 1 dc, * (ch 1, 1 dc in next dc) 6 times, ch 1, (1 dc, ch 3, 1 dc) in next dc (corner made), rep from * 4 times, end with sk 1 dc, (ch 1, 1 dc in next dc) 6 times, ch 1, join with sl st to 3rd dc of starting ch-6.

Round 6: Ch 6, 1 dc in joining sp, * (ch 1, sk 1 dc, 1 dc in next ch-1 sp) 7 times, ch 1, (1 dc, ch 3, 1 dc) in corner ch-3 sp, rep from * 4 times, end with (ch 1, sk 1 dc, 1 dc in next ch 1 sp) 7 times, ch 1, join with sl st to 3rd ch of starting ch-6.

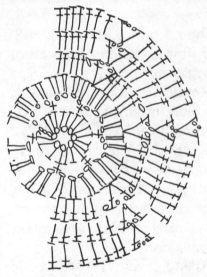

164

30. Flower In Hexagon

Ch 6, join with sl st to form a ring.

Round 1: Ch 4, 23 trc in ring, join with sl st to 4-ch of starting ch-4.

Round 2: Ch 5, (yo, insert hk horizontally from right to left under ch-4 of prev rnd, yo and pull up a long lp) 5 times, yo and pull through 11 lps on hk, ch 1, * sk 1 trc, (2 dc, 1 trc, 2 dc) in next trc, sk 1 trc, (yo, insert hk horizontally from right to left under next trc, yo and pull up a long lp) 5 times, yo and pull through 11 lps on hk, ch 1 (puff st made), rep from * around, end with sk 1 trc, (2 dc, 1 trc, 2 dc) in next trc, sk 1 trc, join with sl st to top of 1st puff st (6 puff sts made)

Round 3: * 1 sc in each of next 2 dc, 3 sc in next trc (corner made), 1 sc in each of next 2 dc, 1 sc in top of next puff st, rep from * around, join with sl st to 1st sc.

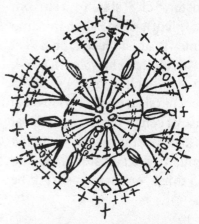

31. Snowflake

Ch 6, join with sl st to form a ring.

Round 1: Ch 4 • yo twice, insert hk into ring, yo and pull up a

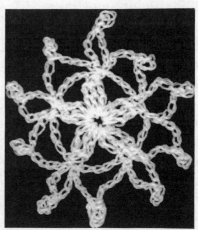

loop, (yo and pull through 2 lps on hk) twice (triple crochet), rep from •, yo and pull through all 3 lps on hk (1 cluster made), * ch 5, (keeping last lp of each trc on hook) 3 trc into ring, yo and pull through all 4 lps left on hook, repeat from * 4 times, ch 5, join with a sl st at top of 1st cluster (6 clusters made).

Round 2: Sl st in center trc of 1st cluster, * ch 8, sl st in 4th ch from hk (picot), ch 4, sl st in same center st of 1st cluster, ch 8 sl st in 4th ch from hk (picot), (ch 4, sl st in 4th ch from hk) twice (3 picot) • (sl st, ch 3, sl st) in ch at base of center picot •, rep • to • at base of next picot, ch 4, sl st in center of next cluster *, rep * to * 5 times, end with a sl st in be ch.

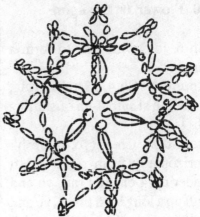

32. Six-Point Snowflake

Ch 15, join with a sl st to form a ring.

Round 1: (Ch 4, trc in ring, ch 4, sl st in ring) 12 times.

Round 2: Sl st in 1st ch 4 at beg of rnd, sc in trc, (ch 11, sk next trc, sc in next trc) 5 times, ch 11, sk next trc, sl st in 1st sc at beg of rnd.

Round 3: Ch 1, (sc in each of the

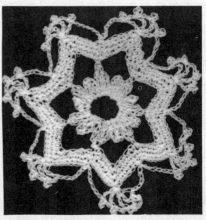

166

1st 5-ch sts, 3 sc in next ch st, sc in each of next 5 ch sts) 6 times. Sl st in 1st sc at beg of rnd.

Round 4: Ch 1, sc in 1st sc where sl st was made, sc in each of next 5 sc, 3 sc in next sc (center sc of the 3 sc group), sc in each of next 6 sc, (sc in each of next 6 sc, 3 sc in next sc, sc in each of next 6 sc) 5 times. Sl st in 1st sc at beg of rnd.

Round 5: Ch 1, sc in 1st sc where sl st was made, sc in each of next 6 sc, 3 sc in next 7 sc, (sc in each of next 7 sc, 3 sc in next sc, sc in each of next 7 sc) 5 times. Sl st in 1st sc at beg of rnd.

Round 6: Ch 1, sc in 1st sc where sl st was made, * ch 6, sk 7 sc, trc in next sc (center sc of the 3 sc group) ch 2 for picot, ch 3, sl st in 3rd ch from hk, ch 2, (trc in same sc, ch 2, picot, ch 2) 3 times, trc in same sc, ch 6, sk 7 sc, sc in each of next 2 sc. Rep from * 5 more times, end with sc in next sc, sl st in 1st sc at beg of rnd.

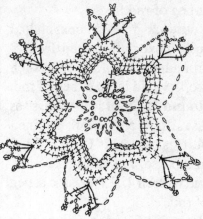

33. Daisy

Ch 6, join with sl st to form ring.
Round 1: Work one 7-loop puff st in ring, ch 3, rep 5 times.(6 puff sts made). Sl st in 1st puff st

at beg of rnd.

Round 2: * 5 sc in next ch lp, 1 sc in next puff st, rep from * around, end with 5 sc in next ch loop, sl st in 1st sc at beg of rnd.

Round 3: Ch 1, 1 sc in same sc as last sl st, * ch 4, work 3 joined puff sts over next 5 sc, ch 4, 1 sc in next sc, rep from * around, end with ch 4, sl st in 1st sc at beg of rnd.

Round 4: Ch 1, 1 sc in same sc as last sl st, * ch 4, 1 sc in same sc as last sc, ch 2, puff st in top of next 3 joined puff st, (ch 1, puff st in same st as last puff st) 3 times, ch 2, 1 sc in next sc, rep from * around, end with ch 2, sl st in 1st sc at beg of rnd.

Round 5: * Ch 5, sk next 2 puff sts, 1 sc in next (ch 1) sp, ch 5, sk next 2 puff sts, 1 sc in next (ch 4) lp, rep from * around, end with ch 5, sl st in 1st sc at beg of rnd.

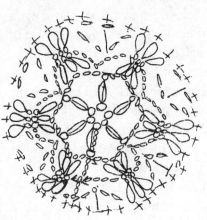

Round 6: Ch 1, 1 sc in same sc as last sl st, * 5 sc in next (ch 5) lp, 3 sc in next sc, 5 sc in next ch lp, 1 sc in next sc, rep from * around, end with 5 sc in next ch lp, sl st in 1st sc at beg of rnd.

Round 7: Sl st in next sc, ch 1, 1 sc in same sc as last sl st, * ch 4, 1 sc in 4th st from hk (this forms picot), sk next 2 sc, 1 sc in next sc, ch 4, 1 sc in 4th st from hk, sk next 2 sc, 1 sc in next sc, ch 4, complete picot, 1 sc in same sc as last sc, work (picot, sk next 2 sc, 1 sc in next sc) twice, picot, sk next sc, 1 sc in next sc, rep from * around, end with picot, sk next sc, sl st in 1st sc at beg of rnd.

34. Wreath

Ch 50, join with sl st to form ring.

Round 1: Ch 3 (counts as dc), ch 2, sk 1 ch, dc in next ch, (ch 2, sk 1 ch, dc in next ch) 23 times, end with ch 2, sk 1 ch, sl st in top of ch 3 at beg of rnd.

Round 2: Sl st in ch 2 sp, ch 3 (counts as dc), 2 dc in same sp, ch 2 (3 dc in next ch 2 sp, ch 2) 24 times, sl st in top of ch 3 at beg of rnd.

Round 3: Ch 4 (counts as a trc), (yo twice, pull up 2 lp in next dc, yo, pull through 2 lps on hk, yo, pull through 2 lps on hk leaving last lp on hk) 2 times, yo, pull through rem 3 lps on hk, ch 4, sc in ch 2 sp, ch 4, * (yo twice, pull up a lp in next dc, yo, pull through 2 lps on hk, yo, pull through rem 4 lps on hk (3 trc clusters made), ch 4, sc in ch 2 sp, ch 4, rep from * 23 times, end with sl st to top of trc cluster at

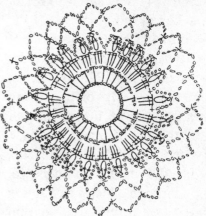

beg of rnd.

Round 4: (ch 6, sl st in top of next trc cluster) 24 time

Round 5: Sl st in next 2 ch of ch 6 sp, (ch 7, sl st in next ch 6-sp, 24 times, end with ch 7, sl st in 3rd sl st at beg of rnd. F.O.

35. Five-Point Snowflake

Ch 2.

Round 1: 10 sc in 1st ch from hk, sl st in 1st sc.

Round 2: Ch 4 (counts as a trc), ch 2 (trc in next sc, ch 2) 9 times, sl st in top of ch 4 at beg of rnd.

Round 3: Ch 3 (counts as a dc) 2 dc in ch 2 sp, dc in trc, 2 dc in ch 2 sp, ch 3, (dc in trc, 2 dc in ch 2 sp, dc in next trc, 2 dc in ch 2 sp, ch 3) 4 times, sl st in top of ch 3 at beg of rnd.

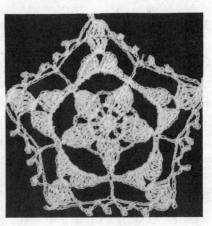

Round 4: Ch 4 (counts as a trc) (yo twice, pull up a lp in next dc, yo, pull through 2 lps on hk, yo, pull through 2 lps on hk leaving last lp on hk) 5 times, yo, pull through rem 6 lps on hk, ch 15, * (yo twice, pull up a lp in next dc, yo, pull through 2 lps on hk, yo, pull through 2 lps on hk leaving last lp on hk) 6 times, yo, pull through rem 7 lps on hk, 6 treble clusters made, ch 15, rep from * 4 times, sl st in top of 1st trc clus-

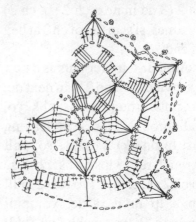

ter.

Round 5: (In ch 15 sp work 3 sc, 3 dc, 4 trc, 3 dc, 3 sc, ch 1) 5 times, sl st in top of 1st sc at beg of rnd.

Round 6: Sl st in last ch 1 sp made, ch 4 (counts as a trc), ch 8, 5 trc in ch 3 sp, ch 8, (trc in ch 1 sp, ch 8, 5 trc in ch 3 sp, ch 8) 4 times, end with sl st in top of ch 4 at beg of rnd.

Round 7: * (Ch 2, for picot ch 3, sl st in 3rd ch from hk, ch 2, sl st in 8 sp) twice, ch 5, 5 trc cluster in the 5 trc, for picot ch 4, sl st in 4th ch from hk, ch 5, (sl st in ch 8 sp, ch 2 for picot, ch 3, sl st in 3rd ch from hk, ch 2) twice, sl st in trc, repeat from * 4 more times. F.O.

36. Eight-Point Snowflake

Ch 12, join with sl st to form a ring.

Round 1: Ch 3 (counts as a dc), work 23 dc, sl st in top of ch 3 at beg of rnd (24 dc).

Round 2: Ch 3 (counts as a dc), dc in each of next 4 dc, ch 6 (sk 1 dc, dc in each of next 5 dc, ch 6) 3 times. Sl st in top of ch 3 at beg of rnd.

Round 3: Sl st in 2nd dc, ch 3, (counts as a dc), dc in each of

next 2 dc, ch 5, sc in ch 6 sp, ch 5 (sk the 1st dc, dc in each of next 3 dc, ch 5, sc in ch 6 sp, ch 5) 3 times. Sl st in top of ch 3 at beg of rnd.

Round 4: Sl st in 2nd dc, ch 3 (counts as a dc), ch 6, dc in same st where sl st was made, ch 4, sc in ch 5 sp, ch 6, sc in next ch 5 sp, ch 4, (dc in 2nd dc, ch 6, dc in same st, ch 4, sc in ch 5 sp, ch 6, sc in next ch 5 sp, ch 4) 3 times, end with sl st in top of ch 3 at beg of rnd.

Round 5: Sl st in 1st and 2nd ch of ch-6 sp, ch 3 (counts as a dc), work 4 dc in same ch 6 sp, ch 8, 2 dc in next ch 6 sp, ch 3, 2 dc in same ch-6 sp, ch 8, (5 dc in next ch-6 sp, ch 8, 2 dc in next ch-6 sp, ch 3, 2 dc in same ch-6 sp, ch 8) 3 times, sl st in top of ch 3 at beg of rnd.

Round 6: Ch 3 (counts as a dc), dc in each of the next 4 dc, ch 8, 2 dc, ch 3, 2 dc in ch 3 sp, ch 8, (dc in each of the next 5 dc, ch 8, 2 dc, ch 3, 2 dc in ch-3 sp, ch 8) 3 times, sl st in top of ch 3 at beg of rnd.

Round 7: Ch 4 (counts as a trc), (yo twice, pull up a lp in next dc, yo, pull through 2 lps on hk, yo, pull through 2 lps on hk leaving last lp on hk) 4 times, yo, pull through rem 5 lps on hk, ch 8, sc over the 2-ch-8 sps below on rnds 5 and 6, ch 8, 2 trc, ch 3, 2 trc in ch 3 sp, ch 8, sc over the next 2 ch-8 sps, ch 8, * (yo twice, pull up a lp in next dc, yo, pull through 2 lps on hk, yo, pull through 2 lps on hk leaving last lp on hk) 5 times, yo, pull through rem 6 lps on hk, (5 treble clusters made), ch 8, sc over 2 ch-8 sps, ch 8, 2 trc, ch 3, 2 trc in ch-3 sp, ch 8, sc over the 2 ch-8 sps, ch 8) repeat from * 2 more times, sl st in 1st trc cluster.

Round 8: Sl st in last ch 8 sp of rnd 7, (ch 4, 8 sc in each of the next 2 ch-8 sps, 2 sc, ch 3, 2 sc in ch 3 sp, 8 sc in each of the next 2 ch-8 sp) 4 times. Sl st in sl st at beg of the rnd.

Round 9: * Work 3 sc in ch 4 sp, for picot ch 4, sl st in 4th ch from hk, 3 sc in same sp, (ch 3, sk 1 sc, sl st in next sp) 9 times, 2 sc in ch 3 sp, ch 2, picot, ch 2, 2 sc in same sp, (ch 3, sk 1 sc, sl st in next sc) 9 times, repeat from * 3 more times, sl st in 1st sc at beg of rnd. F.O.

37. Twelve Petal Flower

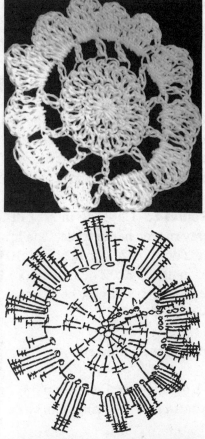

Ch 4, join sl st to form ring.

Round 1: Ch 3 (counts as 1 dc), 11 dc in ring, join with sl st to 3rd ch of starting ch-3 (12 dc).

Round 2: Ch 3 (counts as 1 dc), 1 dc in joining sp, * 2 dc through back lp only of next dc, rep from * around, join with sl st to 3rd ch of starting ch-3. (24 dc).

Round 3: Ch 6, * sk 1 dc, 1 dc through back lp only of next dc, ch 3, rep from * around, join with sl st to 3rd ch of starting ch-6 (12 ch-3 sps).

Round 4: Ch 3, (1 trc, 2 dbl trc, 1 trc, 1 dc) in next 3-ch sp, * (1 dc, 1 trc, 2 dbl trc, 1 trc, 1 dc) in next ch-3 sp, rep from * around, join with sl st to 3rd ch of starting ch-3.

38. Plain Octagon

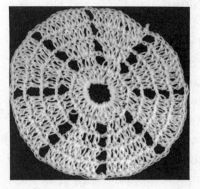

Ch 10, join with sl st to form ring.

Round 1: Ch 2, 23 dc in ring, sl st to top of ch 2 (24 dc).

Round 2: Ch 2, dc in each of next 2 dc, * ch 2, dc in each of the next 3 dc, rep from * 7 times, end with ch 2, join with sl st in top of ch 2 (8 groups).

Round 3: Ch 2, dc in sl st of

173

prev rnd, dc in next dc, 2 dc in next dc, * ch 2, 2 dc in next dc, dc in next dc, 2 dc, in next dc, rep from * 7 times, ch 2, join with sl st in ch 2.

Round 4: Ch 2, dc in sl st of prev rnd, dc in next 3 dc, 2 dc in next dc, * ch 2, 2 dc in next dc, dc in next 3 dc, 2 dc in next dc, rep from * 7 times, ch 2, join with sl st in ch 2.

Round 5: Ch 2, dc in sl st of prev rnd, dc in next 5 dc, 2 dc in next dc, * ch 2, 2 dc in next dc, 1 dc in next 5 dc, 2 dc in next dc, rep from * 7 times, ch 2, join with sl st in ch 2.

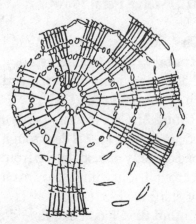

39. Framed Flower

Ch 6, join with sl st to form ring.
Round l: 8 sc in ring, join with sl st.
Round 2: * Ch 9, sk l ch, l sc, l hdc, 5 dc, l hdc, join to ring with sl st in next sc of rnd l, rep from * 8 times, end off.
Round 3: Attach thread to tip of any petal with a sl st, * ch 10, join to tip of next petal with l sc, rep from *, join with sc.
Round 4: l sc in each ch and sc of prev rnd, join with sl st, F.O.

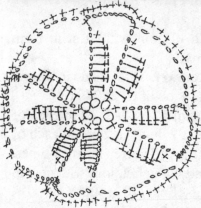

40. Shamrock

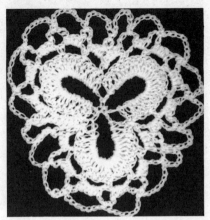

Ch 16.

Round 1: 1 sc in the 1st ch to form a lp, ch 15, 1 sc in same 1st ch as before, twice (3 lps formed).

Round 2: 24 sc in each lp formed in rnd 1, join with a sl st to 1st sc.

Round 3: 1 sc in each sc around all 3 petals, join with sl st to 1st sc.

Round 4: Sl st in next 3 sc, *1 sc, ch 4, 1 sc in 3rd ch from hk, ch 5, 1 sc in 3rd ch from hk, ch 1 (1 picot lp formed), sk 4 sc, 1 sc in next sc, (1 picot lp, sk 4 sc, 1 sc in next sc) twice, 1 picot lp, 1 sc into 5th sc of next petal, rep from * twice, sk last sc and work a sl st in 1st sc of rnd (1 picot lp formed).

Round 5: 4 sl st along edge of 1st picot lp, * 5 sc across picot lp from picot to picot, ch 4, rep from * 11 times more, end with sl st to 4th sl st at beg of rnd.

Round 6: * Ch 8, 1 sc in ch-4 lp, rep from * 11 times more, 2 sl st in next 2 ch of last ch-4 lp.

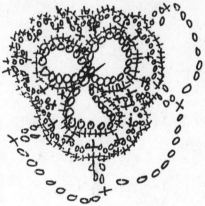

Chapter XVI

Edgings and Trims

1. Start at one end, working lengthwise.

* Ch 6, 1 sl st in 3rd st from hk, 3 trc in same st, ch 3, 1 sl st in same st, repeat from * until length desired.

2. Make a chain slightly longer than length desired.

Row 1: Sc in 6th ch from hk, ch 3, sk 2 ch, sc in next ch, repeat from * across row, end with ch 1, dc in last ch, having number of lps divisible by 3, plus 2. Ch 3, turn.

Row 2: * Sc in next lp, ch 3, repeat from * across row, end with ch 1, dc in last lp, ch 6, turn.

Row 3: Sc in 4th ch from hk (picot made), * ch 2, sc in next lp, ch 3, sc in next lp, ch 6.

3. Make chain the length desired.

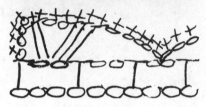

Row 1: Trc in 6th ch from hk, * sk 2 ch, trc in next ch, across row, ending with trc in last ch, ch 4, turn.

Row 2: * ch 4, 2 dtr in 2nd sp, ch 2, 3 dtr in same sp, rep from * across row ending with ch 4, turn.

Row 3: Sl st into ch 4, 2 sc in ch 2, 1 picot, 2 sc in same ch, 5 sc in ch 4, sl st across sp to next dtrc, rep from * across row.

4. Start at end, working crosswise.

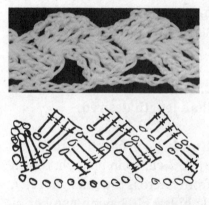

Ch 5, join in row, turn, ch 3, 4 trc in ring, ch 2, 1 sl st in same ring, * turn, ch 3, 4 trc in ch 2, 1 sl st in same ch, repeat from *. When the desired length is made, start at one end in the outside point, * ch 5, 1 sl st in next point repeat from *. This last row is made to sew on to material.

5. Scalloped Design

Ch 5.

Row 1: 3 dc, ch 2, 3 dc in 5th ch from hk (shell made), ch 4, turn.

Row 2: 3 dc, ch 2, 3 dc in ch-2

sp of prev shell, sk 2 dc, trc in next dc, ch 4, turn.

Row 3: Make shell in shell, trc in turning ch-4 loop 2 rows below, ch 4, turn.

Repeat row 3 for desired length.

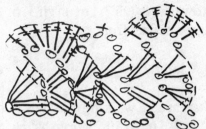

6. Single Rose

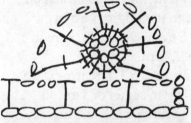

Ch 6, join, 15 sc in ring, turn, ch 5, * repeat until desired length. For top, make a row of sps, 4 sps between each ring. For lower edge, from 1st, make a short knot st, sc into 3rd in ring. Repeat around ring. 6 knot sts around ring, catching last one over the dc of 2nd sp. Repeat around all rings.

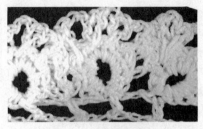

7. Make a chain length desired

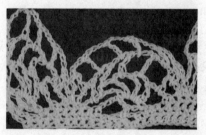

Start at end working lengthwise.

Row 1: * 1 sc in each 11 st of ch, ch 2, sk 2, repeat from *.

Row 2: * 9 sc over 11 sc of prev row, ch 3, 1 trc in ch 2, repeat from *.

Row 3: * 7 sc, ch 3, 1 trc in ch 3, ch 3, 1 trc in ch 3, ch 3, repeat from *.

Row 4: 5 sc, (ch 3, 1 trc in ch 3) 4 times, ch 3, repeat from *.

Row 5: 3 sc, (ch 3, 1 trc in ch 3) 5 times, ch 3, repeat from *.

Row 6: 1 sc (ch 3, 1 trc in ch 3) 6 times, repeat from *.

8. Chain 22

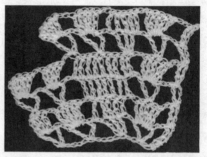

Start at end, working crosswise .
Row 1: 1 trc in 5th ch from hk, ch 2, 1 trc in 3rd ch, ch 2, 1 trc in same ch, ch 2, 3 trc in 3rd ch, ch 2, 1 trc in 5th ch, ch 2, 1 trc in same ch, ch 2, 1 trc in 5th ch, ch 2, 1 trc in same ch, turn.
Row 2: Ch 3, 4 trc in ch 2, 5 trc in next ch 2, ch 2, 1 trc in ch 2, 1 trc in next 3 trc, 1 trc in ch 2, ch 2, 5 trc in ch 2, ch 2, 2 trc in end, ch 2, turn.

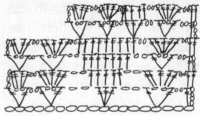

Row 3: Ch 3, 1 trc in next trc, ch 2, 1 trc in center of 5 trc, ch 2, 1 trc in same ch, ch 2, 1 trc in ch 2, 1 trc in each of next 5, 1 trc, ch 2, 1 trc in ch 2, 1 trc in center of 5 trc, ch 2, 1 trc in same st, turn.
Row 4: Ch 3, 1 trc in ch 2, 5 trc in next ch 2, ch 2, 1 trc in ch 2, 1 trc in each next 7 trc, 1 trc in ch 2, ch 2, 5 trc in ch 2, ch 2, 2 trc in end trc, turn.
Row 5: Ch 3, 1 trc in next trc, ch 2, 1 trc in center of 5 trc, ch 2, 1 trc in same st, ch 2, 3 trc in 1st trc of next group, ch 2, 1 trc in 4th trc of same group, ch 2, 1 trc in same st, ch 2, 1 trc in last trc of same group, ch 2, 1 trc in same st.

Repeat rows 2-5 for desired length.

9. Chain 9.

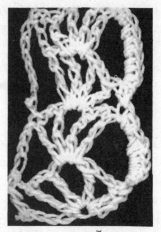

Start at end, working crosswise.
Row 1: 1 trc in 4th ch from hk, ch 2, 1 trc in same st, ch 2, 1 trc in same st, ch 2, 1 trc in same st, ch 2, 1 trc in end ch, ch 5, turn.
Row 2: 1 trc in center ch 2, ch 2, 1 trc in same ch, ch 2, 1 trc in same st, ch 2, 1 trc in same st, ch 5, 1 sl st in end st, turn.
9 sc in ch 5, ch 2.
Repeat last row for rem of work.

10. Chain 4.

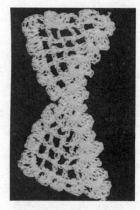

Row 1: In 4th ch from hk, make 2 dc, ch 1, 3 dc, ch 5, turn.
Row 2: Sk 1st 3 dc, 3dc in next ch-1 sp, ch 1, 3 dc, ch 1, turn.
Row 3: Sk 1st dc, sl st in each of next 2 dc, sl st in next ch-1 sp, ch 3, in same sp make (2 dc, ch 1, 3 dc, ch 2), sk 2 dc, dc in next dc, ch 2, dc in 3rd ch of turning ch, ch 5, turn.
Row 4: Sk 1st dc, (dc in next dc, ch 2) twice, sk next 2 dc, (3 dc, ch 1, 3 dc), ch 1, turn.
Row 5: Sk 1st dc, sl st in next 2 dc, sl st in next ch-1 sp, ch 3, (2 dc, ch 1, 3 dc, ch 2) in same sp, sk

181

next 2 dc, dc in next dc, (ch 2, dc in next dc) twice, ch 2, dc in 3rd ch of turning -ch, ch 5, turn.

Row 6: Sk lst dc, (dc in next dc, ch 2) 4 times, sk next 2 dc, (3 dc, ch 1, 3 dc) in next ch-l sp, ch 1, turn

Row 7: Sk lst dc, sl st in each of next 2 dc, sl st in next ch-l sp, ch 3, (2 dc, ch l, 3 dc) in same sp, ch 5, turn.

Repeat rows 2-7 for desired length. Work along pointed edge, attach thread to lst ch-2 sp, in same sp make sc, ch 3, 2 dc, (in next sp make sc, ch 3, 2 dc) 3 times, * in next sp at tip of triangle make (sc, ch 3, 2 dc) 8 times, repeat from * across row.

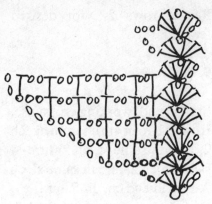

11. Chain 13.

Row l: Make (dc, ch 2, dc) in 7th ch from hk, (shell made) ch 3, dc in each of last 2 chs, ch 3, turn.

Row 2: Dc in 2nd dc, ch 3, shell in ch 2 sp of shell, ch 3, 5 dc in turning ch, ch 4, turn.

Row 3: Sc in lst dc, hdc in next dc, 2 dc in each of next 3 dc, ch 2, dc in next ch-3 sp, ch 2, shell in shell, ch 3, sk next sp, dc in next dc, dc in top of ch-3, ch 3, turn.

Row 4: Dc in 2nd dc, ch 3, shell

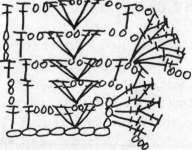

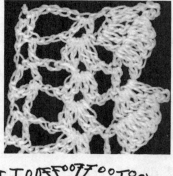

in shell, ch 3, sk next sp, 5 dc in next sp, ch 4, turn.

Repeat rows 3-4 for desired length. End with row 3.

12. Chain 21.

Row 1: Dc in 8th ch from hk, ch 2, sk 2 ch, dc in each of next 4 ch, ch 2, sk 2 ch, dc in next ch, ch 4, sl st in last ch, ch 2, turn.

Row 2: Make 7 dc in ch-4 lp, ch 2, sk dc and ch-2 sp, dc in next dc, ch 2, sk 2 dc, dc in next dc, ch 2, dc in next dc, ch 2, sk 2 ch, dc in next ch, ch 5, turn.

Row 3: Dc in next dc, ch 2, dc in next dc, 2 dc in ch-2 sp, dc in next dc, ch 2, dc in next sp, ch 1, sk next dc, (dc in next dc, ch 1) 6 times, dc in top of ch-2, ch 3, turn.

Row 4: Sc in 1st ch-1 sp, ch 3, (sc in next sp, ch 3) 5 times, sc in next sp, sl st in top of next dc, ch 2, 2 dc in ch-2 sp, dc in next dc, ch 2, sk 2 dc, dc in next dc, 2 dc in ch-2 sp, dc in next dc, ch 2, sk 2 ch, dc in next ch, ch 5, turn.

Row 5: Dc in next dc, ch 2, sk 2 dc, dc in next dc, 2 dc in ch-2 sp, dc in next dc, ch 2, sk 2 dc, dc in top of ch-2, sc in 1st ch-3 sp of scallop to left, ch 3, turn.

Row 6: Repeat row 2.

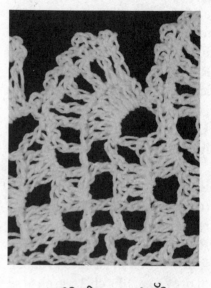

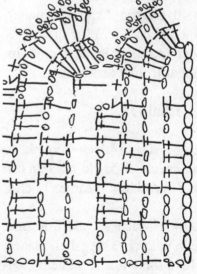

Row 7: Dc in next dc, ch 2, dc in next dc, 2 dc in ch-2 sp, dc in next dc, ch 2, dc in next sp, ch 1, sk dc, (dc in next dc, ch 1) 6 times, dc in top of ch-2, sc in 3rd ch-3 lp of scallop to left, ch 3, turn.

Row 8: Repeat row 4.

Repeat rows 5-8 for desired length. Using row 4 for last row.

13. Chain desired length for item to trim.

Row 1: Sc in 2nd ch from hk, * (ch 5, sk 3 ch, sc in next ch), repeat from * across row.

Row 2: With lp on hk, make the following all in lst ch-5 lp at beg of prev row, (dc, ch 2, dc, ch 5, sc in 4th ch from hk, [picot made], ch 1, dc, ch 2, dc) for shell, * sk next lp, shell in next ch-5 lp, repeat from * across row.

14. Chain 12.

Row 1: Dc in 4th ch from hk, dc in next ch, ch 5, (dc, ch 3) in last ch 3 times, dc in same ch, ch 1, turn.

Row 2: Make (sc, hdc, 3 dc, hdc, sc in next ch-3 sp, (shell made). Make shell in each of next 2 ch-3 sps, ch 5, dc in ch-5 lp, dc in

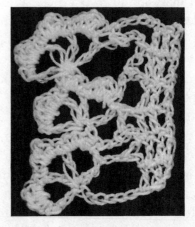

each dc and top of turning ch, ch 3, turn.

Row 3: Dc in 2nd dc and in each rem dc, dc in ch-5 lp, dc in each dc, dc in top of turning-ch, ch 3, turn.

Row 4: Make shell in each of next 3 sps, ch 5, dc in ch-5 lp, dc in each dc, dc in top of turning ch, ch 3, turn.

Rows 5-8: Repeat rows 3-4 (using 1 more dc in each row than prev row) until 8 rows are completed (10 dc in 8th row).

Row 9: Dc in next 2 dc, ch 5, sk 6 dc, in next dc make (dc, ch 3) 3 times, dc in same st, ch 1 turn. Repeat rows 2-9 for pattern.

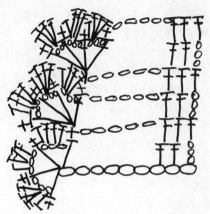

15. Chain ll.

Row l: (3 dc, ch 2, 1 dc) in 7th ch from hk, * sk 1 ch, (3 dc, ch 2, 1 dc) in next ch, repeat from * 1 time, ch 6, turn.

Row 2: * (3 dc, ch 2, 1 dc) in next ch-2 sp, repeat from * twice, ch 6, turn.

Repeat row 2 for pattern for desired length and end last repeat, ch 5.

Finishing: * 1 sc in next ch-6 sp (turning ch of prev row), ch 3, repeat from * across long edge.

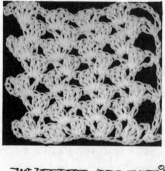

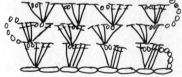

16. Chain 7, join with sl st to form ring.

Round 1: Ch 6, dc in ring, (ch 3, dc in ring) 6 times, ch 3, join to 3rd ch of ch-6 at beg of rnd (8 ch-3 lps).

Round 2: Ch 1, make (sc, 3 dc, sc) in each ch-3 lp around, do not join.

Round 3: (Sl st from the back, around the post of next dc of prev row, ch 6) 8 times, do not join.

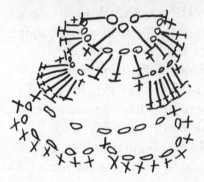

Round 4: Make (sc, hdc, 5 dc, hdc, sc) in each ch-6 lp around, join with sl st to 1st sc.

Make a 2nd rose through rnd 3, then join to 1st rose as follows: In ch-6 lp make sc, hdc, 2 dc, sl st to center st of any petal of 1st rose, make 3c, hdc, and sc in same lp on rose in progress, make sc, hdc, 2 dc, in next lp, join to center st of next petal on 1st rose, made 3 dc, hdc, sc in same lp and finish rose same as 1st rose. Continue to make roses and join in same way leaving 2 free petals on each side for desired length.

17. Chain 6.

Begin at narrow edge.

Row 1: (2 dc, ch 2, 2 dc) in 6th ch from hook, ch 5, turn.

Row 2: (2 dc, ch 2, 2 dc) in ch-2 sp (shell made), ch 5, turn. Repeat row 2 for pattern until desired length, end with odd number of ch-5 sps on 1 long edge, and 1 more ch-5 sp on opposite edge.

Finish: Ch 5, yo twice, insert hk in next ch-5 sp (on long edge with odd number of ch-5 sps), yo and pull through, (yo and pull through 2 lps on hk), twice, [yo twice, insert hk in same ch-5 sp, yo and pull through, (yo and pull through 2 lps on hk)] twice, yo and pull through last 4 lps on hk (cluster made), * (ch 6, 1 dc in top of last cluster made, 1 cluster in same ch-5 sp) twice, ch 3, 1 sc in next ch-5 sp, ch 3, 1 cluster in next ch-5 sp, repeat from * across 1 long edge and end (ch 6, 1 dc in top of last cluster made, 1 cluster in same ch-5 sp) twice, ch 5, 1 sc at base of 1st shell. F.O. Attach yarn to 1st ch-5 sp on opposite long edge, 1 sc in same ch-5 sp, * ch 7, 1 sc in next ch-5 sp, repeat from * across row.

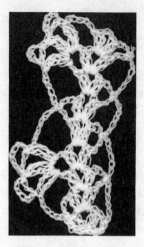

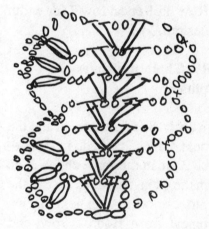

18. Chain multiples of 5 plus 4.

Row 1: Make 2 dc in 6th ch from hk, * ch 1, 2 dc in 6th ch, make 2 dc in the 5th ch, repeat from * across row, end with last set and dc in the 2nd and last ch, ch 3, turn.

Row 2: * Make 2 dc in the ch 1 sp, ch 1 and work 2 dc in the same 1-ch, ch 2, repeat from * across row, end with last set and 1 extra dc in the last ch, ch 3, turn.

Row 3: Repeat row 2 for width desired.

19. Chain multiples of 20 plus 6.

Row 1: Sc in the 2nd ch and the next 4 chs, * ch 2, dc in the 3rd, ch 2, dc in the same ch, ch 2, dc in the ch just used, ch 2, sc in the 3rd ch, sc in the next 4 chs, repeat from * across row, end with sc in each of the last 5 chs.

20. Chain multiples of 12 plus 2.

Row 1: Sc in the 2nd ch from hk and in each ch across the row, ch 3, turn.

Row 2: Ch 4, make 3 dc back in the 1st sc, * make 3 dc in the 6th

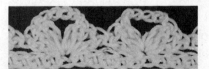

sc, ch 5, make another 3 dc in the sc just used, repeat from * across row, end with 3 dc in the last sc, ch 4, sl st in last ch.

21. Chain multiples of 16 plus 2.

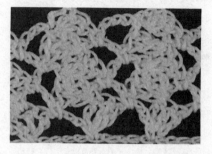

Row 1: Sc in the 2nd ch from hk, * ch 4, sc in the 4th ch, ch 3, make 2 dc back in the sc just formed, repeat from * across row, end with sc in the last ch, ch 5, turn.

Row 2: * Sc around the middle of the 4-ch, ch 4, sc around the top of the 3-ch, ch 3, make 2 dc in the base of the sc just formed, repeat from * across row, end with dc in the last sc, ch 1, turn.

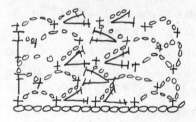

Row 3: Sc in the top of the dc, * ch 4, sc in the top of the 3-ch, ch 3, make 2 dc back in the sc just formed, sc around the middle of the 4-ch, repeat from * across row, end with sc in the last ch, ch 5, turn.

Row 4: * Sc around the 4-ch, ch 4, sc in the top of the 3-ch, ch 3, make 2 dc back in the base of the sc, repeat from * across row, end with dc in the last sc, ch 1, turn.

Row 5: Sc in the dc, * ch 4, sc in the top of the 3-ch, ch 3, make 2 dc back in the sc just formed, sc around the middle of the 4-ch, repeat from * across row, end with sc in the last ch.

22. Chain multiples of 32 plus 6.

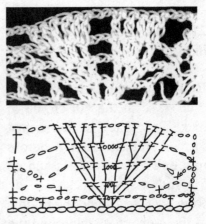

Row 1: Dc in the 8th ch from hk, * ch 3, dc in the 3rd ch, ch 2, make 2 dc in the 3rd ch, ch 1, 2 dc in the next ch, ch 2, dc in the 3rd ch, ch 3, dc in the 3rd ch, ch 3 and dc in the 3rd ch, repeat from * across row, end with dc in the last ch, ch 1, turn.

Row 2: Sc in the 1st dc, ch 3, sc in the 2nd 3-ch, * ch 2, dc in the 2nd dc, make 2 dc in the next dc, ch 2, make 2 dc in the next dc, dc in the next dc, ch 2, sc in the next 3-ch, ch 3, sc in the next 3-ch, repeat from * across row, end with sc in the last ch, ch 6, turn.

Row 3: * Sc around the 3-ch, ch 3, 1 dc in the next dc, 2 dc in the next dc, 1 dc in the next dc, ch 3, dc in the next dc, make 2 dc in the next dc, dc in the next dc, ch 2, sc around the 3-ch, ch 3, repeat from * across row, end with sc, ch 3, dc in the last sc, ch 1, turn.

Row 4: Sc in the dc, ch 3, * dc in each of the next 2 dc, make 2 dc in the next dc, dc in the next dc, ch 4, dc in the next dc, make

2 dc in the next dc, dc in the next
2 dc, ch 2, sc in the middle of the
3-ch, ch 2, repeat from * across
row, end with 3 chs, 1 sc in the
last ch, ch 6, turn.

Row 5: * Dc in the next 2 dc, 2
dc in the next dc, dc in the next 2
dc, ch 5, dc in the next 2 dc, 2 dc
in the next dc, 1 dc in the next 2
dc, ch 2, repeat from * across
row, end with last set, 2 chs, dc in
the last sc.

23. Chain 28.

Begin at narrow edge.

Row 1: 1 dtr in 16th ch from hk,
ch 2, sk 2 ch, 1 dtr in next ch, ch
2, sk 2 ch, 1 trc in next ch, ch 2, sk
2 ch, 1 dc in next ch, ch 2, sk 2 ch,
1 sc in last ch, ch 1, turn.

Row 2: * 1 sc in next st, ch 2, sk
ch-2, repeat from * 3 times, end
with 1 sc in last st, ch 1, turn.

Row 3: 1 sc in 1st sc, ch 2, 1 dc in
next sc, ch 2, 1 trc in next sc, ch
2, 1 dtr in sc, ch 2, 1 dtr in last sc,
ch 1, turn.

Row 4: Repeat row 2, ch 15,
turn.

Row 5: 1 dtr in 1st sc, ch 2, 1 dtr
in next sc, ch 2, 1 trc in next sc, ch
2, 1 dc in next sc, ch 2, 1 sc in last
sc, ch 1, turn.

Repeat rows 2-5 for pattern for

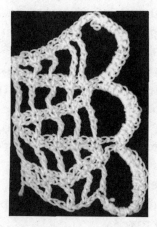

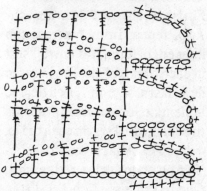

191

desired length.

Finish: Attach yarn to 1st ch-15 sp, ch 3, 2 dc in same sp, * 15 dc in same ch-15 sp, 3 dc in next ch-15 sp, repeat from * across row, end with 15 dc in same ch-15 sp.

24. Chain 4.

Begin at narrow edge.

Row 1: 1 dc in 4th ch from hk, ch 5, (yo, insert hk in same ch, yo and pull through, yo and pull through 2 lps on hk) twice, yo and pull through last 3 lps on hk (cluster made), ch 7, turn.

Row 2: Sk (1 cluster, 2 ch), (1 cluster, ch 5, 1 cluster) in next ch, ch 15, turn.

Row 3: Sk (1 cluster, 2 ch), (1 cluster, ch 5, 1 cluster) in next ch, ch 7, turn.

Repeat rows 2-3 for pattern for desired length, end last repeat with row 3.

Finish 1st row: * 9 dc in next ch-7 sp, repeat from * across top long edge, turn. **2nd row:** 1 sl st in each of next 5 dc, 1 sc in same dc as last sl st, * ch 7, sk 8 dc, 1 sc in next dc, repeat from * across row, end with 1 sl st in each of last 4 dc. F. O. Attach yarn to 1st ch-15 sp on opposite long edge, ch 3, 6 dc in same sp, * ch 4, 1 sl st in

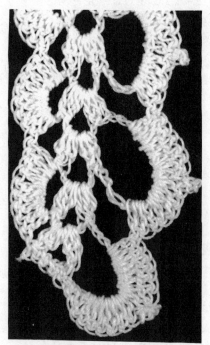

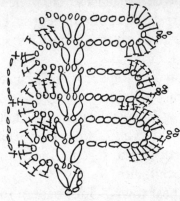

4th ch from hk (picot made), 7 dc in same ch-15 sp, 7 dc in next ch-15 sp, repeat from * across row, end 1 picot, 7 dc in same ch-15 sp.

25. Chain 6.

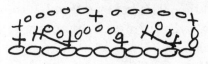

Begin at narrow edge.

Row 1: 1 sc in 3rd ch from hk, ch 2, sk 2 ch, 1 dc in next ch, * (ch 5, 1 dc in last dc worked) twice, ch 5, 1 sc in 3rd ch from hk, ch 2, 1 dc in last dc made (picot made), repeat from * until desired length, ch 8, turn.

Finish: * Sk next picot, 1 sc in next ch-5 sp, ch 3, 1 sc in next ch 5, ch 7, repeat from * across row, end with sk last picot, 1 sc in same ch as 1st dc.

26. Chain multiples of 30 plus 15.

Row 1: Sc in the 2nd ch from hk and across row, ch 5, turn.

Row 2: Dc in the 4th sc, * ch 2, dc in the 3rd sc, repeat from * across row, end with dc in last sc, ch 1, turn.

Row 3: Sc in each st across row, ch 6 turn.

Row 4: Trc in the dc, ch 2, trc in next dc, ch 2, trc in next dc, ch 2, trc in next dc, * make another trc in the next dc, ch 4, make 5 trc around the trc just made at a perpendicular angle, make a trc in the 2nd dc, ch 4, make 5 trc at a perpendicular angle around the trc just formed, trc in the 2nd dc, ch 4, make 5 trc around the trc just formed, at a perpendicular angle, trc in next dc and ch 2, 4 times, trc in last dc, ch 1, turn.

Row 5: 1 sc in each st across row, ch 6.

Row 6: (Trc in trc, ch 2), 3 times, trc in the next trc, trc in the top of the 4-ch, ch 4, make 5 trc around the trc at a perpendicular angle, make trc in the top of the next 4-ch, ch 4, make 5 trc at a perpendicular angle around the last trc formed, make trc in the next 4-ch, ch 4, make 5 trc around the last trc at a perpendicular angle, (trc in the next trc and 2 chs), 4 times, trc in the last trc.

Row 7: 1 sc in each st across row, ch 6 turn.

Row 8: Ch 4, make 5-ch picot, ch 2, trc in next trc, make 5-ch picot with 2 chs 3 times, trc in next trc, * trc in top of the next 4-ch, ch 4, make 5 trc around the last trc at a perpendicular angle, make trc in the top of the next 4-ch, ch 4, make 5 trc around the last trc at a perpendicular angle, 5 trc around the last trc at a perpendicular angle, trc in the next trc, make 5-ch picot, ch 2 (4 times) in each of the next trc, trc in the last trc.

27. Chain multiples of 24 plus 5.

Row 1: Dc in the 7th ch from hk, * make 5 dc in the 3rd ch, dc in the 3rd ch, ch 1 and dc in the 2nd ch, ch 1 and dc in the 2nd ch, ch 1 and dc in the 2nd ch, repeat from * across row, end with 1 ch, 1 dc in the last ch, ch 5, turn.

Row 2: Sk 1st dc, * dc in the next 7 dc, (ch 1, dc in the next dc) 2 times, ch 1, repeat from * across row, end with 1 ch, 1 dc in the last ch, ch 5, turn.

Row 3: Sk 1st dc, * dc in the 2nd dc, dc in the next 4 dc, ch 2, dc in the 2nd dc, ch 1 and dc in the next dc, ch 2, repeat from * across row, end with 2 chs, 1 dc in the last ch, ch 6, turn.

Row 4: Sk 1st dc, * dc in the 2nd dc and next 2 dc, ch 3, dc in the 2nd dc, ch 1 and dc in the next dc, ch 3, repeat from * across row, end with dc in the last ch, ch 7, turn.

Row 5: Sk 1st dc, * dc in the 2nd dc, ch 4, dc in the 2nd dc and the ch 1, dc in the next dc, ch 4, repeat from * across row, end with dc in last ch.

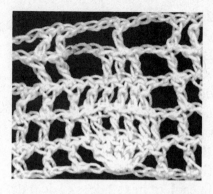

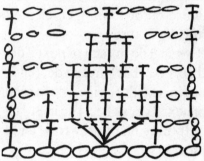

28. Chain 12.

Begin at narrow edge.

Row 1: 1 dc in 4th ch from hk, 1 dc in next ch, (1 dc, ch 2, 1 dc) in next ch, ch 2, sk 2 ch, 1 dc in each of the next 4 ch, ch 3, turn.

Row 2: 1 dc in each of next 3 dc, (1 dc in next dc, ch 2) twice, 1 dc in each of next 2 dc, sk 1 dc, 1 dc in 3rd ch of turning ch of prev row, ch 3, turn.

Row 3: 1 dc in each of next 2 dc, (1 dc, ch 2, 1 dc) in next dc, (ch 2, 1 dc in next dc) twice, 1 dc in each of next 2 dc, sk 1 dc, 1 dc in 3rd ch of turning ch of prev row, ch 3, turn.

Row 4: 1 dc in each of next 4 dc, (2 dc in next ch-2 sp, 1 dc in next dc) 3 times, 1 dc in each of next 2 dc, 1 dc in 3rd ch of turning ch of prev row, ch 3, turn.

Row 5: 1 dc in each of next 2 dc, (1 dc, ch 2, 1 dc) in next dc, ch 2, sk 2 dc, 1 dc in each of next 4 dc, ch 3, turn.

Repeat rows 2-5 of pattern for length desired, end last repeat with row 4.

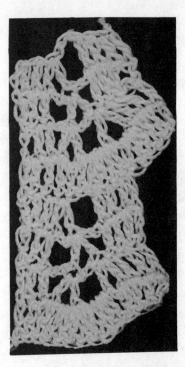

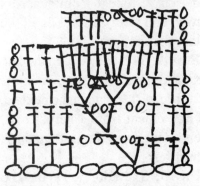

29. Chain multiples of 17 plus 15.

Row 1: Ch 3, 1 dc in 4th ch from

hk, * 1 dc in next ch, repeat from * across row, ch 3, turn.

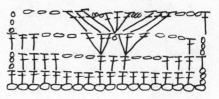

Row 2: 1 dc in each of next 4 dc, * ch 3, sk 3 dc, 3 dc in next dc, ch 3, sk 3 dc, 1 dc in each of next 10 dc, repeat from * across row, end with 1 dc in each of last 4 dc, 1 dc in last ch of prev row, ch 3, turn.

Row 3: 1 dc in each of 1st 3 dc, * ch 3, sk (2 dc, ch-3), 3 dc in next dc, ch 3, sk 1 dc, 3 dc in next dc, ch 3, sk (ch-3, 2 dc), 1 dc in each of next 6 dc, repeat from * across row, end with ast repeat with 1 dc in each of last 2 dc, 1 dc in last ch of prev row, ch 6, turn.

Row 4: Sk (3 dc, ch-3), 1 dc in each of next 3 dc, ch 3, sk 1 ch, 3 dc in next ch, ch 3, sk 1 ch, 1 dc in each of next 3 dc, * ch 3, sk (ch-3, 2 dc), 1 dc in each of next 2 dc, ch 3, sk (2 dc, ch-3), 1 dc in each of next 3 dc, ch 3, sk 1 ch, 3 dc in next ch, ch 3, sk 1 ch, 1 dc in each of next 3 dc, repeat from * across row, end with ch 3, sk (ch-3, 3 dc), 1 dc in last ch of prev row.

30. Chain 16

Begin at narrow edge.
Row 1: (3 dc, ch 2, 3 dc) in 4th ch from hk (shell made), ch 9, sk 11 ch, 1 shell in next ch, ch 2, turn.
Row 2: 1 shell in 1st ch-2 sp, ch

ll, 1 shell in next ch-2 sp, ch 2, turn.

Row 3: 1 shell in lst ch-2 sp, ch 7, insert hk under chs of last 3 rows, yo and pull through, yo and pull through 2 lps on hk, ch 1, turn, 1 sc in each of next 7 ch, * ch 1, turn, (1 sc through back lp only of next sc) 7 times, repeat from * 4 times (square made), 1 shell in next ch-2 sp, ch 2, turn.

Row 4: Repeat row 2.

Row 5: 1 shell in lst ch-2 sp, ch 9, 1 shell in next ch-2 sp, ch 2, turn.

Row 6: Repeat row 2.

Row 7: 1 shell in lst ch-2 sp, ch 7, 1 sc in corner of last square made (working over chs of last 3 rows), ch 1, turn, 1 square over next 7 ch, 1 shell in next ch-2 sp, ch 2, turn.

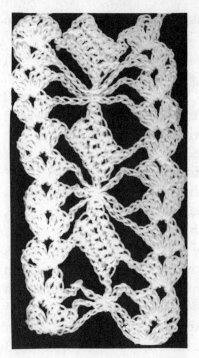

Repeat rows 4-7 for pattern until desired length and end last repeat with row 6 working last row as follows: 1 shell in lst ch-2 sp, ch 5, 1 sc in corner of last square made (working over chs of last 3 rows), ch 5, 1 shell in next ch-2 sp.

Finish: Ch 5, * 1 sc in next turning ch-2 sp on one long edge, ch 4, repeat from * across row.

Attach yarn to lst ch-2 sp on opposite edge, repeat last row

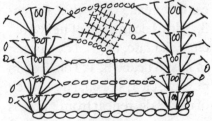

across row.

31. Make a chain the length desired.

Begin at one end working lengthwise.

Row 1: * Make 1 dc, ch 2, repeat from * across row, ch 3, turn.

Row 2: * Sl st into 1st sp, 3 dc in next sp, * sk next sp, 3 dc in next sp, repeat from * across row.

Row 3: Start in sp, * ch 5, 3 sc in next sp, repeat from * across row.

Row 4: * 8 sc in ch 5 lps, 1 sc in center of 3 sc in prev row, repeat from * across row.

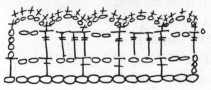

32. Make a chain the length desired.

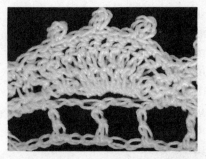

Begin at one end working lengthwise.

Row 1: * Make 1 trc, ch 2, repeat from * across row, ch 4, turn.

Row 2: Start in trc, * ch 10, 1 sl st in 2nd trc, ch 2, 1 sl st in next trc, turn, 12 trc in ch 10, turn, 1 sc in each 1st 3 trc, (1 picot in each next 3 trc), 1 picot, 1 sc in each next 3 trc, 1 picot, 1 sc in each next 3 trc, repeat from * across row.

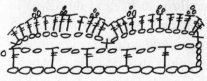

33. Chain 12, join with sl st to form ring.

Begin at one end, working crosswise.

Round 1: * sc in ring, turn, ch 6, 1 dtr in 1st sc (ch 2, 1 dtr in next sc st) 6 times, turn.

Round 2: (1 sc in dtr, 2 sc in ch 2) 7 times, turn.

Round 3: Ch 12, 1 sl st in 3rd sc, turn, repeat from * around.

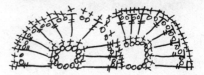

34. Chain 15, join with sl st to form ring.

Begin at center of scallop .

Round 1: Ch 1, work 25 sc in ring, join with sl st to 1st sc.

Round 2: Ch 5, (sk next sc, dc in next sc, ch 2) 5 times, sk next sc, in next sc make (dc, ch 3, dc [tip of scallop]), (ch 2, sk next sc, dc in next sc) 6 times, ch 1, turn.

Round 3: Sc in 1st dc, (2 sc in next ch-2 sp, sc in next dc) 6 times, 3 sc in ch-3 sp at tip of scallop, sc in next dc, (2 sc in next ch-2 sp, sc in next dc) 5 times, end with 3 sc over turning ch, ch 1, turn.

Round 4: Sk 1st sc, sc in each sc to center sc at tip of scallop, 3 sc in center sc, sc in each sc to end, ch 1, turn.

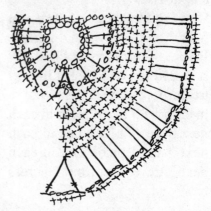

Round 5: Sk 1st st and work same as rnd 4.

Round 6: Repeat rnd 4.

Round 7: Repeat rnd 4.

Round 8: Sc in 1st sc, then work as for rnd 4.

Round 9: Sl st in 1st sc, ch 4, trc in same sc, (ch 3, sk 2 sc, holding back the last lp of each trc, work 2 trc in next sc, yo, and pull through 3 lps on hk (trc cluster made) 7 times, ch 3, in center sc work (trc cl, ch 3, trc cl), ch 3, sk sc, trc cl in next sc, (ch 3, sk 2 sc, trc cl in next sc) 7 times, ch 1, turn.

Round 10: In each ch-3 sp around, work scallop of sc, 3 dc and sc.

35. Chain multiples of 12 plus 7.

Row 1: Sc in the 10th sc and in the next 6 chs, ch 7, sc in 6th ch, repeat from * across row, end with sc in each of the last 4 chs, ch 1, turn.

Row 2: Sc in the 1st sc, * ch 1, make 3-lp cl around the beg of the 7-ch and ch 2, make another 3-lp cl and 2 chs, 3 times, make another 3-lp cl around the end of the 7-ch and 1 ch, sc in the 4th sc, repeat from * across row, end

with a cl, 2 chs, a cluster, 2 chs, dc in the last ch, ch 1, turn.

Row 3: Sc in the dc, * sc in the 2-ch, ch 3, sc in the next 2-ch, ch 3, sc in the 1-ch, sc in the next 1-ch, ch 3, sc in the 2-ch, ch 3, sc in the next 2-ch, ch 3, repeat from * across row, end with sc in the last sc.

36. Chain multiples of 16 plus 5.

Row 1: Dc in the 5th ch from hk, * ch 3, make 4-lp popcorn st in 4th ch, (ch 1 and popcorn st in the 2nd ch) 4 times, ch 3, dc in the 4th ch, repeat from * across row, end with dc in each of the last 2 chs, ch 3, turn.

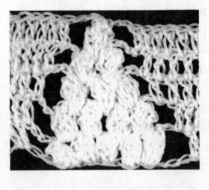

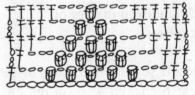

Row 2: Dc in the 2nd dc, * dc in the 1st ch, ch 3, make 4-lp popcorn st in the next 1-ch, ch 1, 4-lp popcorn st in next 1-ch, ch 1, 4-lp popcorn st in next 1-ch, ch-1, 4-lp popcorn st in next ch-1, ch 3, dc in the last of the 3-ch, dc in the dc, repeat from * across row, end with dc in the last ch, ch 3, turn.

Row 3: Dc in the 2nd dc, dc in next dc, * dc in the 1st of the 3-ch, ch 3, make 4-lp popcorn in the 1-ch, ch 1, make 4-lp popcorn st in the 1-ch, ch 1, and make another popcorn st in the next 1-ch, ch 3, dc in the last of the 3-ch, dc in the next 3 dc, repeat from * across row, end with 3 dc and 1 dc in the last ch, ch 3, turn.

Row 4: Dc in the 2nd dc, dc in the next 2 dc, * dc in the beg of the 3-ch, ch 3, make 4-lp popcorn st in the 1-ch, ch 1, make 4-lp popcorn st in the next 1-ch, ch 3, dc in the last of the 3-ch, dc in the next 5 dc, repeat from * across row, end with 4 dc and 1 dc in the last ch, ch 3, turn.

Row 5: Dc in the 2nd dc and the next 3 dc, * dc in the beg of the 1–ch, ch 3, make 4-lp popcorn st in the 1-ch, ch 3, dc in the last of the 1-ch, dc in the next 7 dc, repeat from * across row, end with 5 dc and 1 dc in last ch.

37. Chain multiples 6 plus 2.

Row 1: Sc in the 2nd ch from hk, * ch 3, make 5-lp popcorn st in the 3rd ch, ch 3, 1 sc in the 3rd ch, repeat from * across row, end with sc in last ch, ch 3, turn.

Row 2: Dc in the 1st sc, make 3-ch picot, * sc in the top of the popcorn st, make dc in the sc, make 13-ch picot (4 times), repeat from * across row, end with 1 dc, 1 picot and 1 dc in last sc.

38. Chain multiples of 6 plus 2.

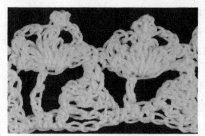

Row 1: Sc in the 2nd ch, sc in the 3rd ch, * ch 6, turn, make sc in the 2nd ch from end, hdc in the next ch, make 1 dc in the next 3 chs, sc in the 4th ch, sc in each of the next 2 sc, repeat from * across row, end with sc in each of the last 2 chs, ch 7, turn.

Row 2: * Sc in the last ch of the set, ch 2, dtr in the middle of the 3 sc, ch 2, repeat from * across row, end with dtr, ch 3, turn.

Row 3: Make dc in top of the dtr, * make 3-ch picot, ch 3, make 3-lp puff st in the same st just used, sc in the next sc, make 3-lp puff st in the top of the next dtr, ch 3, make 3-lp puff st, repeat from * across row, end with 2-lp puff st in the last ch and 3 picot.

39. Chain multiples of 14 plus 4.

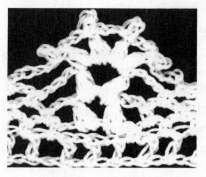

Row 1: 1 dc in 5th ch from hk, * ch 1, dc in the 2nd ch, repeat from * across row, end with dc in 2nd ch and an extra dc in the next ch, ch 1, turn.

Row 2: Sc in the 1st dc, ch 3, sc in the next 1-ch, ch 3, sc in the next 1-ch, * ch 7, 1 sc in the 3rd 1-

ch, ch 3, sc in the next 1-ch, ch 3, sc in the next 1-ch, ch 3, sc in the next 1-ch, ch 3, sc in the next 1-ch, repeat from * across row, end with sc, 3 chs, sc, 3 chs and 1 sc in the last ch, ch 4, turn.

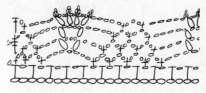

Row 3: Sc in the 3-ch, ch 3, sc in the next 3-ch, * ch 3, make (1) 2 lp puff st in the middle of the 7-ch, ch 3, make 2-lp puff st in the same ch just used, ch 3, sc in the 3-ch, ch 3, sc in the next 3-ch, ch 3, sc in the next 3-ch, ch 3, sc in the next 3-ch, repeat from * across row, end with sc in last 3-ch, ch 1, 1 dc in the last sc, ch 1, turn.

Row 4: Sc in the 1st dc, ch 3, sc in the next 3-ch, * ch 4, make 2-lp puff st in the ch after the puff st from the prev row, ch 4, make puff st in the ch just before the puff st in the prev row, ch 4, sk next 3-ch, sc in the next 3-ch, ch 3, sc in the next 3-ch, ch 3, sc in the next 3-ch, repeat from * across row, end with sc in the last ch, ch 4, turn.

Row 5: Sc in 3-ch, * ch 5, make 2-lp puff st in 4-ch after puff st of prev row, make 3-ch picot, ch 3, make another 3-ch picot, 2-lp puff st in the same 4-ch, ch 3, make another 2-lp puff st in the 4-ch, make 3-ch picot, ch 3, make 2-lp puff st in the 4-ch, make 3-ch picot, ch 5, sc in the next 3-ch, ch 3, sc in the next 3-ch, repeat from * across row, end with last set, ch 1, dc in last sc.

40. Chain multiples of 8 plus 4.

Row 1: Dc in 5th ch from hk, and in each ch across the row, ch 1, turn.

Row 2: Sc in the 1st dc, * ch 3, make 3-lp puff st in the 4th dc, ch 3, make 3-lp puff st in the dc just used, ch 3, sc in the 4th dc, repeat from * across row, end with sc in the last ch, ch 3, turn.

Row 3: Dc in the beg of the 3-ch, * ch 3, make 3-lp puff st in the next 3-ch, ch 1, make 3-ch picot, ch 1, make 3-lp puff st in the same 3-ch, crochet 2 dc tog in the next 3-ch, and the next 3-ch, repeat from * across row, end with 2 dc crochet tog in the last 3-ch and the sc.

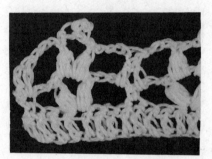

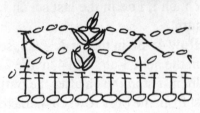

41. Chain multiples of 3 plus 2.

Row 1: Sc in the 2nd ch from hk and in each ch across row, ch 4, turn.

Row 2: Make 3-lp puff st in the 1st sc, * crochet together with a 3-lp puff st in the 3rd sc, ch 2,

make 3-ch picot, ch 1, make 3-lp puff st in the sc just used, repeat from * across row, end with after last set with, 1 dc in the same sc as the last puff st.

42. Chain multiples of 22 plus 2.

Row 1: Sc in the 2nd ch from hk and in each ch across row, ch 5, turn.

Row 2: Dc in the 4th sc, * ch 2, dc in the 3rd sc, repeat from * across row, end with dc in the last sc, ch 3, turn.

Row 3: Make 3 dc in the next (3) 2-chs, * ch 13, sk (1) 2 chs, make 3 dc in the next (6) 2-chs, repeat from * across row, end with 1 extra dc in the last ch, ch 4, turn.

Row 4: Make 3 dc between the 1st 2 sets of 3 dc, make 3 dc between the next 2 sets of dc, * ch 6, sc in the middle of the 13-ch, ch 6, make 3 dc between the next 2 sets of 3 dc, repeat 4 times, repeat from * across row, end with 2 dc in the last ch, ch 3, turn.

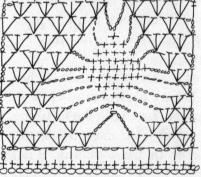

Row 5: Make 3 dc after the 1st 2 dc, make 3 dc between the next 2 sets of 3 dc, * ch 6, sc in the last of the 6-ch of the prev row, sc in the sc, sc in the 1st of the next 6-

ch, ch 6, make 3 dc after the next set of dc, repeat 3 times, repeat from * across row, end with 1 extra dc in the last ch, ch 4, turn.

Row 6: Dc in the top of 2 dc, make 3 dc between the next 2 sets of 3 dc, * ch 6 and sc in the last of the 6-ch, sc in each of the next 3 sc, sc in the beg of the next 6-ch, ch 6, make 3 dc after the next 3 dc, repeat twice, repeat from * across row, end with 2 dc in the last ch, ch 3, turn.

Row 7: Make 3 dc after the 2 dc, * ch 6 and sc in the last of the 6-ch, sc in each of the next 5 sc, sc in the 1st of the next 6-ch, ch 6, make 3 dc after the 1st set of 3 dc, make another 3 dc after the next set of 3 dc, repeat from * across row, end with dc in last ch, ch 4, turn.

Row 8: Dc in the 1st dc, * ch 6 and sc in the last of the 6-ch, sc in the next 7 sc, sc in the 1st of the next 6-ch, ch 6, make 3 dc in the middle of the 2 sets of 3 dc, repeat from * across row, end with 2 dc in the last ch, ch 3, turn.

Row 9: 3 dc in the 2nd dc, * ch 6 and sc in the 2nd sc, sc in the next 6 sc, ch 6 and 3 dc in the next dc, 3 dc in the 2nd dc, repeat from * across row, end with dc in last ch, ch 4, turn.

Row 10: Dc in the 1st dc, make 3 dc in the last 3 dç of set, * ch 6 and sc in the 2nd sc and in each of the next 4 sc, ch 6, 3 dc in the next dc, make 3 dc in middle of the 2 sets of 3 dc, make 3 dc in the 3rd dc, repeat from * across row, end with 2 dc in last ch, ch 3, turn.

Row 11: Make 3 dc after the 2 dc, make 3 dc in the 3rd dc, * ch 6, sc in the 2nd, sc in the next 2 sc, ch 6, make 3 dc in the next dc, make 3 dc in the middle of the next 2 sets, make 3 dc in the last dc, repeat from * across row, end with 1 dc in the last ch, ch 4, turn.

Row 12: Dc in the 1st dc, make 3 dc in between the 2 sets, make 3 dc in the 3rd dc, * ch 6 and sc in the 2nd sc, ch 6 and make 3 dc in the next dc, make 3 dc in between the sets of 3 dc (3 times), 3 dc in the 3rd dc, repeat from * across row, end with 2 dc in last ch, ch 1, turn.

Row 13: Sc in 1st dc, ch 2, sc between next 2 sets of 3 dc, ch 4, sc between the next set of 3 dc and ch-4, sc in last dc, * ch 7 and sc in last dc, ch 4 and sc between the sets (4 times), ch 4 and sc in the last dc, repeat from * across row, end with sc between last sets, ch 2, sc in the last ch.

43. Make chain the length desired.

Begin at one end, working lengthwise.

Row 1: Trc in 4th ch from hk, * sk 2 ch, trc in next ch, repeat from * across row, sl st into sp.

Row 2: Ch 5, 1 sc in next sp, * ch 3, 1 trc in 2nd sp, ch 4, 1 trc in same sp, ch 3, 1 sc in 2nd sp, repeat from * across row, ch 1, turn.

Row 3: Sc in sc, * ch 3, 3 trc in ch 4, ch 2, 3 trc in same ch, ch 2, 3 trc in same ch, ch 3, 1 sc in sc, repeat from * across row.

Row 4: * 1 popcorn st in 2nd trc, ch 3, 1 popcorn st in ch 2, ch 3, 1 popcorn st in 2nd trc, ch 3, 1 popcorn st in ch 2, ch 3, 1 popcorn st in 2nd trc, repeat from * across row.

Row 5: * 2 sc in ch 2, 1 picot, 2 sc in same ch, repeat from * across row.

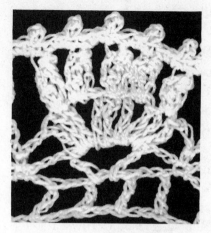

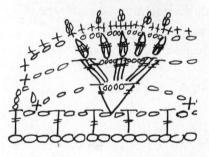

44. Chain even multiple of stitches.

Row 1: Ch 4, sk 1, 1 sc *, repeat * to *.

Row 2: Ch 6, * sc in ch 4-sp, ch 4, repeat * to * across row.

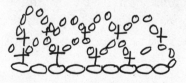

45. Chain 5.

Begin at one end, working cross-wise.

Rows 1-9: Make 1 dc in each st across row.

Row 10: On the side edge of work into row 5, (ch 2, 1 trc) 5 times in same st, ch 1, sl st in row 1, turn, in each ch 2 sp make (1 sc, ch 3, 1 sc).

Repeat these 10 rows for the desired length, working the fans on one side or alternate side edges.

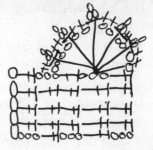

46. Chain 4.

Begin at narrow edge.

Row 1: 2 dc in 4th ch from hk, (ch 2, 2 dc) in same ch, ch 5, turn.

Row 2: Sk 2 dc, (2 dc, ch 2, 2 dc) in ch-2 sp, ch 5, turn.

Repeat row 2 of pattern for length desired.

Finish: After last row is completed, * ch 5, 1 sc in next ch-5 sp, repeat from * across 1 edge, end with ch 5, 1 sc in 4th ch of foundation ch-4, F.O.

Attach yarn to 1st turning ch opposite edge, * ch 5, 1 sc in next ch-5 sp, repeat from * across row, F.O.

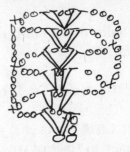

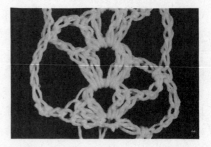

47. Chain 7.

Begin at narrow end.

Row 1: In 7th ch from hk, (dc, ch 1, dc), ch 4, turn.

Row 2: Dc in ch-1 sp, ch 7, turn.

Row 3: In turning ch-4 sp, make (dc, ch 1, dc), ch 4, turn.

Repeat rows 2-3 for desired length, end with row 3. Ch 1, turn. Now work across long side as follows: * in ch-7 lp make (2 sc, ch 3) 3 times, 2 sc in same lp, sc in side of next dc, repeat from * across row, F.O.

48. Chain multiples of 15 plus 2.

Row 1: Sc in 2nd ch from hk and in each of the next 5 chs, * ch 5, sc in the 5th ch, sc in the next 10 chs, repeat from * across row, end with sc in the last 6 chs, ch 1, turn.

Row 2: Sc in the next 5 sc, * make 3-lp cl in the 5th ch, ch 3, make 3-lp cl, (4 more times), sc in the 2nd sc and the next 8 sc, repeat from * across row, end with sc in the last 4 sc, ch 3, turn.

Row 3: Make dbl X-st in 1st and next sc, * make 3-lp cl after the sc, ch 1, make another 3-lp cl in the same st, ch 3, sc in the 3-ch,

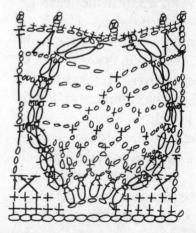

211

ch 3, sc in the next 3-ch (3 more times), ch 3, make 3-lp cl just before the sc, ch 1, 3-lp cl in same st, make dbl X-st in the 3rd sc and the next sc, make another X-st in the next 2 sc, make another X-st in the next 2 sc, repeat from * across row, end with dc in the last sc, ch 4, turn.

Row 4: Make (dc, ch 1, dc) in the 1-ch, ch 2, sc in 3-ch and sc in the next 3-ch, (4 times), ch 3, make (dc, ch 1, dc) in the ch-1, ch 2, repeat from * across row, end with dc in the last ch, ch 5, turn.

Row 5: * Make (dc, ch 1, dc) in the 1-ch, ch 3, sc in the 2nd 3-ch, ch 3, sc in the next 3-ch (3 times), ch 3, make (dc, ch 1, dc) in the 1-ch, ch 3, repeat from * across row, end with trc after the last cl, ch 5, turn.

Row 6: * Make (dc, ch 2, dc) in the 1-ch, ch 3, sc in the next 3-ch, ch 3, sc in the next 3-ch, ch 3 and sc in the next 3-ch, ch 3, make (dc, ch 2 dc) in the next 1-ch, ch 6, repeat from * across row, end with last dc group and ch 1, dc in the last ch, ch 8, turn.

Row 7: * Make (dc, ch 2, dc) in the 1-ch, ch 3, sc in the 2nd 3-ch, ch 3, sc in the next 3-ch, ch 3, make (dc, ch 2, dc) in the next 1-ch, ch 8, repeat from * across row, end with last group of dc, ch 3, trc in the last ch, ch 8, turn.

Row 8: * Make (dc, ch 3, dc) in the 1-ch, ch 3, sc in the 2nd 3-ch, ch 3, make (dc, ch 3, dc) in the 1-ch 10, repeat from * across row, end with 5 chs and dc in the last ch, ch 3, turn.

Row 9: Dc in the 2nd ch, * ch 3, crochet 2 dc tog, in the same ch as the last dc, and the 3rd ch, ch 3, make (dc, ch 3, dc) in the 1-ch, ch 1, make another (dc, ch 3, dc), ch 3 and crochet 2 dc tog in the 1st ch and the 3rd ch, ch 3, crochet another 2 dc tog, in the last ch used and the 3rd ch, repeat from * across row, end with 3 chs and dc in the last ch, ch 1, turn.

Row 10: Sc in the dc, work 4-ch picot, 3 sc in the 3-ch and 4-ch picot, * make 4 sc in the next 3-ch, sc in the 1st (dc, ch 3 dc) group, sc in the 1-ch, make 4-picot, sc in the 1-ch, sc in the next (dc, ch 3, dc) group, 4 sc in each 3-ch and 4-ch picot 3 times, repeat from * across row, end with picot and sc in the last ch.

49. Chain multiples of 14 plus 7.

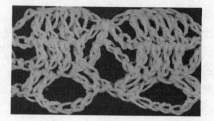

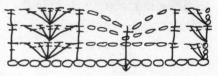

Row 1: 2 dc in the 4th ch from hk, * dc in the 3rd ch, ch 7, dc in the 8th ch, 5 dc in the 3rd ch, repeat from * across row, end with 3 dc in the last ch, ch 3, turn.
Row 2: 2 dc in the 1st dc, dc in the 3rd dc, * ch 7, dc in next dc, make 5 dc in the 3rd dc, dc in 3rd dc, repeat from * across row, end with 3 dc in last ch, ch 3, turn.
Row 3: 2 dc in the 1st dc, * dc in the 3rd dc, ch 3, sc made around the 3 rows of chs of prev rows, ch 3, dc in the next dc, make 5 dc in the 3rd dc, repeat from * across row, end with 3 dc in the last ch.

50. Chain multiples of 16 plus 2.

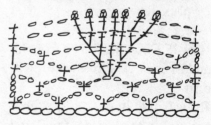

Row 1: Sc in the 2nd ch from hk, * ch 5, sc in the 4th ch, repeat from * across row, end with sc in the last ch, ch 7, turn.
Row 2: Sc around the center of the 5-ch, ch 5, repeat from * across row, end with sc, ch 3, dc in the last sc, ch 1, turn.
Row 3: Sc in the dc, * ch 5, sc around the center of the 5-ch, ch 3, make 3 dc in the center of next 5-ch, ch 3, sc around the center

of the next 5-ch, ch 5, sc around the center of the next 5-ch, repeat from * across row, ending with sc in the last ch, ch 6, turn.

Row 4: * Sc in the center of the 5-ch, ch 3, make 2 dc in the next dc, dc in the next dc, 2 dc in the next dc, ch 3, sc in the center of the next 5-ch, ch 5, repeat from * across row, end with sc, ch 3 and dc in last sc, ch 1, turn.

Row 5: Sc in the 1st dc, * ch 3, make 2 dc in the next dc, dc in the next 3 dc, make 2 dc in the next dc, ch 3, sc in the center of the next 5-ch, repeat from * across row, end with sc in the last ch, ch 1, turn.

Row 6: * Sc in the sc, ch 3, dc in the next dc, make 3-ch picot (6 times), dc in the next dc, ch 3, repeat from * across row, end with sc in the last sc.

51. Chain multiples of 29 plus 4.

Row 1: Dc in the 5th ch from hk and in each ch across row, ch 5, turn.

Row 2: Dc in the 4th dc, (ch 2 and dc) in the 3rd dc, (ch 2 and dc) in the 3rd dc, * (ch 5 and trc) in the 5th dc, (ch 5 and dc) in the 5th dc, (ch 2 and dc) in the 3rd dc

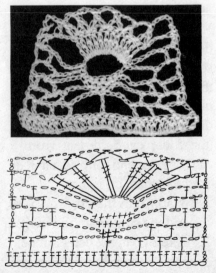

214

(6 more times), repeat from * across row, end with dc in the last ch, ch 4, turn.

Row 3: Dc in the center of the 2-ch, (ch 2 and dc) in the center of the next 2-ch, (ch 2 and dc) * (ch 5 and sc) in the last of the 5-ch, sc in the trc, sc in the beg of the 5-ch, (ch 5 and dc) in the 2-ch, (ch 2 and dc) in the next 2-ch (5 more times), repeat from * across row, end with 2 dc in last ch, ch 5, turn.

Row 4: Dc in the 2-ch, (ch 2 and dc) in the next 2-ch, * (ch 5 and sc) in the last of the 5-ch, sc in each of the next 3 sc, sc in the beg of next 5-ch, (ch 5 and dc) in next 2-ch, (ch 2 and dc) in next dc (4 more times), repeat from * across row, end with dc in the last ch, ch 4, turn.

Row 5: Dc in the 2-ch, (ch 2 and dc) in the next 2-ch, * (ch 6 and sc) in the end of the 5-ch, sc in the next 5 sc, sc in the beg of the next 5-ch, (ch 6 and dc) in the 2-ch, (ch 2 and dc) in the next 2-ch (3 more times), repeat from * across row, end with 2 dc in last ch, ch 5, turn.

Row 6: 1 dc in the 2-ch, * (ch 6 and sc) in the last of the 6-ch, (ch 7 and sc) in the beg of the next 6-ch, (ch 6 and dc) in the 2-ch, (ch 2 and dc) in the 2-ch (2 more times), repeat from * across row, end with dc in the last ch, ch 4, turn.

Row 7: Dc in the 2-ch, * ch 2, make 2 dtr in the 7 ch, ch 1, make 2 dtr in the 7-ch, (5 more times), (ch 2 and dc) in the 2-ch, (ch 2 and dc) in the 2-ch, repeat from * across row, end with 2 dc in last ch, ch 7, turn.

Row 8: * Crochet 2 dc tog in the 2-ch and the next 1-ch, ch 3, crochet 2 dc tog in the last 1-ch and the next 1-ch (5 more times), (ch 3 and dc) in the 2-ch, ch 3, repeat from * across row, end with dc in the last ch.

52. Chain multiples of 16 plus 2

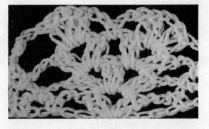

Row 1: Sc in the 2nd ch from hk, * ch 5 and sc in the 4th ch, repeat from * across row, end with sc in last ch, ch 7, turn.

Row 2: * Sc around the center of the 5-ch, ch 5, repeat from * across row, end with sc, (ch 3, dc) in the last sc, ch 1, turn.

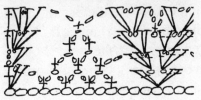

Row 3: Sc in the dc, * (ch 5, sc) around the center of the 5-ch, ch 3, make 3 dc in the center of the next 5-ch, (ch 3, sc) around the center of the 5-ch, repeat from * across row, end with sc in the last ch, ch 6, turn.

Row 4: * Sc in the center of the 5-ch, ch 3, make 2 dc in the next dc, dc in the next dc, 2 dc in the next dc, (ch 3, sc) in the middle of the next 5-ch, ch 5, repeat from * across row, end with sc, ch 3 and dc in the last sc, ch 1, turn.

Row 5: Sc in the 1st dc, * ch 3, make 2 dc in the next dc, dc in the next 3 dc, make 2 dc in the next dc, (ch 3, sc) in the center of the next 5-ch, repeat from * across row, end with sc in the last ch, ch 1, turn.

Row 6: * Sc in the sc, ch 3, dc in the next dc, make 3-ch picot, (6 times), dc in the next dc, ch 3,

216

repeat from * across row, end
with sc in the last sc.

53. Chain multiples of 16 plus 4.

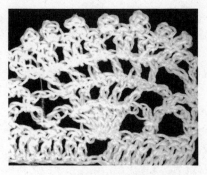

Row 1: Dc in the 5th ch from hk,
dc in the next 6 chs, * (ch 1, dc) in
the 2nd ch, dc in the next 14 chs,
repeat from * across row, end
with 1 dc in each of the last 8 chs,
ch 1, turn.

Row 2: Sc in the dc, * (ch 5, sc)
in the 4th dc, ch 3, make 5 dc in
the 1-ch, (ch 3, sc) in the 4th dc,
(ch 5, sc) in the 4th dc, repeat
from * across row, end with sc in
the last ch, ch 5, turn.

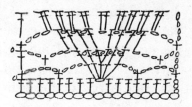

Row 3: * Sc in the 5-ch, ch 3, dc
in the dc, ch 1, dc in the dc, ch 1,
dc in the dc, ch 1, dc in the dc just
used, ch 1, dc in the next dc, ch 1,
dc in the next dc, ch 3, sc in the
next 5-ch, ch 5, repeat from *
across row, end with sc, ch 2, dc
in the last sc, ch 1, turn.

Row 4: Sc in the dc, * (ch 3, dc)
in the 3-ch, (ch 1, dc) in the 1-ch
(5 times), (ch 1, dc) in the beg of
the next 3-ch, (ch 3, sc) in the
center of the 5-ch, repeat from *
across row, end with sc in the
last ch, ch 4, turn.

Row 5: * Make 2 trc in the 3-ch,
make 3-ch (picot 6 times), 2 trc

217

in the next 3-ch, repeat from *
across row, end with trc in the sc.

54. Chain multiples of 25 plus 6.

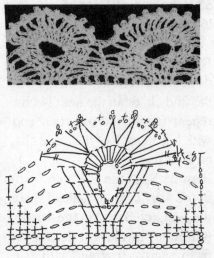

Row 1: Dc in the 8th ch from hk,
* (ch 1 and dc) in the 2nd ch,
repeat from * across row, end
with dc in the last ch, ch 1, turn.
Row 2: Sc in the 1st dc, next ch,
next dc, next ch and next dc, *
(ch 3, dc) in 3rd dc, dc in the next
ch, the dc, the ch and the dc, the
ch the dc, the ch and the dc,
repeat from * across row, end
with sc in the last dc, ch and dc in
the last ch, ch 1, turn.
Row 3: Sc in the 1st 4 sc, * ch 3,
dc in the next 3 dc, ch 2, dc in the
dc just used, dc in the next 2 dc,
ch 3, sc in the 2nd sc and sc in the
next 6 sc, repeat from * across
row, end with sc in the last 4 sc,
ch 1, turn.
Row 4: Sc in each of the 1st 3 sc,
* (ch 3, dc) in each of the next 3
dc, (ch 2, sc) in the 2-ch, (ch 2,
dc) in next 3 dc, (ch 3, sc) in 2nd
sc, sc in next 4 sc, repeat from *
across row, end with sc in each
of the last 3 sc, ch 1, turn.
Row 5: Sc in each of the 1st 2 sc,
* (ch 3, dc) in next 3 dc, (ch 1, sc)
in dc prev used, ch 10, sc in next

dc, (ch 1, dc) in dc prev used, dc in each of next 2 dc, (ch 3, sc) in 2nd sc and next 2 sc, repeat from * across row, end with sc in each of the last 2 sc, ch 1, turn.

Row 6: Sc in the 1st sc, * ch 3, dc in next 3 dc, make 16 dc in the center of the 10-ch, dc in the next 3 dc, (ch 3, sc) in the 2nd sc, repeat from * across row, end with sc in the last sc, ch 9, turn.

Row 7: Sk 1st 3 dc, * make 1 trc in the next dc, make another trc in the 2nd dc, ch 2, make trc in the dc prev used, make trc in 2nd dc, (repeat 6 more times), ch 2, dc in the sc, ch 2, repeat from * across row, end with dc in last 3-ch, ch 1, turn.

Row 8: Sl st in dc, sl st in 2-ch, sl st in 1st trc, * sc in 2-ch, make 4-ch picot, (repeat 5 more times), sc in next 2-ch, sl st, repeat from * across row, end with last set and sl st 3 times in the last ch.

55. Chain multiples of 43 plus 4.

Row 1: Dc in the 5th ch from hk and across row, ch 4, turn.

Row 2: Dc in the 3rd dc, * (ch 4, dc) in 6th ch, (ch 1, dc) in 2nd dc, repeat from * across row, end

with (dc, ch 1, dc) in last ch, ch 6, turn.

Row 3: Make 1 dc in next 4-chs, (ch 4, 1 dc) in next 4-chs, (ch 1, make 9 trc) in next 4-ch, (ch 1, 1 dc) in each of the next 4-ch, (ch 4, 1 dc) in next 4 chs, (ch 3, dc) in last ch, ch 4, turn.

Row 4: Make 2 dc in 3-ch, (ch 4, 1 dc) in the next 4-chs, (ch 1, trc) in trc, (ch 1, trc in the trc 8 times), (ch 1, 1 dc) in each of the 4-chs, (ch 4, 3 dc) in the last ch, ch 6, turn.

Row 5: Make 1 dc in each of the 4-chs, (ch 1, work 2 trc) in the 2nd 1-ch, (ch 2, 2 trc in next 1-ch, 7 times), (ch 1, make 1 dc) in next 4-chs, ch 3, dc in last ch, ch 4, turn.

Row 6: 2 dc in 3-ch, ch 2, make 3-ch picot, make 1 trc in 2-ch, make 3-ch picot and make 2 trc in same 2-ch, make another 3-ch picot, make trc, picot, 2 trc, picot, (6 more times), ch 2, 3 dc in last ch.

56. Chain multiples of 22 plus 2.

Row 1: Sc in 2nd ch from hk and across row, end with ch 1, turn.
Row 2: Sc in 1st sc, sc in next 3 sc, make another sc in sc just

220

used, * ch 6, dc in 6th sc and next 3 sc, ch 6, make 2 sc in 6th sc, sc in next 6 sc, make another sc in sc just used, repeat from * across row, end with 5 sc, ch 1, turn.

Row 3: Sc in 1st 4 sc, * ch 6, 2 dc in 1st dc, dc in next dc, ch 3, dc in next dc, 2 dc in next dc, ch 6, sc in 2nd sc, sc in next 6 sc, repeat from * across row, end with sc in the last 4 sc, ch 1, turn.

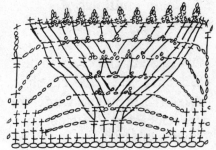

Row 4: Sc in 1st 3 sc, * ch 6, 1 dc in each of 1st 3 dc, ch 3, dc in 3-ch, ch 3, dc in 3-ch just used, ch 3, dc in next 3 dc, ch 6, sc in 2nd sc and next 4 sc, repeat from * across row, end with 3 sc, ch 1, turn.

Row 5: Sc in 1st 2 sc, * ch 6, dc in next 3 dc, ch 3, dc in next dc, ch 3, dc in next 3-ch, ch 3, dc in 3-ch just used, ch 3 dc in dc, ch 3, dc in next dc, dc in next 2 dc, ch 6, sc in 2nd sc and next 2 sc, repeat from * across row, end with 2 sc, ch 1, turn.

Row 6: Sc in the 1st sc, * ch 6, dc in next 3 dc, ch 3, dc in next dc (2 times), ch 3, dc in 3-ch, ch 3, dc in the 3-ch just used, ch 3, dc in the next dc 3 times, dc in the next 2 dc, ch 6, sc in the 2nd sc, repeat from * across row, end with sc, ch 8, turn.

Row 7: * Dc in the next 3 dc, (ch 3 and dc) in next dc 3 times, (ch 3, dc) in 3-ch, (ch 3, dc) in 3-ch just used, ch 3, dc in next dc (4 times), dc in next 2 dc, ch 3, repeat from * across row, end with dbl trc in last sc, ch 5, turn.

Row 8: Dc in 1st dc, * dc in next 2 dc, (ch 3, dc in dc 4 times), (ch 3, dc) in 3-ch, (ch 3, dc) in the 3-ch just used, (ch 3 and dc in next dc 5 times), dc in next dc, crochet it tog with a dc in 3-ch, dc in next dc, repeat from * across row, end with 2 dc crocheted tog in last dc and turning ch, ch 1, turn.

Row 9: Sc in each of 1st dc, * make 2 sc around beg of 3-ch, make 3-ch picot, make 2 other sc around same 3-ch, sc in each dc in between sets, repeat from * across row, end with sc in last 3 dc and turning ch.

57. Chain multiples of 14 plus 2.

Row 1: Sc in 2nd ch, sc in next ch, * ch 2, sc in 2nd ch, ch 2, make (4) 3-lp puff sts with 3 chs between each st in 4th ch, ch 2, sc in 4th ch, ch 2, sc in 2nd ch, ch 2, sc in 2nd ch, repeat from * across row, end with sc in last ch, ch 1, turn.

Row 2: Sc in 1st sc, * ch 2, make 1 dc in next 3-ch, ch 1, dc in 3-ch just used, ch 1, dc in 3-ch just used, ch 1, dc in next 3-ch, ch 1, dc in 3-ch just used, ch 1, dc in 3-ch just used, ch 1, dc in next 3-ch, ch 1, dc in 3-ch just used, ch 1, dc in 3-ch just used, ch 2, sc in 3rd 2-ch, repeat from * across row, end with sc in last sc, ch 4, turn.

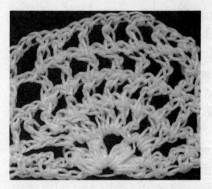

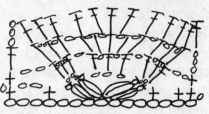

Row 3: Dc in 1st dc, * (ch 1, dc in next dc 3 times), (ch 1, dc) in next 1-ch, (ch 1, dc) in next dc, (ch 1, dc) in the next 1-ch, (ch 1, dc in next dc 3 times), ch 2, crochet 3 dc tog 1 in next dc, 1 in sc and 1 in dc, repeat from * across row, end with 2 dc crochet tog in last dc and sc, ch 3, turn.

Row 4: Sk 2 dc, crochet tog, dc in next dc, ch 2, * dc in next dc, ch 1 (3 times), dc in 1-ch, ch 1, dc in next dc, ch 1, dc in 1-ch, ch 1, dc in next dc, ch-1, 2 times, dc in next dc, ch 2, crochet 3 dc tog in next dc, the 3 dc crochet together and next dc, repeat from * across row, end with 2 dc crocheted together, the last in the last ch.

58. Chain multiples of 24 plus 4.

Row 1: Make 4 dc in 4th ch from hk, * (ch 1, sc) in 5th ch, (ch 3, sc) in the 4th ch, (ch 4, sc) in 5th ch, (ch 3, sc) in 4th sc, ch 1, make 9 dc in 5th ch, repeat from * across row, end with 5 dc in last ch, ch 4, turn.

Row 2: Sk 1st dc, dc in each dc, ch 1 (4 times), * make 2 dc in 2nd sc, (ch 1, 2 dc) in the same sc, make 2 dc in next sc, (ch 1, 2 dc) in same sc, (ch 1, dc in dc, ch 1, 9 times), ch 1, repeat from * across row, end with dc in last dc, ch 4, turn.

Row 3: Sc in 1-ch, ch 3 (4 times), * 2 dc in 2nd 1-ch, (ch 1, 2 dc) in next 1-ch, (ch 3, sc) in the 2nd 1-ch, (ch 3, sc in next 1-ch 7 times), ch 3, repeat from * across row, end with (sc, ch 1, dc) in last ch, ch 1, turn.

Row 4: Sc in dc, ch 3, sc in the 3-ch (3 times), * (ch 3, 2 dc) in 1-ch, ch 1, 2 dc in 1-ch just used, ch

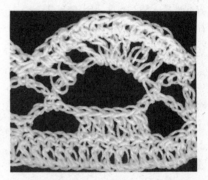

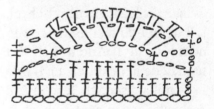

3, (sc in 3-ch 7 times) repeat from * across row, end with sc in last ch, ch 4, turn.

Row 5: Sc in 3-ch, (ch 3, sc) in sc, (ch 3, sc) in sc, * (ch 3, 2 dc) in 1-ch, (ch 1, 2 dc) in the 1-ch just used. (ch 3, sc) in 2nd 3-ch, (ch 3, sc in next 3-ch 5 times), repeat from * across row, end with sc in last 3-ch, ch 1, dc in sc, ch 1, turn.

Row 6: Sc in dc, (ch 3, sc) in 3-

ch, (ch 3, sc) in next 3-ch, * (ch 3, 2 dc) in 1-ch, (ch 1, 2 dc) in 1-ch just used, (ch 1, 2 dc) in 1-ch just used, (ch 3, sc) in 2nd 3-ch, (ch 3, sc in next 3-ch 4 times), repeat from * across row, end with sc in last ch, ch 4, turn.

Row 7: Sc in 3-ch, (ch 3, sc) in next 3-ch, * (ch 3, 2 dc) in 1-ch, (ch 1, 2 dc) in 1-ch just used, (ch 1, 2 dc) in next 1-ch, (ch 1, 2 dc) in 1-ch just used, (ch 3, sc) in 2nd 3-ch, (ch 3, sc in next 3-ch, 3 times), repeat from across row, end with sc in the last 3-ch, ch 1, dc in last sc, ch 1, turn.

Row 8: Sc in dc, ch 3, sc in next 3-ch, * ch 3, 2 dc in next 1-ch, ch 1, 2 dc in 1-ch just used, 2 dc in next 1-ch, ch 1, 2 dc in 1-ch just used, 2 dc in next 1-ch, ch 1, 2 dc in 1-ch just used, ch 3, sc in 2nd 3-ch, ch 3, sc in next 3-ch, ch 3, sc in next 3-ch, repeat from * across row, end with sc in last ch, ch 4, turn.

Row 9: Sc in 3-ch, * ch 3, 2 dc in next 1-ch, ch 1, 2 dc in 1-ch just used, ch 2, 2 dc in next 1-ch, ch 1, 2 dc in 1-ch just used, ch 2, 2 dc in next 1-ch, ch 1, 2 dc in 1-ch just used, ch 3, sc in 2nd 3-ch, ch 3, sc in next 3-ch, repeat from * across row, end with sc in last 3-ch, ch 1, dc in last sc, ch 1, turn.

Row 10: Sc in dc, * ch 3, 2 dc in next 1-ch, ch 1, 2 dc in 1-ch just used, ch 2, 9 dc in next 1-ch, ch 2, 2 dc in next 1-ch, ch 1, 2 dc in the 1-ch just used, ch 3, sc in 2nd 3-ch, repeat from * across, end with sc in last ch.

59. Chain multiple of 8 plus 5.

Row 1: 1 dc in 7th ch from hk, * ch 1, 1 dc in 2nd ch, repeat from * across row, end with dc in last ch, ch 5, turn.

Row 2: * 1 sc in 2nd dc, ch 5, repeat from * across row, end with sc in last dc, ch 2, 1 dc in last ch, ch 1, turn.

Row 3: Sc in dc, * ch 3, dc in next 5-ch, ch 4, make 4-ch picot, 3 dc in 1st of 4-ch just made, ch 3, sc in next 5-ch, repeat from * across row, end with sc in last ch.

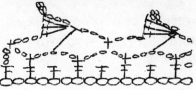

60. Chain multiples of 6 plus 5.

Row 1: Dc in 5th ch from hk, * ch 1, dc in 2nd ch, repeat from * across row, end with 1 dc in last ch, ch 3, turn.

Row 2: 1 sc in 2nd dc, * sc in next 1-ch, sc in next dc, sc in next 1-ch, sc in next dc, ch 3, sc in next dc, repeat from * across row, end with last set, ch 1, 1 hdc in last ch, ch 1, turn.

Row 3: Sc in hdc, * ch 7, 1 dc back in the sc, ch 3, 4 dc back in top of dc, sc in top of 3-ch, sl st back in each of 4 dc, ch 3, dc in sc, repeat from * across row, end with sc in last ch.

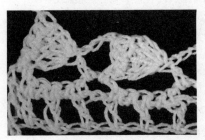

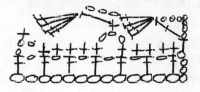

61. Chain multiples of 4 plus 2.

Row 1: Sc in 2nd ch from hk, * ch 2, 4 dc in 2nd ch, sc in 4th ch, repeat from * across row, end with sc in last ch, ch 3, turn.

Row 2: 2 dc in sc, * sc in top of next 2-ch, ch 2, 4 dc in sc between 4 dcs of prev row, repeat from * across row, end with 2 dc in last sc.

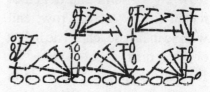

62. Chain multiples of 7 plus 4.

Row 1: Dc in 5th ch from hk, dc in next ch, * ch 2, sc in 2nd ch, ch 2, dc in 2nd ch and next 4 chs, repeat from * across row, end with dc in last 3 chs, ch 1, turn.

Row 2: Sc in 1st dc, * ch 1, dc in sc, ch 3, dc in same sc, ch 1, sc in 3rd dc, repeat from * across row, end with sc in last ch, ch 3, turn.

Row 3: * 3 dc in beg of 3-ch, 3-ch picot, 3 dc in center of same 3-ch, 3-ch picot, 3 dc in same 3-ch, repeat from * across row, end with dc in last sc.

63. Chain multiples of 7 plus 2.

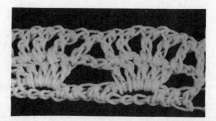

Row 1: Sc in 2nd ch from hk and next 2 chs, * ch 3, sc in 4th ch and next 3 chs, repeat from * across row, end with sc in last 3 chs, ch

4, turn.

Row 2: * 5 dc in next 3-ch, ch 3, repeat from * across row, end with 1 ch and 1 dc in last ch, ch 3, turn.

Row 3: Sk 1st dc, * dc in next dc, ch 1 (4 times), dc in next dc, repeat from * across row, end with extra dc in last ch.

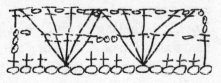

64. Chain multiples of 10 plus 2.

Row 1: Sc in 2nd ch from hk, * ch 1, 1 dc in 5th ch, ch 1, (7 times), sc in 5th ch, repeat from * across row, end with dc and ch in last ch, 3 times, 1 extra dc in last ch, ch 1, turn.

Row 2: Sc in 1st dc, * ch 1, dc in sc 7 times, ch 1, sc in 4th dc, repeat from * across row, end with dc and 1 ch 3 times, 1 extra dc in last sc, ch 1, turn.

Row 3: Sc in 1st dc, * ch 1, dc in sc 7 times, ch 1, sc in 4th dc, repeat from * across row, end with dc and 1 ch 3 times, 1 extra dc in last sc.

65. Chain multiples of 5 plus 1.

Row 1: 1 sc in 2nd ch from hk and each ch across row, ch 1, turn.
Row 2: 1 sc in 1st sc and each sc

across row, ch 1, turn.

Row 3: Sc in 1st sc, * ch 2, dc in next sc, ch 3, 5 dc around dc just made (making perpendicular angle), sc in 4th sc, repeat from * across row, end with sc, ch 1, turn.

Row 4: Sc in 1st sc, ch 2, * sc in 3rd dc, ch 2, sc in next dc, ch 2, sc in next dc, ch 2, sc in center of the 3-ch, ch 2 sc in top of the perpendicular dc, repeat from * across row, end with dc in last sc.

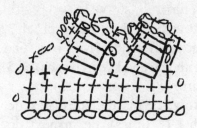

66. Chain multiples of 10 plus 4.

Row 1: Dc in 4th ch from hk and in each ch across row, ch 1, turn.

Row 2: Sc in next 3 dc, * ch 3, 2 dc in 3rd dc, ch 2, 2 dc in same dc, ch 3, sc in 3rd dc, ch 2, 2 dc in same dc, ch 3, sc in 3rd dc and each of next 4 dc, repeat from * across row, end with sc in each of last 3 dc, ch 1, turn.

Row 3: Sc in 1st sc and 2nd sc, * ch 3, 3 dc in 2-ch, ch 2, make 3 dc in same 2-ch, ch 3, sc in 2nd sc and in each of next 2 sc, repeat from * across row, end with 2 sc, ch 1, turn.

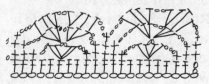

Row 4: Sc in 1st sc, * ch 3, 4 dc in 2-ch, ch 2, 4 dc in same 2-ch, ch 3, sc in 2nd sc, repeat from *

across row, end with sc in last sc.

67. Chain multiples of 8 plus 5.

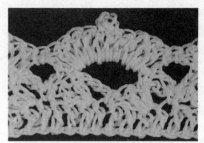

Row 1: Dc in 5th ch from hk, and in each ch across row, ch 1, turn.
Row 2: Sc in 1st dc, * 2 dc in 3rd dc, ch 3, sc in next dc, repeat from * across row, end with sc in turning ch, ch 5, turn.
Row 3: * Sc in top of 3-ch, dc in next sc, ch 3, dc in sc just used, sc in next 3-ch, ch 6, repeat from * across row, end with sc in top of last 3-ch, ch 2, make 1 trc in last sc, ch 3, turn.

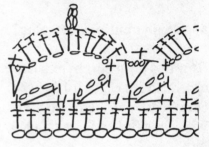

Row 4: 3-ch picot, 5 dc in 2-ch, * sc in center of 3-ch, make 5 dc in 1st half of 6-ch, 5-ch picot, 5 dc in last half of 6-ch, repeat from * across row, end with (5 dc, ch 2, 1 trc) in last ch.

68. Chain multiples of 8 plus 5.

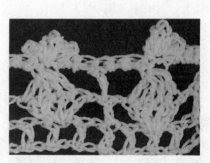

Row 1: 1 dc in 7th ch from hk, * ch 1, dc in 2nd ch, repeat from * across row, end with dc, ch 4, turn.
Row 2: 5 dc in 3rd dc, * ch 1, dc in 2nd dc, ch 1, 5 dc in 2nd dc, repeat from * across row, end with dc in turning ch, ch 6, turn.
Row 3: Sk 1st dc, * crochet 5 dc tog, 1 in each of the next 5 dc, ch

3, dc in next dc, ch 3, repeat from * across row, end with dc in turning ch, ch 1, turn.

Row 4: Sc in 1st dc, * 1 sc in each of the 3 chs, 1 sc in top of 5 dc, crochet tog, make (3) 5-ch picot in sc just formed, sl st tog, sc in each of next 3 chs, repeat from * across row, end with 1 extra sc in last ch.

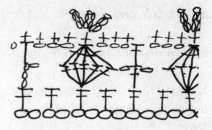

69. Chain multiples of 6 plus 5.

Row 1: 4 dc in 8th ch from hk, * ch 1, dc in 3rd ch, ch 1, 4 dc in 3rd ch, repeat from * across row, end with dc in 3rd and last ch, ch 5, turn.

Row 2: Sk 1st dc, * crochet 4 dc tog in each of next 4 dc, ch 2, dc in next dc, ch 2, repeat from * across row, ending with 2 chs, 1 dc in turning ch, ch 3, turn.

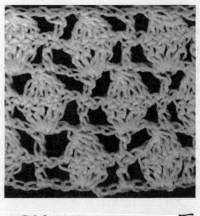

Row 3: Dc in 1st dc, * ch 1, dc on top of 4 dc, crochet tog, ch 1, 4 dc in next dc, repeat from * across row, end with 2 dc in turning ch, ch 3, turn.

Row 4: Dc in 2nd dc, * ch 2, dc in next dc, ch 2, crochet 4 dc tog, 1 in each of next 4 dc, repeat from * across row, end with dc in last dc and dc in turning ch, ch 4, turn.

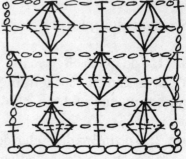

Row 5: Sk 1st 2 dc crocheted

tog, * 4 dc in next dc, ch 1, dc in top of 4 dc crocheted tog, ch 1, repeat from * across row, end with dc in turning ch, ch 5, turn.

Row 6: Sk 1st dc, crochet 4 dc tog, 1 formed in each of next 4 dc, ch 2, dc in next dc, ch 2, repeat from * across row, end with dc in turning ch.

70. Chain multiples of 8 plus 5.

Row 1: Crochet 2 dc tog, 1 in the 5th ch and 1 in the 4 ch, * ch 3, crochet 2 dc tog, 1 in the ch just used and 1 in the 4th ch, repeat from * across row, end with last group, (ch 1, dc) in ch just used, ch 3, turn.

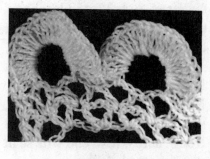

Row 2: Dc in top of 2 dc crocheted tog, * ch 3, crochet 2 dc tog (1 in the top of the last 2 dc crocheted tog, 1 in top of the last 2 dc crocheted tog), repeat from * across row (end with 2 dc crocheted tog in top of last 2 dc and last ch), ch 1, turn.

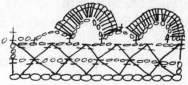

Row 3: Sc in top of 1st 2 dc crocheted tog, ch 2, * sc in center of 3-ch, ch 8, sc in center of next 3-ch, ch 5, repeat from * across row, end with (sc, ch 2, sc) in last sc.

Row 4: * Make 23 dc around 8-ch, sc in center of 5-ch, repeat from * across row, end with sc in last sc.

71. Chain multiples of 4 plus 2.

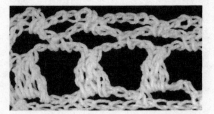

Row 1: Sc in 2nd ch from hk, * ch 5, sc in 4th ch, repeat from * across row, end with sc, ch 5, turn.

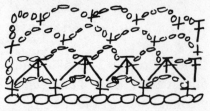

Row 2: * (1 trc in 1st sc, 1 dc in center of 5-ch, 1 trc in last ch of ch-5), crochet all just used st tog, ch 5, repeat from * across row, end with (1 ch, 1 trc) in last sc, ch 1, turn.

Row 3: Sc in the 1st trc, * ch 5, sc around center of 5-ch, repeat from * across row, end with sc in turning ch, ch 6, turn.

Row 4: * Sc around center of 5-ch, ch 5, repeat from * across row, end with sc, ch 2, trc in last sc.

72. Chain multiples of 12 plus 7.

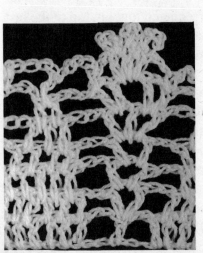

Row 1: Dc in 10th ch from hk, dc in next 7chs, * (ch 2, dc) in 3rd ch, (ch 2, dc) in the 3rd ch, dc in next 6 chs, repeat from * across row, end with ch, ch 3, turn.

Row 2: Dc in 1st dc, * ch 2, dc in the sp between the 1st and next dc, make 1 dc between each of next 5 sets of dc, (ch 2, dc) in 2nd dc, (ch 2, dc) in dc just used, repeat from * across row, end with dc in turning ch, ch 4, turn.

Row 3: Dc in 2-ch, * (ch 3, dc) after next dc, make 4 more dc between the next 4 sets of dc, (ch 3, dc) in 2nd 2-ch, (ch 2, dc) in same 2-ch, repeat from * across row, end with dc, 2 chs, dc in turning ch, ch 3, turn.

Row 4: Dc in 2-ch, (ch 2, dc) in 2-ch just used, * (ch 4,dc) in sp after 2nd dc, 1 dc in sp between each of next 3 sets of dc, ch 4, dc in 2-ch, (ch 2, dc) in 2-ch just used, repeat from * across row, end with dc, ch 2, dc in the turning ch, ch 3, turn.

Row 5: Dc in 2-ch, ch 2, dc in 2-ch just used, * (ch 4, dc) in sp after next dc, dc in between next 2 sets of dc, (ch 4, dc) in next 2-ch, (ch 2, dc) in 2-ch just used, (ch 2, dc) in 2-ch just used, repeat from * across row, end with ch 5, after last set, turn.

Row 6: Dc in 3rd dc, ch 2, dc in dc just used, * (ch 4, dc) in sp after next dc, dc after next dc, (ch 4,dc) in 2nd dc, (ch 2, dc) in dc just used, repeat from * across row, end with ch 5, after last set, turn.

Row 7: Make 4-ch picot, dc in

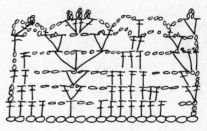

1st dc, ch 2, * sc in 2nd dc, ch 5, dc in sp between next 2 dc, ch 5, sc in 2nd dc, ch 2, dc in 2nd 2-ch, 4-ch picot, dc in 2-ch just used, 4-ch picot, dc in the 2-ch just used, 4-ch picot, dc in 2-ch just used, ch 2, repeat from * across row, end with dc, picot, dc in turning ch.

73. Chain multiples of 21 plus 2.

Row 1: Sc in 2nd ch from hk, * ch 5, sc in the 5th ch, repeat from * across row, end with sc in last ch, ch 6, turn.

Row 2: * Sc in center of 5-ch, ch 5, repeat from * across row, end with sc, ch 2, dc in last sc, ch 1, turn.

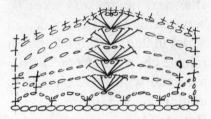

Row 3: Sc in dc, * ch 5, 3 dc in 2nd 5-ch, ch 2, 3 dc in 5-ch just used, ch 5, sc in 2nd 5-ch, repeat from * across row, end with sc in last ch, ch 1, turn.

Row 4: Sc in sc, * ch 5, 3 dc in 2-ch, ch 2, 3 dc in 2-ch just used, ch 5, sc in next sc, repeat from* across row, end with sc in last sc, ch 1, turn.

Row 5: Same as row 4.

Row 6: Same as row 4.

Row 7: * sc in sc, ch 7, 3 dc in 2-ch, ch 3, 3 dc in 2-ch just used, ch 7, repeat from across row, end with last sc, ch 1, turn.

Row 8: Sc in the 1st sc, * make 7 sc around 7-ch, 1 sc in each of 3 dc, 2 sc in 3-ch, sc in each of 3-dc, 7 sc around 7-ch, repeat from * across row, end with sc in last sc.

234

74. Chain multiples of 19.

Begin at narrow edge.

Row 1: 1 dtr in 10th ch from hk, ch 2, sk 2 ch, 1 trc in next ch, ch 2, sk 2 ch, 1 dc in next ch, ch 2, sk 2 ch, 1 sc in last ch, ch 1, turn.

Row 2: 1 sc in 1st sc, ch 2, 1 sc in next dc, ch 2, 1 sc in next trc, ch 2, 1 sc in next dtr, ch 2, 1 sc in turning ch of prev row, ch 1, turn.

Row 3: 1 sc in 1st sc, ch 2, 1 dc in the next sc, ch 2, 1 trc in next sc, ch 2, 1 dtr in next sc, ch 2, 1 dtr in next sc, ch 1, turn.

Row 4: 1 sc in next dtr, ch 2, 1 sc in next dtr, ch 2, 1 sc in next trc, ch 2, 1 sc in next dc, ch 2, 1 sc in next sc, ch 7, turn.

Row 5: Sk 1st sc, 1 dtr in next sc, ch 2, 1 trc in next sc, ch 2, 1 dc in next sc, ch 2, 1 sc in next sc, ch 1, turn.

repeat rows 2-5 for pattern, end last repeat with row 3.

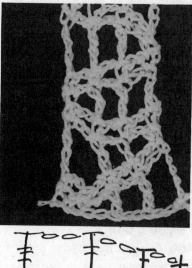

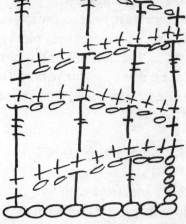

75. Chain multiples of 8.

Begin at narrow edge.

Row 1: 1 sc in 2nd ch from hk, * 1 sc in next ch, repeat from * across row, ch 1, turn.

Row 2: 1 sc in 1st sc, (1 sl st, ch 4, 1 sl st) in next sc (picot made), 1 sc in each of next 3 sc, 1 picot in next sc, 1 sc in last sc, ch 1, turn.

Row 3: 1 sc in 1st sc, ch 1, sk 1 picot (keep picots in front of ch-1's), 1 sc in each of next 3 sc, ch 1, sk 1 picot, 1 sc in last sc, ch 1, turn.

Row 4: 1 sc in 1st sc, 1 sc in next ch-1 sp, 1 sc in next sc, 1 picot in next sc, 1 sc in next sc, 1 sc in next ch-1 sp, 1 sc in last sc, 1 ch 1, turn.

Row 5: 1 sc in each of next 3 sc, ch 1, sk 1 picot, 1 sc in each of last 3 sc, ch 1, turn.

Row 6: 1 sc in 1st sc, 1 picot in next sc, 1 sc in next sc, 1 sc in next ch–1 sp, 1 sc in next sc, 1 picot in next sc, 1 sc in last sc, ch 1, turn.

Repeat rows 3-6 for pattern for desired length, end last repeat with row 5.

76. Chain multiples of 11.

Begin at narrow edge.

Row 1: [yo twice, insert hk in 11th ch from hk, yo and pull through, (yo and pull through 2 lps on hk) twice] 3 times, yo and pull through last 4 lps on hk (cluster made), ch 10, turn.

Row 2: 1 cluster in 10th ch from hk, ch 10, turn.

Repeat row 2 for pattern and desired length (having an even number of clusters), ch 5.

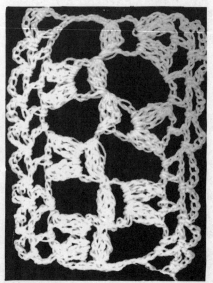

Finish:

Row l: * Sk l cl, (l cl, ch 3, l cl) in next ch-l0 sp, ch 4, repeat from * across long edge, ch 4, turn.

Row 2: * l dc in ch-3 sp, ch 2, (l dc, ch 2, l dc) in ch-4 sp, ch 2, repeat from * across edging, and end with (l dc, ch 2, l dc) in turning ch of prev row, ch 7 turn.

Row 3: Sk (l dc, ch 2, l dc), * l sc in next ch-2 sp, ch 5, repeat from * across edging and end with l sc in turning ch of prev row, F. O.

Attach to llth ch of foundation ch, ch 5, and repeat rows 1-3 along opposite edge.

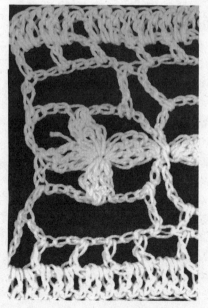

77. Chain 5.

Begin at narrow edge.

Row l: * [yo twice, insert hk in 5th ch from hk, yo and pull through, (yo and pull through 2 lps on hk) twice] 3 times, yo and pull through last 4 lps on hk (cluster made), ch 5, repeat from * for pattern and desired length (using even number of clusters), ch 7.

Finish:

Row l: * [yo twice, insert hk in same ch as next cl, yo and pull through 2 lps on hk) twice] 4 times, yo and pull through last 5 lps on hk, ch 7, 1 sc and 1 cl in next ch, ch 7, repeat from * around the whole piece, end with 1 sc in top of last cl.

Row 2: 1 sl st in each of next 3-ch, 1 sc in same ch-7 sp, ch 11, * (1 trc in next ch-7 sp) twice, ch 7, repeat from * across 1 long edge, end with 1 trc in last ch-7 sp, ch 5, turn.

Row 3: * Sk 2 sts, 1 dc in next st, ch 2, repeat from * across edge, leaving last 4 sts free, ch 3, turn.

Row 4: * 2 dc in next ch-2 sp, 1 dc in next dc, repeat from * across edge, F.O. Repeat rows 2-4 along opposite edge.

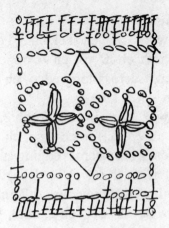

78. Chain 25, join with sl st to form a ring.

Round 1: Ch 3, 49 dc in center of ring, join with sl st to 3rd ch of starting ch-3. FO.

Round 2: Ch 25, insert ch through center of last ring made, join with sl st to form a ring. Ch 3, 49 dc in center of 2nd ring, join with sl st to 3rd ch of starting ch-3, F. O.

Make rings in same manner as 2nd until desired length is reached.

Finish: Attach yarn to any dc on

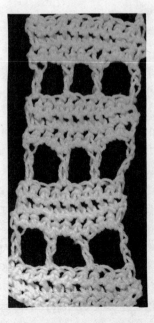

last ring, ch 6, * sk 2 dc, 1 dc in next dc, ch 2, sk 2 dc, yo twice, insert hk in next dc, insert hk through any dc of next ring, yo and pull through both sts, (yo and pull through 2 sps on hk) 3 times, ch 2, sk 2 dc on 2nd ring, 1 dc in next dc, ch 2, repeat from * across edge, end with sk 2 dc, 1 dc in next dc, ch 2, sk 2 dc, 1 dc in next dc, F.O.

Sk 19 dc on last ring, attach yarn, work across opposite edge in same manner.

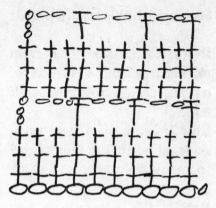

79. Chain multiples of ll.

Row 1: 1 sc in 2nd ch from hk, * 1 sc in next ch, repeat from * across row, ch 1, turn.

Row 2: * 1 sc in next sc, repeat from * across row, ch 1, turn.

Row 3: * 1 sc in next sc, repeat from * across row, ch 6, turn.

Row 4: Sk 3 sc, * 1 dc in next sc, ch 2, sk 2 sc, repeat from * once, end with 1 dc in last sc, ch 1, turn.

Row 5: * 1 sc in next dc, 2 sc in ch-2 sp, repeat from * once, end with 1 sc in next dc, 3 sc in turning ch of prev row, ch 1, turn. Repeat rows 2-5 for pattern and desired length, end with last repeat row 3.

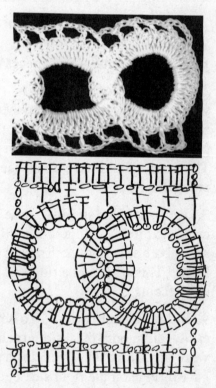

80. Chain multiples of 4 plus 1.

Row 1: Ch 5, 1 dc in 6th ch from hk, * ch 1, sk 1 ch, 1 dc in next ch, repeat from * across row, ch 1, turn.

Row 2: 1 sc in 1st ch-1 sp, * ch 6, sk next ch-1 sp, 1 sc in next ch-1 sp, repeat from * across row, ch 3, turn.

Row 3: 4 dc in 1st ch-6 sp, * ch 1, 4 dc in next ch-6 sp, repeat from * across row.

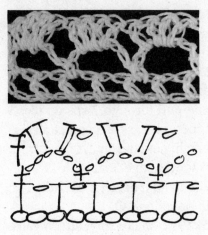

Four Ways to Join Crochet Items

1. Smooth Seams — Sew pieces together with an overcast stitch.

2. Smooth Decorative Seam — Use a blunt needle and the same yarn or thread used in the crocheted item. Join with an overcast or whip stitch in back loop or both strands of stitches, whichever pleases you best. Don't pull yarn or thread too tightly as you sew. The seam should have about the same amount of "give" as the crocheted item.

3. Ridge on Underside — Use a hook one size larger than the crocheted item. Align work; slip stitch in every crochet stitch under both strands of both pieces being joined, or only in the back loops. This will form a ridge on the underside. Work with right sides facing.

4. Ridge on Right Side — To obtain a seam that can be observed easily, align both pieces of crochet with wrong sides facing and work single crochet stitches in back loops of both pieces. You will have a ridge on the right side between both pieces being joined.